Philosophy and m

GW01316220

Philosophy and Mystification is both a book of philosophy and a book about philosophy. It is a reflection on the nature, methods and resources of philosophic enquiry, one that is grounded in concretely discussed central problems. The problems discussed are ones which have dogged Western philosophy in the modern era: logical necessity, machine intelligence, the relation of science and religion, determinism, skepticism, as well as the search for foundations and origins that has so characterized our time.

Guy Robinson argues that a conception of philosophy was adopted in the Seventeenth Century which brought with it projects, goals and methods that required us to see the world upside-down, creating abstract and mystified entities to explain the ordinary and concrete, requiring us to explain the social in terms of the individual, and the human and purposive in terms of the mechanical, and not only to see nature as a vast mechanism but science as a mechanical activity whose rules it was the business of philosophers to discover.

Robinson has made an unusual alliance between Aristotle, Marx and Wittgenstein in trying to re-focus our views on these problems and in locating philosophy itself in a wider historical context. His thesis is that the historical tasks of a revolutionary transition in Europe made the new conceptions of philosophy, of nature and of humanity seem both natural and necessary and hid from the philosophers the inversions and incoherences involved. If we are to escape from the confusions and blind-alleys we were led into then, we are going to have to go back not only to question the agenda but to understand how the historical context made that agenda seem both natural and necessary. The aim of *Philosophy and Mystification* is to make a start on that project.

Guy Robinson was senior lecturer in philosophy at the University of Southampton until his early retirement in 1982 and then research professor at MIT and the University of Boston. He now lives and works in Dublin.

Philosophy and mystification

A reflection on nonsense and clarity

Guy Robinson

FORDHAM UNIVERSITY PRESS
New York • 2003

Library of Congress Cataloging-in-Publication Data

Robinson, Guy, 1927–
  Philosophy and mystification : a reflection on
nonsense and clarity /
Guy Robinson.— 1st paperback ed.
    p. cm.
  Originally published: London : Routledge, 1998.
  Includes bibliographical references and index.
  ISBN 0-8232-2291-8 (pbk. : alk. paper)
  1. Methodology. 2. Philosophy. I. Title.
BD241.R594 2003
101—dc21   2003006062

Printed in the United States of America
07 06 05 04 03   5 4 3 2 1
Fordham University Press edition 2003

Contents

Preface

The discussions that make up this book have a history going back almost forty years, but it is a consequence of the view of philosophy they embody that I have not found myself having seriously to revise or recant. Their aim has been clarity of thought and vocabulary, and while this aim always leaves a space for improvement, it does not have a place for the notion of "being wrong" that goes with the activity of setting out theories and doctrines.

Those discussions that have previously been published have therefore been left more or less as they were and simply clarified where I could see they needed it. They have also been left in the order of their first writing, with the exception of chapter 1, not previously published, which attempts an overview of the method, resources and the conception of philosophy they exhibit.

I would like here to thank the editors and publishers of the following journals for permission to use material from articles and symposium papers for the following chapters: chapter 2, "Following and Formalization," *Mind* (1964); chapter 3, "Infinity," *Proceedings of the Aristotelian Society*, supplementary vol. (1964); chapter 4, "Miracles," *Ratio* (1967); chapter 5, "How to Tell Your Friends from Machines," *Mind* (1972); chapter 6, "Nature and Necessity," *Royal Institute of Philosophy Lectures* (1974); chapter 7, "Skepticism about Skepticism," *Proceedings of the Aristotelian Society*, supplementary vol. (1977); chapter 8, "Fool's Intelligence," *Universities Quarterly* (1982); chapter 9, "Language and the Society of Others," *Philosophy* (1992); chapter 10, "*Deus sive Natura*, Science, Nature and Ideology," *Philosophy* (1993); chapter 11, "On Misunderstanding Science," *International Journal of Philosophical Studies* (1996).

Acknowledgements

Properly, acknowledgements should reach back to what Graham Greene so beautifully describes as "that moment in childhood when a door opens and lets the future in." For me that was not so much a moment as a period, the period of several years from the age of eight when my father and I would walk a mile to the railway station in Douglaston, Long Island, he to take the train to work in New York City, and I to go in the opposite direction to school in Port Washington. During those walks he would often explain scientific ideas to me and gave me a sense of the physical world and how things worked. He was himself a biochemist and as a graduate student had been asked by Frederick Banting to be his assistant in the work of isolating and refining insulin. Declining, he offered his roommate Charlie Best in his place.

Those talks gave me an interest and a sense of being at home in the sciences that I have carried with me even though I never pursued that interest. But it is something I have to acknowledge as part of my philosophical formation.

Another important part of that formation was being introduced to philosophy through Aristotle and not through Descartes. This gave me an outsider's perspective, one that will be evident throughout this book. Lincoln Reis was the teacher who helped me to see Aristotle as a living philosopher and not merely a historical figure whose ideas had to be studied rather than used. But on the other hand, it was perhaps more important that I came to see that Aristotle was not to be taken as an ultimate authority whose words could save one thought. Those words, or the words of any other, can only be starting points and suggestions to be critically examined. If they are to have life and substance, one has to think them for oneself and make them one's own.

For another element I have to thank Elizabeth Anscombe, who generously lent me the galley proofs of Wittgenstein's *Remarks on the Foundations of Mathematics* in 1955 when I was struggling with the problem of "the actual infinite" that was thought to be generated by set theory and by Cantor's "transfinite arithmetic." In the further struggle to understand the *Remarks* and to bring it to bear on the problem, I came to see the depth and the radical nature of Wittgenstein's criticism not only of Cantor and Russell, but of some of the deepest currents in the philosophy of the modern era. Entry by that port helped me avoid the canonical interpretation of the "private language" argument, one that attempted to draw the sting of Wittgenstein's criticism of the individualistic assumptions of the modern era by making his argument bear only against a language that "could not be taught to another." I have tried to set out my own versions of those criticisms in what follows.

To my late colleague A. R. Manser I owe the recognition of the philosopher in Karl Marx. That philosopher is at times sketchy and only suggestive, perhaps, but offers many insights if read sympathetically. That influence will be seen also in some of the discussions following.

I have tried to repay my debt to the writing of T. S. Kuhn in chapter 11, and since writing that chapter, and following his generous reaction to it, I benefited much from discussion and correspondence with him, though I am pretty sure that he would not have agreed with everything that I have drawn from those discussions. His death left many issues unsettled.

From my old colleague Tony Palmer, I have had the incalculable benefit of sharp criticism and a dogged opposition that forced me to argue my corner and clarify my ideas. At the same time, when those ideas had been clarified and objections met, he was generously able to accept new ideas and a different point of view and to acknowledge that. One could hardly ask for more.

From Bernard Harrison I have had a combination of support and criticism that I can hardly overvalue. His criticisms have been valuable and his support enthusiastic and practical.

Alasdair MacIntyre has been an enthusiastic and supportive reader over many years and has given practical and critical help that I am more than glad to acknowledge.

Robin Andersen has given a close and careful reading to some chapters and has made criticisms that have been especially valuable in being made from the point of view of a non-specialist. My son Guy Robinson has been helpful in that way too.

Finally, from my wife, Bee Ring, a writer herself, I have had not just support (that would be too passive a word) but rather, pushing to create a single book out of the thought and the writing of a lifetime.

Guy Robinson
Dalkey, Dublin, 1997

Introduction: Philosophy and mystification

There are two currents that run through this book, both of which set it in opposition to a practice and conception of philosophy that can be traced back to the seventeenth century and is exemplified most clearly in Descartes. One current flows from the view that the business of philosophy is not with some special kind of truth, such as Descartes sought, a truth higher and more elusive than that found in the everyday world, a truth requiring special techniques for its discovery. The contrary view informing this book is that the object of philosophy ought to be clarity and putting order into our thoughts and our ways of talking about the everyday. These thoughts often enough get tangled when ways of talking that have been developed in one area or field get transferred to another, or come up against ways of talking devised for entirely different subject matter and for different purposes. That view of philosophy and the resources it can appeal to is discussed in chapter 1 and is exemplified throughout the following treatments of particular tangles and confusions endemic to the modern era.

But there is also, beyond this, a view about the source of the tangles and confusions that have been characteristic of that era (which is our era), their source in certain moves, certain assumptions and projects that seemed natural and necessary to the philosophers of the seventeenth century, seemed so for very good historical reasons. But good historical reasons, as their name implies, have a shelf life, and in any case, while they may be motivating, they are not compelling with the universal, timeless and abstract force that philosophers generally set themselves to pursue, and often think they have found. And this brings the discussion into a deeper conflict with the self-image of philosophy that has been particularly sharply drawn in the modern era, the image of it as the pursuit of the absolute and the timeless and what is unconditioned by circumstance and history.

One of the tasks on which I have tried to make a start is that of identifying some of those false assumptions and mistaken projects that initiated the modern era, while at the same time giving at least a sketch of a concrete historical analysis of the circumstances in which they came to seem natural, justified and even necessary assumptions to make and projects to undertake. The inclusion of historical discussions and analysis will seem strange to many and unwarranted to some, but it is only a concrete historical analysis that can give any substance to claims about "the historicity of knowledge." Without such a concrete account, general claims of that sort are abstract, weightless and of little use. We would have no way of assessing them.

In several of the chapters that follow I have done what I can to give a concrete account of the historical conditions that in the seventeenth century gave a plausibility to its individualistic assumptions and an apparent urgency to the project of seeking "absolute" foundations that was undertaken then. Because I can hardly claim authority as a historian, what I have done in that line will have to speak for itself. I would welcome further discussion of, and even instruction in, the business of historical accounting for the adoption of those projects and those assumptions that have set modern philosophy on its particular course.

But now I need to say something about my title, because the word "mystification" that appears there is not being used in a loose and general sense to cover muddles and confusions of every kind, even deliberate or interested ones. It is used in a very specific sense to indicate those confusions and that bafflement which arises out of a failure to separate carefully the secular, concrete and conditioned from the transcendent, the absolute and the unconditioned. That particular sort of bafflement and confusion is involved in almost every one of the problems tackled in the following chapters, and the discussions in those chapters are perhaps the best guide to the nature of the particular sort of confusion and senselessness caused by the attempt to give a transcendental role to words and notions[1] that are to all appearances secular in character. Still, it is important to say something, however sketchy, to indicate what to look for in those later discussions.

The seeking of foundations, for example, is a perfectly sensible project, if by that is meant looking for a good firm place to build, a place that is adequate to the building you have in mind. We apply the principles of geology and soil mechanics, make test bores, and consult records of earthquakes and flooding. If necessary, we sink piles or create rafts that work with the natural conditions to create a foundation that will withstand the forces that it will be subjected to through wind loading or flood, through earthquakes or the pounding of traffic.

It is quite another thing to look for a foundation that is "absolute" and "unconditioned," one that needs no support from anything else, and is not only adequate in itself, but adequate at the same time, to any building however high, or load however great, that you may want to place on it. The latter search, by contrast to the first, is a senseless enterprise. Such a foundation is not to be found in this world – or on it. Looking for such a thing is like looking for the rainbow's end, for "Tír na nOg," for "El Dorado," Prester John, or the place where parallels meet.

Searching for impossible things may, of course, lead you through interesting country and teach you much. Or on the other hand, it may lead you into a shadowland where nothing is real. In chapter 7 I argue that Descartes's "Method of Hyperbolical Doubt" leads us into just such a shadowland, that the "doubts" that are the basis of the "method" are unreal. Because there is nothing really going on in the so-called "doubting," what this pseudo-process is thought to reveal is just as unreal and insubstantial as the "doubts" themselves. In setting out on this impossible quest for the absolute, for foundations that, while needing no support themselves can support anything whatever, Descartes employs means that are just as unreal and delusive as the elusive and impossible goal he is pursuing. But that view has to be argued for.

Contrast the Aristotelian dialectic with this search for "absolute" foundations. When Aristotle looks for a place to begin the investigation of any topic he suggests that we begin with "the opinions of the many or the wise." This is hardly because those opinions are thought to be infallible. We need not have a mystical view about "the collective wisdom of humanity" to think it sensible to start there. It simply makes more sense than wasting our time with random fanciful or extraordinary views, views that have come out of nowhere and are likely only to lead nowhere, the wild suppositions of impossible happenings: colors that change on a certain date, universes that consist only of sounds or of one object, and so forth. Under the influence of Descartes's method, these imaginings have been thought to reveal "conceptual boundaries." (That belief also gets discussed in chapter 7.)

To be worth examining, Socrates required that views be seriously held. And that seems a good place to start. (It is also where Socrates and Descartes part company. Descartes, by contrast, tells us not to take seriously the doubts that are to be the basis of his philosophical method.) But the Socratic and the Aristotelian examination will be a critical examination of those seriously held views: have they doubtful antecedents? Have they unacceptable consequences? Do they make sense? How do they square with other deeply held or important views? Can they be incorporated into a larger picture that makes sense and is fruitful? The views may have to be modified before they can be so incorporated, but for Aristotle, the views of "the many" and "the wise" are unlikely to be rejected outright. Again, this is not because of some mystical collective wisdom, but rather because, collectively, the speakers of a language ("the many") have a role in forming that language (in which "the wise" also have a special role, as can be seen by the special place they are given, for example, in the *Oxford English Dictionary*).

The language that "the many" and "the wise" form through what they say and through what they accept as true will be one that will reflect, and at the same time be incorporated in, the collective practices of a whole way of life. The words of that language will get their sense from their role in those practices and that way of life.

Though "the many" and "the wise" collectively determine the language, the two are distinguished here because "the wise" may have a leading role in summing up and expressing currents that are there in the common life that they share with "the many." The greatness of Shakespeare or of Chaucer and their ability to leave their imprint on the language can be seen as lying in their sensitivity to, and ability to articulate, deep changes in human life in their time and culture. They were in that way "speaking for" us all in that culture, for "the many," helping us to see who we were and giving us a vocabulary and stories that would help us think about our lives.

However, while taking this on board we have at the same time to keep in mind Hobbes' great discovery that when a society is itself divided there may be those who pretend to speak for all but really only speak on behalf of an interested section, even when they think they speak for all. That is, they are providing a vocabulary and ways of looking that help us to see ourselves in certain ways that benefit the one segment and prevent us from seeing ourselves and understanding our life in ways that would damage the interests of that segment.

But now we come to the deepest and most difficult point. We have to understand and come to terms with the charge of "relativism" and with the charge of "cultural relativism" that will be made against the suggestion that "the many" and "the wise" collectively determine what is sayable, and even what is accepted within the culture. These are not irresponsible charges, but they are not helpful either.

The charge of "relativism" is not helpful in two separate ways. Firstly, it counterposes a "written in the sky" absolutism to an anarchic and unfettered freedom of a culture to make up a language and a view of the world, offering us only these two possibilities. Secondly, what is particularly unhelpful about the accusation of "relativism" is that it suggests some kind of philosophical or moral wickedness, an abdication of all judgment, order or constraint. The problem is not wickedness, but incoherence and senselessness. The notion of a culture with no constraints on its language formation or on its practices and accepted patterns of behavior is simply incoherent. The "language" would be no language. Without shaping forces and constraints it would be an arabesque of sound and no more. If it were arbitrary and unconstrained, there would be no connection with the life and world of the people. There would be no meaning for its words and no sense in its institutions, rituals and practices. The notion of *sense* would have evaporated.

There is something here that bears on whole cultures in a way that has analogies to, but is different from, the way the "private language argument" bears on individuals. Many Wittgensteinians have concentrated only on the fact that the individual confronts the social as part of a shaping environment which through its constraints makes possible significant speech and action. But, though whole cultures don't face the *social* constraints of the sort that confront the individual, there are, nevertheless, a whole range of shaping forces that, in being recognized and responded to by the culture, give weight and substance and point both to its language and to its social forms and practices. The adequacy or inadequacy of a culture's response to those forces it comes to recognize, and the tension between its responses to different forces will give the culture a history. That history may be slow-moving and almost imperceptible or so fast-moving that one generation can hardly recognize the world of the next, or know how to operate in it.

But understanding the "externality" of those forces and constraints facing a whole culture is difficult enough, and we may be tempted to what looks like a simple, natural and even necessary solution – that of making their externality absolute and timeless, something that stands them outside the whole of humanity, outside humanity as such, humanity not considered as a collection of definite individuals belonging to definite cultures at particular times, but humanity as some abstract and timeless universal. What is proposed as standing opposite such an abstract and timeless, abstract and universal "humanity" will necessarily be an equally timeless and abstract set of "constraints" and "forces." What we can't understand is how such abstractions are meant to act on one another, or what either of them have to do with actual concrete individual human beings, nor can we see how they are meant to produce actual recorded history. What we can't understand is what role they are meant to have in the understanding of anything.

Every definite, historical culture faces constraints that are not of its own choosing, but it is not helpful to imagine these as something entirely separate, external, abstract and timeless, something in fact transcendental and lying outside their world and its history. To picture the constraints in that way is to mystify them entirely. We can give no intelligible account of the existence, the nature or the manner of operation of those transcendental abstractions that are pictured as separate from the human world and separate for all eternity. How would such abstracted and separated things carry out their constraining and affect our choices?

We can make sense of those constraints if we drop that picture of them. "The many" and "the wise" of any culture are made up of concrete individuals who have grown up within the culture and are constrained by its history, its historically developed language, its accumulation of skills and artifacts, its social structures and ways of looking, its moral formation, its traditions and its devotion to those traditions, or its ability to accept change, and the pressures of environment which may call for change.

And in our own time we have to see that perhaps the most important feature of the environment of any culture will be the possibility of the destructive intrusion of another powerful and dominating culture that can change the landscape of its life overnight, turning peasants, for example, into wage workers supplying the needs of the developed world and hankering after its "goods," while at the same time turning the culture's artifacts and sacred relics into commodities and emptying its rituals of sense.

Those are actual and concrete constraints that can be identified and located, not in the sky, where they become mysterious, but in the concrete historical situation of a people, where they can be understood. And we can see too how the world-views, the institutions and the ways of talking are a part of the way a culture interacts with its environment. In part they collectively define and limit the world of the people of that culture, but not in a way that precludes modification of language, world-view, institutions and way of life through the interaction of all those elements.

And if we start there amongst those concrete and identifiable constraints, we can make sense of the notions of progress and development without being entangled in the unintelligible picture of progress as an approach to some "goal" which, because it is ideal and transcendental, is neither attainable nor, if we think about it carefully, even approachable. (That notion of progress gets analyzed more fully in chapter 11, "On Misunderstanding Science.")

Once they are defined out of reach as absolutes and transcendentals, notions such as "reality" and "truth" can no longer even define a direction. They can be made to look as though they define a direction only by appeal to the sort of analogical reasoning that theology uses to "reach out to" God. But in a secular context, this appeal merely misleads us because those idealized notions are in fact being characterized by just that already sensed direction which they are pretending to characterize and define. These matters are discussed in several places in what follows, again, particularly in chapter 11.

But our present purposes are understanding the particular role of "the many" and "the wise" in the Aristotelian dialectic as a good starting point for a discussion of any topic, a starting point that is in no way privileged and a foundation but is subject to correction, modification and improvement. The important point that we have to hold on to is that we can make sense of those notions of *improvement* and *correction* without the attempt to appeal to transcendental, eternal and separated "ideals."

It is in this sense, and for this language-forming reason, that the views of "the many" and "the wise" cannot be rejected out of hand. But this is not to say that they may not be modified, as a language may be modified, and a culture may develop. Modifications need not come only from large historical changes in the culture and its practices, but may come even from the kind of critical analysis that a philosopher might undertake. Aristotle forged a vocabulary that reflected, but at the same time modified, ways of talking current in his time, and that vocabulary of "substance," "nature," "cause,," "matter," "axiom," and many other terms has had its influence down to the present, even (unfortunately) in the inverted and mystified versions that were set before us in the seventeenth century.

In the case we have just been looking at, the word *archē* ("beginning" or "starting point") in this context means for Aristotle "the place where *we* begin" in our investigations or the place where our analysis ends. His *archē* is not an "absolute foundation" taken as "the place where all things begin" or all knowledge begins, the absolute origin of existence or of knowledge. The latter was the sort of starting point that was being sought by the rationalists and the empiricists. That notion of an "absolute foundation" or starting point is a theological notion, one that necessarily reaches outside the world and all that is in it.[2] Only something that is essentially transcendental and mysterious, and not to be known with secular knowledge, will fill that particular bill. And this

is my justification for using the word "mystified" to describe the fate
that overtook the Aristotelian vocabulary in the seventeenth century.

In more than one place below I discuss the mystification of the
notion of *Nature* in the seventeenth century through the theological
role that was given to it then. That theological role was explicitly recognized by Spinoza in his repeated phrase *Deus sive natura.* Some of
Spinoza's contemporaries saw the equation of God and Nature in the
opposite sense, as bringing God within the world rather than as
exporting Nature out of it, and branded him a "pantheist." But it is
pretty clear that the role that was given to the notion of *Nature* at that
time had the effect of projecting it out of the world, making it into a
mysterious, quasi-theological entity that stood "over and above" the
world. The talk of "Nature's laws" gives us that. These were thought of
as "absolute and inviolable" and not subject to the change and development that characterize the things of this world.[3] And that metaphor
of "laws" suggests a separation of "governor" and "governed" that
places the governor outside the world, as Christian theology had God
standing outside the world and governing according to His Plan. That
mystified, theologized notion of "Nature" and its metaphorical "laws"
has caused its share of confusion down the centuries.

Perhaps one further sketched example of what I would describe as
"mystification" will be helpful not only in understanding what I mean by
that term but in seeing what I have been trying to do in the discussions
that follow, by way of "demystifying" a number of notions. Another
notion that got mystified in the seventeenth century as the result of
being given transcendental or theological work to do is that of *substance.*

Aristotle had forged the notion as part of an attempt to provide a
perspicuous vocabulary to give order to our talk about change, among
other things, and the distinction that we make between change and
destruction. Where there was change and not destruction and disappearance it had to be possible to identify something that changed and
therefore something that could be identified through and after the
change and to which the change could be attributed.

In his proposed vocabulary there were, firstly, substances, the particular things that underwent change: this horse that got trained, that
schedule that got changed, the house that got enlarged, the child who
grew up, the city that was bombed and rebuilt. (Though Carthage was
destroyed, ploughed up and the site sown with salt, and so it disappeared.)

In contrast to this, there were the aspects of the thing which
changed. These simply disappeared and were replaced: the wildness of
the horse, the chaos or injustice of the schedule, the immaturity of the

child, the uninhabitable desolation of the bombed city that disappeared with rebuilding.

This prompted a distinction between the enduring thing that changes and the attributes which have no separate existence from the thing to which they were attributed and whose disappearance and replacement constitutes the change. Attributes (this temperature, that shade of green, the sweetness) disappear absolutely with the change. That to which they are attributed is something on which they are dependent for their existence, something which, by contrast, has an existence that is independent of the attribute. ("'Well! I've often seen a cat without a grin,' thought Alice; 'but a grin without a cat!'") Despite Lewis Carroll's fancy, and Alice's dream, when the cat leaves off smiling, there is no smile left to leave behind.

But the independence of the cat from the attribute of smiling is not an absolute independence of the kind that was being sought by the new seventeenth-century philosophers (the "Reformers," Leibniz called them). It is certainly true that Aristotle made it a mark of being a substance that anything identified as a substance could not be attributed to anything else. A substance was in some sense "primary." But an Aristotelian substance was primary only in relation to its attributes. Its primacy was not absolute. He was pointing out that those attributes depended for their existence on the substance to which they were attributed. The cat's grin required the cat and could not be parted from it. The grin could not be transferred to another cat, or to a crocodile or a human. Only in a joke or in a fanciful manner of speaking could we talk about the grin passing to another face.

So the substance (the cat) is independent of the attribute (the grin) and the attribute dependent. If we stick to the Aristotelian usage that applies the word "substance" to the myriad of individual things that can be identified through a change of attributes, we shall stay on firm ground with a useful and intelligible vocabulary. But the seventeenth-century philosophers (for reasons I try to make out in chapter 14) had another project to which they wanted to recruit the notion of *substance*. That was the project of finding foundations, and absolute ones. They were not content with trying to find a perspicuous vocabulary with which to talk about the things of this world. They wanted to talk about this world *as a whole*, to find the basis of the whole, its origins, the stuff of which *everything* was made, to find the beginnings of *everything*. (The belief which some cosmologists have that this is a sensible project, and a scientific one into the bargain, gets discussed later.)

My claim is that this is essentially and necessarily a theological project (taking the word "theological" as being used to refer to what lies outside the world as a whole, to the transcendent.) I argue in chapter 4 that the attempt to talk about "the world as a whole" is already to engage in a theological project, that the notion of a *whole* makes sense only from a position outside. In addition, I would go on to say that it is the recruitment to this essentially theological project of the search for absolutes that has mystified the once useful Aristotelian vocabulary of "cause," "substance," "matter," "nature," and the rest.

Let's return briefly to the mystification of the notion of "substance." It was, of course, that relation of independence and dependence that made the ,substance/attribute, distinction a natural target for takeover and incorporation into the new project of finding absolute foundations. To receive that role of absolute foundation for existence, however, "substance" had to be wrenched loose from the reference to the ordinary, the particular and the concrete that it had with Aristotle. With him, to say that the cat is independent of the grin is to say no more than that the cat need not be grinning, that grinning is not part of our way of identifying the cat. And to say that the grin is not independent of the cat is to say no more than that this cat's grin cannot be transferred to some other cat, that we cannot identify the grin through the fanciful "transfer" in the way that we can identify the cat through its change from grinning to scowling. There is nothing mysterious in all that. But we have to be clear that the cat, as a substance, is not an absolutely independent being. The cat has come into being and is continually dependent on air and water and food, on not being run over or thrown into the lake. That sort of "substance" would hardly answer the requirements of the new project.

To use the term "substance" for the new purposes, it had to be made into a purely abstract notion identified by that relation of dependence and independence alone. And the "substance/attribute" distinction had to be abstracted and detached from the context of change and the understanding of change in which it had been forged and from which it drew its sense. It had to be taken, that is, out of the context in which it was meant to function and had its point. The new conception could not be allowed, like the Aristotelian notion, to refer to concrete individuals identifiable through change. Those concrete changing individuals could hardly fulfil the role the seventeenth-century philosophers had in mind for "substance," namely, that of underpinning the whole of existence.

It is important to take note of the fact that the role of underpinning the whole of existence was one that had in scholastic theology been reserved to God.[4]

In this transformation, the notion of *substance* shared the fate of the notion of *nature*, which had also been transformed and made to take over another role that the scholastics had assigned to God, that of external source of order and development in the world. Needless to say, Aristotle never talked of any such external source of order or change. His concept of *nature* was of something internal to the individual changing thing (internal to it, however, only as belonging to some particular species). But of course, Aristotle was not trying to answer theological questions with his notion of *nature*.

The scholastics, on the other hand, *were* asking theological questions, questions about an external and transcendent source of the order that we seem to find in the world. The new philosophers of the seventeenth century took on board the scholastic question and felt that it had to be answered, but answered in a new way that took it out of the hands of the theologians and the scholastics. They thought that by offering the name "Nature" in answer to that question about an external source of order, they were secularizing the question and handing it over to study by the sciences that were just then emerging.

But that move was capable neither of secularizing the question about an external source of order nor of handing that question over to the scientists for study. The sciences have no means of studying what is "external to the world," and they have no means of studying how that proposed external source of order is meant to operate, how it is supposed to bring about the order within the world, of which it is being offered as the source and the "explanation." As I suggest later in the book, any scientist who proposed studying the means by which nature or its "laws" enforced an order on the world would soon find themselves shown the door (perhaps one they couldn't open from the inside). We are dealing with a picture only, a metaphor, and not with a genuine explanation. In so far as this has not been understood, the notion of *nature* has simply been mystified, given a role it cannot play and status it cannot have. (More is said about this in chapter 12.)

The discussions that make up this book have three chief aims: one is the demystification of that vocabulary which was transformed and mystified in the seventeenth century. The second is to try to understand how those notions came to be mystified in the first place, what the project was that forced impossible roles onto them. Finally, and most controversially, the aim is to try to see historically how that project came to seem possible, sensible and necessary to the founding fathers of modern philosophy.

I have done what I can to avoid or to explain technicalities so that the discussions will be available to non-specialists who are willing to put in the work to follow their arguments. The view of philosophy that informs this work is that philosophy is not a specialist subject separated off from life and history. On the contrary, its conceptions and its problems have historical roots and historical consequences that are the concern of us all and affect our ability to think clearly about the world around us.

1   Understanding nonsense

I would like in this first chapter to articulate the conception of philosophy that runs through this book. It is a conception that owes much to Wittgenstein on the one hand and to Aristotle on the other. From Wittgenstein comes chiefly the idea that philosophy has no subject matter, nothing that it studies and seeks to describe and to theorize, the idea that the business of philosophy is with clarity and not with truth of some special kind such as Descartes sought with his method and persuaded following generations to seek. Wittgenstein's conception of the task of philosophy brings to the center the notions of *sense* and *nonsense* that assume the kind of importance that *truth* and *falsehood* had for Descartes's conception of philosophy as theorizing and seeking a higher order of truth.

To see Aristotle's contribution to this conception and its connection with Wittgenstein's, let's begin with the distinction of inexhaustible usefulness that Aristotle makes between the *exo logos* (the "outer words"), the words of a person's mouth, and the *eso logos*, the "inner words" that represent what someone really assents to, the genuine beliefs to which that person is commited, words that are connected to their life and implicit in their acts. There are, Aristotle says, things which someone may seem to affirm or deny with the mouth, but which cannot be made their *eso logos,* cannot be *lived.* And we all know too well the sort of public-bar philosophers (and some professionals) who put forward propositions purely for the nuisance value they may have, without at all believing in them.[1] Wittgenstein makes a similar point in the *Remarks on the Foundations of Mathematics* (I, §116): "And there is even something in saying: he can't *think* it. One is trying e.g. to say: he can't fill it with personal content; he can't really *go along with it* – personally, with his intelligence." Wittgenstein might have added "He can't *act on it* or *live* it."

I make my own use of that distinction between *exo* and *eso logos* later in the discussion of the notion of "artificial" or "mechanical" *intelligence* in chapter 5, "How to Tell Your Friends from Machines." The suggestion there is that the professions of belief in the possibility of mechanical or artificial intelligence are mere *exo logos*, mouthed words, and that the demeanor required by a serious belief in the intelligence of a machine would amount to madness. The same madness would be evidenced by Descartes's "hyperbolical doubts" if they were serious beliefs and not mere words of the mouth, and Descartes is aware of that. It prompts his "dreaming" argument as a defense against accusations that his cerebellum may be "clouded by black bile." It also prompts his requiring of us a fatal separation between thought and action, a requirement that empties each of those two notions of any content, and has caused such confusion in philosophy. Chapter 7, "Skepticism about Skepticism," also puts that distinction to use in examining what I regard as the emptiness of the "hyperbolical" doubt and the counter-productiveness of the "method" of pseudo-doubting that Descartes recommends.

Aristotle makes a crucial use of that distinction between "mouthed" words with nothing behind them and words expressive of genuine beliefs in the very special sort of argument he brings against those, like Cratylus and the Heracleiteans, who profess to deny what he regards as the deepest principles of all – the law of contradiction and the law of the excluded middle. That form of argument he calls *apodeixai elentikos* (roughly: "argument by cross-examination"), and it is concerned to show that the professed denials are only mouthed words, *exo logos*, and *cannot* be *eso logos*. That is, it aims to show that the words cannot represent the genuine beliefs of those out of whose mouths the words are coming. The nature of the "cannot" is here crucial and shows Aristotle's philosophy and conception of philosophy to be something quite different from those of Plato and utterly apart from Descartes's conception and method. That is, the "cannot" that stands between the words of the profession and genuine belief is not a "logical" or "conceptual" *cannot* of the sort that Descartes or his modern followers might look for and require. Not at all. And the form of the argument here is one that most moderns cannot understand, steeped as they are in the method of Descartes and the requirement of demonstration of a logical or conceptual impossibility as the only type of impossibility that they will recognize as relevant to philosophy.

The "cannot" that Aristotle aims to bring out is a practical one, not a logical or conceptual one. The person who professes to deny the law of contradiction and the law of the excluded middle cannot put that profession into practice. In the first place, the denial and offering it as having sense already rests on and involves the law. Even those who pretend to give it up and make a pretense of avoiding statement and judgment – Cratylus sitting and wagging his finger and (later) Carneades being led about by the slave boy – have not succeeded in "acting out" their professions of disbelief in the axioms. Aristotle says of the demeanor that would be bound up with a genuine denial of those laws that such a person would be "no better than a vegetable."

Most people pass over this rapidly, thinking perhaps that Aristotle has lapsed into invective, having run out of argument. But that is not it at all. He has shown by argument and analysis what behavior would be required of someone to show that the mouthed words of denial represented a genuine denial of the law of contradiction and were not empty mouthings with nothing behind them. But these words of denial *are* empty. They have no life or sense. They do not connect with anything or indicate anything. They might as well be nonsense words. They only imitate real speech with content.

There is a view here that is utterly opposed to and subversive of Descartes's method of "hyperbolical" doubt. As I try to bring out in chapter 7, Descartes is enjoining us in his method to work exclusively in philosophizing with *exo logos*, with empty mouthings that are not to connect with real belief or action. The "doubt" is empty and the "method" can do no real work. There is in Aristotle's argument a view also of how words get sense and substance and a suggestion of one way in which they may lack it.

But here we are beginning to define two deeply opposed views of philosophy. Before we go on to develop and examine the differences we need to stop, notice and inscribe in stone the fact that, when he comes to his most basic principles, Aristotle does not argue for their *truth*, or suggest an external or eternal source for them. His argument is that those principles cannot be meaningfully denied by actual humans – that is, no one can put meaning into the words of a denial; those words could not be given sense, be connected to anything, be made part of life, could not rise above the status of mere sounds, could not *say* anything.[2]

MAKING SENSE OF NONSENSE

On one view of philosophy, the notions of *sense* and *nonsense* lie at its heart. That is, those notions are implicated in its tasks, its methods and the resources it can call on. On that view of philosophy its main business could be described as "getting a clear view of what we know already," what we know in one way but can't grasp well or express clearly. On that view the business of philosophy is not with theories or discoveries but with clarifications. Even the Greek word that nowadays invariably and inevitably gets translated as "truth," the word *aletheia*, seems to concur with this view in its root sense of "waking up." That picture tempts us less to "theories" of truth of whatever kind, correspondence, coherence, or other.

But the determined will find the material for theorizing anywhere, and so we have Plato inverting the old mythical picture of the passage through the river Lethe after death and in his theory of *anamnesis* interposing the river Lethe, the river of oblivion, between a posited preexistence with a direct knowledge of the Forms and a present in which we have lost and have to recover that knowledge. That is his "theory" to account for the sense that we have of the things that we know in some way or other but can't quite grasp or "put into words." Of course, no one takes it seriously as a philosophical theory, and philosophers hardly set about looking for other evidence for that preexisting state of clarity and understanding that was wiped away by the trauma of passage into this world. The closest that the modern world has come to Plato's theory is in positing something called "innate ideas" which have been variously thought of as having been implanted in the newborn or the pre-born by God or by nature.

We have no business at the moment with the question whether the theory of innate ideas advances things at all or leaves us where we were.[3] All we want is to notice that both it and Plato's theory of *anamnesis* at least testify to the sense we have of things that we know in one way, but cannot quite grasp, or grasp clearly enough to express or explain. That leaves it open to us to suggest that the business of philosophy is in bringing out, clarifying and elucidating those things that are imperfectly grasped. That is one task. Another quite distinct task is accounting for the existence of those things which are glimpsed or sensed but not grasped. The theories of *anamnesis* and *innate ideas* both have this aim. Both are called theories, but Plato's might be better described as a "picture." No one would take it seriously as a "theory" or regard it as telling us more than we knew at the outset. It is a picture only, a way of arranging what we know. But the arrangement is such as to send us off in the wrong direction.

I shall give notice here of my own view that the things that we have a sense of but have difficulty making explicit and expressing clearly do not lie in some "other realm" (as the Forms were supposed to), or constitute some "ultimate reality" that is always beyond grasp, but are implicit in practices we engage in – either individually or as a group or as a whole culture. I see them as at hand, as embodied in practices and not "out of this world" in some other realm. But teasing out those embodied principles and describing the rule implicit in a practice is a task that may be full of difficulty, and we may make mistakes enough. But I only give notice of that view. I am not going to develop it here or rely on it. It can lie in the background of the discussion of the notion of *nonsense* and the discussion of the importance, the centrality of that notion on one view of the nature of philosophical investigations.

There are, in effect, two rival conceptions of philosophy: one that aims to set out theories and theses and makes *truth* and *falsehood* as its guide and test. It regards itself as seeking after a special sort of truth. The other conception of philosophy turns on a *sense/nonsense* axis and takes *clarity* as its aim together with the exhibiting of the emptiness of certain notions or claims the unmasking of nonsense.

Descartes held to the first conception and offered us his method of "hyperbolical doubt" for use in "contemplating the truth." I see Aristotle and Wittgenstein as regarding philosophy and practising it in the second way. In Aristotle's case, that comes out of a careful examination of the nature and role of the *apodeixis elentikos* form of argument which he uses to prove (i.e. "test") his basic principles. Those arguments are not abstract ones as Descartes's doubts are, but are addressed to a definite respondent (anyone who professes to deny the laws). More importantly, those arguments don't aim to establish the "truth" of the laws. The *apodeixis elentikos* arguments aim only to show that the laws are implicated in practices that the respondent engages in and has no intention of giving up – *could not* give up without abdicating their humanity and becoming "like a vegetable."

As I point out in chapter 2, "Following and Formalization," it does not even make sense to talk of someone "giving up" their rationality to become like a vegetable ("catatonic," if you like). That would be mere play-acting. *Losing* one's rationality would be another matter. If I were to lose my rationality, that would not be an act or choice of mine, as the attempt or pretense of relinquishing or repudiating my rationality would be. As an *act* of mine the attempt and pretense of giving up rationality would be issuing from, connected to and evidence of my rationality. And so my would-be "repudiation" would be only show. Cratylus, Carneades and the others were, of course, merely play-acting. There was no more reality and meaning in their actions than in their words.

There are correspondences and resonances between Aristotle's form of argument here and Wittgenstein's suggestion that the only givens are "forms of life." One could put it that Aristotle's argument is that those two basic principles are bound up with one's humanity itself, with that form of life called "rationality." Those axioms are not "given" in any other way – by God, by nature, by the "structure of the world." They are simply constituents of that rationality which itself constitutes our humanity.

Now I want to turn attention to the notion of *nonsense* itself, because, though I have cast it in the role of an essential tool for philosophy, the notion throws up a variety of difficult problems and itself needs clarification. No doubt clarifying the notion of *nonsense* will involve clarifying the notion of *sense* as well.

The question we can start with is: is nonsense simply the absence of sense? Or is it something positive (so to speak)? One way of taking that question is as asking whether the notion of *nonsense* involves an *illogical thought*, something *unthinkable* or merely *no thought*, that is, a failure to give sense to an expression. An associated question is: how is it possible to embrace, propound or believe nonsense? Seemingly this happens all the time, and that raises the problem of how to describe what is going on when someone professes, or professes to believe, or believes they believe, something which we see, or come to see, is nonsense. Great passion may be involved in the profession and great resistance made to anyone's attempts to show that the embrace is an embrace of air and sound and nothing more.

A young poet I once knew (she was six) made a poem that went:

Words are whispers and whistles
And all made out of air
With something else hard in them
That makes them be.

We are concerned with that "something else hard" – how it gets to be there, how it fails to be there and leaves nothing but air and whistles.

On the question of whether nonsense is a simple absence of sense or a kind of "counter-sense," Cora Diamond takes a firm position: "Anything that is nonsense is so merely because some determination of meaning has *not* been made; it is not nonsense as the logical result of determinations that *have* been made."[4] There are echoes in that of Wittgenstein's description in *Tractatus* 6.53 of the correct method in philosophy as involving showing someone who "wanted to say something metaphysical . . . that he had failed to give a meaning to certain signs in his propositions." And she links it with the powerful remark of Wittgenstein's that: "after all, it is not the *sense* that is *senseless*." (That would be nonsense, indeed!)

Still, it is not clear what the nature and source of the failure is when someone fails to give sense to an expression. Perhaps the person simply didn't try. A new word was introduced and no attempt made to define it. Edward Lear's adjective "runcible" applied to the spoon with which the owl and the pussycat ate their mince and slices of quince (applied later by Eliot to his hat) is like that: a mellifluous emptiness. No attempt was made to give it content. And no one takes it as having any. That is precisely its point.

Sometimes empty but impressive expressions have a less innocent use. In the mouths of ideologues, demagogues, con-men and salesmen they may be given the job of confusing and manipulating an individual or an audience, firing up a crowd or swaying a vote. Real sense is not needed, wanted or attempted. Drafters of reports, agreements or treaties may sometimes search hard for phrases with no more than the appearance of meaning so that parties with irreconcilable interests or views will each think they have been given what they want, or at least the signatories will be able to use the empty expression to persuade their supporters they have been given what they want.

The nonsense with which philosophers have to contend is generally not like that. Expressions are used, explanations given, doctrines set out in the belief that they have sense and advance things when in fact they do not. On the one hand, we have to try to understand the belief in their meaningfulness, which may be obsessive, even fanatical; on the other hand, we have to say something about the sources of the emptiness (if that is not too paradoxical a way of putting it). What is the nature of the failure of sense, and the reason for it, when the person or group clearly intends it to have sense and thinks it does?

And then there is the threat to the whole notion of *nonsense* posed by what has been dubbed the "conference theory of meaning" by those who take it to be itself a piece of nonsense. That theory takes its stand on Wittgenstein's phrase "the game is played," a phrase meant to indicate the place where explanations come to an end. One can't ask for explanations of all the rules. The gloss put on that by the "conference theory" is that the most one can ask of an expression is that it be used in a uniform way by some group. In the particular case that earned it that title, it was suggested that because certain expressions were used regularly and in a regular way at philosophical conferences, that was enough to give them a meaning. The notion of *nonsense* seems to have no place in that theory.

It would be easy enough to jump up and down and shout "Relativism!" at the "conference theory," but I don't think that would advance things much. That charge itself is one of those empty "smear words" that are of great use to those who want to avoid the hard work of careful analysis. The "conference theory" may have something fatuous about it; however, it does pose some interesting questions, and we would lose something by ignoring them. The "conference theory" is a sort of analogue for *meaning* of the "coherence theory of truth" and has some of the same attractions – "seductions" if you prefer. Taken seriously, it leads to serious questions about meaning and, with luck, important insights.

Take its connection with Quine's view that the unit of meaning is a whole language. The "conference theory" shares with Quine the view that words and even propositions get the meaning they have from being embedded in a whole system of practices and uses, the sort of system that we call a language. (Quine might prefer to talk of "rules" and "principles" and not of "practices" and "uses," as I have done. Of that, more later.) What the "conference theory" shies away from is Quine's talk of the "meaning" of a language as a whole.

What can be meant by that talk of Quine's is in any case hard to see. Even to put such a question about the "meaning of a whole language," to take it as having sense, is to generate a temptation to call up a dummy referent with the name "Reality" tagged onto it. But the expression "reality" functions much like a variable in quantificational logic. It is a place-holder and nothing more. It can have no content. And one cannot ask for the meaning or reference of that expression without starting to turn in a circle of not large dimensions. This leaves us with the question of the motivation for wanting to take a whole language as "the unit of meaning" when we can make no sense of the phrase "the meaning of a language."

Quine comes to his view by an expansion of Frege's "context principle": "Never to ask for the meaning of a word in isolation, but only in the context of a proposition." It was Wittgenstein who first turned that commandment from a procedural principle and guide into a substantive claim about meaning. In *Tractatus* 3.3 and 3.314, he says that "An expression has meaning only in a proposition." And it is really this substantive claim that Quine has expanded, though it would be possible to see the expansion as already implicit in Wittgenstein's dark saying at 3.311: "An expression presupposes the forms of all the propositions in which it can occur. It is the common characteristic mark of a class of propositions."

In any case, the unexpanded and unadorned claim that an expression has meaning only in the context of a proposition puts us into a difficulty: how can those severally meaningless bits come to constitute a context, a meaningful whole that bestows meaning on the parts? They must have *something* that they bring with them to the whole. They can't be complete blanks, for blank + blank = blank. We need something like those "presupposed forms of all the propositions in which the expression can occur" to rescue us here. Something like them, perhaps, but what are they? What can we mean by a "presupposed form?"

So long as we picture language as an abstract system that is approached by humanity and used by humans as something external to humanity, preexisting and formed, we are going to be in difficulties. But if we accept and make use of the fact that language is a human historical product, that perhaps human history and the history of language are co-terminous, then there may be a way out. Still, we have to give some account of that externality of language we all feel and submit to, and which is essential to our individual use of language if it is not to be idiot babbling with no form.

The language of a people may be bound up with the existence of that people and not something external to it that it came upon, but clearly it is external to any individual. By being born among that people, into that linguistic community, the individual comes on the language as something preexisting and formed all right. Though, we should add, not fixed and formed forever. An individual might even contribute to its formation and further development, perhaps deeply and importantly at certain historical moments – as Chaucer, Tyndall, or Shakespeare did for English, Luther for German, Homer for Greek and other literary figures on a historical scale have done for the language of their culture.

"But," say those who want to theorize about language, "we don't want to talk about particular languages like English, Chippewa or Pushtu; we want to talk about *language itself.*" The reply to that is, "There is no such thing and we can't talk about it." If we want to talk about language itself, the notion of *language,* we are going to have to do so through talking about particular, historical, human languages, languages that came into being, have been modified and may disappear. There are no others. There are no languages in the abstract, external to humanity, and no existing thing called *language itself* ranged up there with Plato's Forms, known by the faltering memory of a previous existence.

And we have to keep before our minds the fact that the existing languages exist and are kept in being by the practices of a linguistic community. Without that community and its practices, the language becomes a "dead" one. It may be recorded in a literature and have a kind of existence, one that depends on present understanding of that literature. Where there is no literature or record that can be the basis of a secondary practice and the language is known by rumor and report only, the language will have ceased to exist along with the linguistic community that gave it being.

Where there is enough of a record it may be possible to set about trying to reestablish a language as a living one and to create a linguistic community to give it life – as people have tried to do with Cornish. But that linguistic community of Cornish speakers will tend to be something of an artifact, a bit like a club, because the lives of the people who make it up are more deeply shaped by their membership in a more inclusive and dominating social formation whose language is English. The revived Cornish will be riddled with borrowings to make it capable of dealing with that larger world in which the speakers are embedded. They will find it impossible to secede completely to reestablish the form of life that existed when Cornish was a living language. The revived language will in part be a coded form of English because the society of the speakers will not have a separate dynamic that could give the basis for a language truly separate from that of the embedding society.

The aim of this elaborated detour has been to bring into prominence the dependence amounting to an equivalence between a language and the practices of a linguistic community, and to give some understanding of the sense in which the language is external to each of us without being external to all (where that "all" is to be taken historically and diachronically, sweeping up all the speakers throughout history). Seeing language, any language, as based on concrete practices of a definite period and people, rather than as an abstract system of rules embodied nowhere, will help us to deal with some of the problems we have been facing. To find our way through those problems and make sense of the notion of *nonsense* we shall have to come down from the sky, where there are no languages, to the ground where people and their languages actually live and work.

But we first have to face an objection that might be made in the name of Frege, an objection that in making the practices of people the heart and basis of language we are going against one of his founding principles: "Always to separate sharply the psychological from the logical, the subjective from the objective." This objection helps us to make an important point about the notion of a *practice*, namely, that a practice is public and social in character, and in that way, objective and external to the individual, something that the individual meets and is trained in or inducted into. It is the reverse of the private, internal, subjective or idiosyncratic. The practice as public, social, objective, and external is in fact a *condition* of the private, internal, subjective or idiosyncratic, what I suppose Frege meant by "the psychological."

But we shall have to say more about the dependence of the private and subjective on the social and objective because the opposite has been almost an article of faith in the modern era. The conception of the task of philosophy that has dominated our era is that we have to start with the individual and work outwards. This picture has got things backwards, and defining the tasks of philosophy in terms of it has sent philosophers off on impossible quests. What we really have to understand is the historical evolution of the possibility of individuality, the distillation of the individual out of what Marx describes as the "herd existence" of our early pre-tribal ancestors. That is the actual historical problem. The contrary assumption of primal individualism is part of what is no more than a picture or model, a picture whose function and use is not very clear.[5]

There are, of course, individual and idiosyncratic habits, and practices which are perhaps practiced by one person only. Out of the materials provided by the practices of my culture and society I can construct a practice and rule that may in fact be adhered to by no one else – say, never to greet anyone whose name contains a "th" until they have greeted me. But that can be a rule for me, a rule that is something objective against which I can measure my practice only where there is a social and objective practice I can appeal to in making up the rule and in following it, a practice that I have been inducted into.

Because of the strength of our era's characteristic determination to make the individual the base and material, and the social the construct and product, there have been attempts to show how a rule could be given objectivity and made an objective measure of the practice of an individual in the complete absence of social practices external to the individual. These attempts invariably appeal to the objectivity of "nature" and of "natural" regularities. (I have some things to say about these attempts in chapter 9, "Language and the Society of Others." There is much more to be said about the notion of *nature* as the would-be paradigm of the external and the objective.) What we need to notice is that the attempt to make a natural regularity into an objective measure or test of the regularity of a practice *requires* a regularity of practice (the practice of testing). It does not create one.

Here we are facing the great gulf that is riven between the natural and the social, a gulf that has generated a fascination and almost scenic awe since the seventeenth century and sent philosophers off on quests for a bridge and a moment of transition. These quests always end in myth: the Social Contract, the Original Position and suchlike. That they run out into myth should make us suspicious of the question and the enterprise.

However fascinating these matters are and however necessary it is in the end to deal with them, they are drawing us away from our primary concern with the notion of *nonsense* and with the problems that arose about it.

With a cool head and a firm grip on the rootedness of a language in the practices of a people and the connection between the meaning of its words and their role in those practices, we may be able to steer a safe course through the difficulties and even draw on what is useful in the "conference theory" and in Quine without being stuck with trying to make sense of the notion of the *meaning* of a whole language. Before we could even begin to make sense of that notion, we would have to settle some questions about the meaning of the word "whole" in the phrase "whole language," because it is not so clear as might be thought just how any real language does form a whole.

This has not struck many philosophers as a problem because they have operated with a conception of language that has come from a project and a program rather than the consideration of any actual language. The program was that of constructing an "ideal language," a program that has never emerged from its comfortable programmatic chrysalis to be carried through and realized, for the simple reason that it is unrealizable. Whatever those philosophers might construct that had the logical unity they aimed for would not be a language, could not be the language of any living people. Even as an "ideal" it would have been something more like an attempt at a comprehensive unified theory or description of the physical world of the sciences rather than anything that could be called a "language." A language does not of itself "describe the world" or even attempt to. People use a language in the enterprise of living in a world and in the process develop their own descriptive terms which help define their world for them.

In taking up this question about the "wholeness" of a language, the first thing to notice is the "motley" of those practices that give sense to the words of any actual language. They do not form a seamless whole. On the contrary, the vocabularies of many of those practices are "incommensurable" – to use Kuhn's invaluable term. They cannot be translated into one another. We cannot translate the vocabulary of musical counterpoint and harmony into that of quantum electrodynamics or *vice versa*. There is no point of contact. However, that may not prevent us using the vocabulary of one field or practice in a poetic, allusive and metaphorical way to illuminate the other. But we shall only get into trouble and risk nonsense if we mistake that metaphorical use for the literal. We can then be led to ask of a picture questions that are alien to its purpose and function, like someone trying to determine distances between the stops by measuring on a London Underground map. That is not the function of such maps, and they can't be used that way.

To take a different example: the great and sad mistake of the "creationists" is that they can't see that religious understanding and scientific explanation are two incompatible enterprises with different functions in human life and incommensurable vocabularies. In trying to get a share of the prestige of science for the Bible, they only succeed in debasing the Bible and emptying it of all richness and depth. As a scientific explanation the Bible story is not up to much and would soon be knocked out of contention if anyone took it as a serious contender in that field. The value of the Bible is quite other and is not to be measured in that way. The creationists have been seduced by the grand ideological claim that has been hung round the neck of the sciences – that they give the only correct and true view of things. Even the author of the *Tractatus* seems, at first sight anyway, to give voice to that view in identifying "what can be said" with "the propositions of natural science."

In any case there has been from the early days of the modern era a view and a hope and a project to make a seamless whole out of language, largely on the basis of a vocabulary provided by the sciences (seen as the purveyors of the truth of things). It is this Grail and philosopher's stone that Quine is talking about in saying that the unit of meaning is "a whole language." No actual language forms a whole of that kind, and the seamless "ideal language" pursued so vigorously by many philosophers could not be the language in which any living people conducted their lives. Could not, that is, be an actual language. For all its elusiveness, the Holy Grail of Arthurian legend had some claim to historical actuality as the cup used at the Last Supper. The elusiveness of the "ideal language" lies in the fact that it could never be an actual language used by real people to conduct their life. It has never been, and can never be, more than a shimmering myth on the philosophical horizon.

Any language used by real people for the conduct of life in a developed society will contain a tumbling welter of vocabularies that are incommensurable, not reducible or mutually translatable. Their sense and force will come from practices, activities, and projects that are not aimed at the same thing or measurable on the same scale. Those activities and their vocabularies may be political, legal, religious, medical, literary, artistic, historical, scientific, sporting or commercial, together with all the subdivisions of human activity of a complex society, including the various crafts, skills and trades, and many etceteras. Many of these forms of activity may have within them a range of rival practices and outlooks each of which involves a vocabulary that is incompatible with the others. But here we are getting into an incompatibility of a different sort, because these practices may actually be *rival.* That is, the practices may be competing for more or less the same ground and the practitioners may regard the vocabulary of the rivals as meaningless and the practice fraudulent. Neo-liberal political theorists may so regard the vocabulary of Marxist theorists, or conventional medical practitioners may so regard the vocabulary of homeopathy.

There is no such rivalry between the vocabulary of a legal system and its practice and that of medicine, politics or sport. And yet they are incommensurable and not mutually translatable.[6] Because the sense of those different vocabularies arises out of and is rooted in the separate practices of say, bee keeping and water skiing, there is no more logical relation between them than there is between those practices themselves. Those practices may be in competition for our time and our commitment, but that is about their only relation. One of those vocabularies is not "more accurate," "more comprehensive," or "deeper" than the other – any more than the activities themselves.

Here we come face to face with the "conference theory of meaning," seeming to have sold it a whole defensive armory which would allow it to claim philosophy conferences or philosophy publication as an activity that gives sense to a certain vocabulary.

"The game is played," said Wittgenstein, and set us up for some misunderstanding. What we have to ask is not whether the vocabulary has sense within the conference regarded as a self-contained activity, a "game." We have to ask, rather, what the place of that "game" is in our life. Considering it simply as a game, we can't criticize its conduct or ask for the meaning of its terms. But philosophy is not – had better not be – a self-contained activity of that sort. That would make it into a type of recreation, a sort of intellectual Scrabble.[7]

And this pushes us back to the question with which we started about the point and function of philosophy. Is it clarity and the elimination of nonsense and confusion? Or is it the pursuit of some special kind of truth as the Cartesian/Platonic tradition holds? The first view, which I hold to, still owes us an account of nonsense. Though now, maybe we are in a better position to give it.

We have to insist on and keep in mind two things: one is the dependence of the sense of an expression on a practice in which it is embedded and within which it has a role. The words "tort" or "tumor" get what sense they have and bring to any proposition from their established role within a whole set of practices, the one within a whole set of techniques and categories of diagnosis and treatment, the other within a set of assessments of behavior involving notions such as *negligence* and *fraud* and a context of litigation and awarding of damages. Those words can have no meaning for a people who lack those practices and can have no place in their language. (Here I am aware that I am setting my face against the whole Cartesian project, which starts from an explicit, conscious and enjoined divorce in Descartes's "hyperbolical" doubting between word and idea, on the one hand, and life, action, and practice on the other. The result is that his "hyperbolical doubt" can have no content and empties all that it touches.)

The second thing that is going to be important for us in untangling the notion of *nonsense* is that the life of any actual society will involve a jumble of incommensurable practices, like law, sport, medicine or religion, which generate and give sense to a collection of incommensurable vocabularies that are part of the one language because they are part of the practices of what can loosely be called one society. I know English, but have little or no knowledge of many of its vocabularies, for example, those associated with practices such as mountaineering, the financial markets, maritime law or dressage. Nevertheless they are all part of English and will have their equivalents in the languages of other countries with the same practices, countries such as France, Sweden or Germany, though not, perhaps, in the languages of quite different cultures such as Pushtu or Chippewa.

What we have to insist on is both the incommensurability of those various vocabularies and that they belong to one language. It is just this that makes metaphor possible. Metaphor could be described as the border traffic between provinces of the same language, and it is mistaking the metaphorical for the literal, taking a visiting expression for a native of the area, that makes nonsense possible. That is one source, anyway, and we shall have to develop that point further. (I'm not sure that a general account of nonsense is available. All I can say for sure is that I have not got one and so can only propose looking at a number of particular cases to see what can be learned from them.)

The notion of *nonsense* provides philosophy both with tools and with problems. As a tool, the notion of *nonsense* can operate in a way analogous to the way Descartes's method of "clear and distinct ideas" was supposed to. That is, a good ear for nonsense can show us where we have "gone over the edge." In that way, it helps us to see where the edge is, to make out what Wittgenstein would call the "grammar" of the expression. The nonsense of Lewis Carroll is of this kind –

philosophical nonsense aimed at showing edges and how some philosophers' doctrines have gone over them. His works are full of brilliant, teasing nonsense and paradoxes for philosophers to learn from.

There is much to be said about the kind of nonsense that Lewis Carroll rejoices in, nonsense which comes from treating something as belonging to an inappropriate category, such as the Cheshire cat that leaves its smile behind and the dog that loses its temper and so fails to take that away when it runs off. Though this kind of category mixup is an important source of the nonsense which falls to philosophers to deal with, the discussion of it would involve a clarification of the notion of a *category*, something which is far beyond anything I want to attempt here.

Though an ear for nonsense may be an important organ for philosophizing, not everyone's ear is the same, and not every piece of nonsense strikes the ear with the same force. And so expressions and theses get into circulation and are accepted as having sense when they have none. This provides the problems, and not always easy ones. The sources of emptiness may lie so deep and seem so innocuous that it may take long and careful analysis to exhibit that emptiness and to track down the false move that left the expression without sense. And it may be hard work to get the false move accepted as a *false* move. It may seem such a natural move to make, one that has been accepted into the habits of a time. And the understanding of that seeming naturalness may take us into another dimension of analysis, one with a historical cast.

Taking Einstein's relativity theory as an example of the kind of analysis that leads to the unmasking of the senseless may seem a bizarre choice. But it can be seen as an example of philosophical analysis; and it is useful to look at it that way. After all, its function was to show the emptiness of a notion that had been accepted as sensible and natural and with which people had worked and were working with some confidence. (The "conference theorists" need to sit up and take special notice here because that confidence and that apparent agreement in use were not enough to guarantee sense.) A lot can be learned about philosophy and about nonsense by looking at Einstein's enterprise as just such a paradigm.

The notion in question was that of *absolute simultaneity*, which was the subject of analysis in the special theory of relativity. It seemed perfectly natural to the generations that followed Newton, and many before him, to think that of any two events in the Universe it was a determinate fact that one had occurred at the same time as the other, or else before or after. This was seen as a fact that was independent of human observers and simply "there" to be discovered. And for a great many of those generations, within the limits of theory and instrumentation available to them, this belief was perfectly innocent, even if of no practical use, and caused no problems. However, by Einstein's time both theory and instrumentation had developed to the point that he could be struck, as he tells us, by the fact that we never find light waves moving slowly past us, or standing still. That is, when we measure the velocity of light from whatever source, we always get the same value. The motion of the source toward us or away from us may cause a change in color, but not in velocity.

The object of Einstein's analysis was to unravel and remove the extraordinariness of this seemingly extraordinary and counter-intuitive fact. If the facts go against our intuitions, the intuitions have to be reexamined and realigned. As Aristotle said, philosophy begins in wonder and ends in seeing that it would be the cause of wonder if things were any other way.

There will be some relief at the news that we do not here really have to follow through the details of Einstein's analysis, even though there might be much value in that. Einstein has himself set it out perspicuously for a lay audience in his little book *Relativity*, published by Methuen in 1920 and reissued several times since.

From the vantage point that Einstein has secured for us we can identify the source of the trouble, the hole out of which sense drained. It lay in a certain way of taking Newton's notions of *absolute space* and *absolute time*. From that new vantage point, we can see how that way of taking those notions made them into what could be described as "transcendental conceptions," conceptions that involved a "God's-eye" point of view. That transcendental viewpoint did not have, and could not be given, a concrete role within the secular enterprise of describing and analyzing dynamic changes among objects. That essentially theological picture could in the end have no role in scientific investigation and those absolute notions no final place in the picture and the method of analysis that Newton was offering in the *Principia*, even though they may have been some help in grasping a new framework and getting it to work.

But at the time of writing the *Principia* this could not have been seen, and it was in fact necessary for the development of dynamics that a distinction between relative and absolute motion be available.[8] This was necessary in putting the heavens at the disposal of terrestrial physics as the great workshop in which frictionless motion could be studied. The motion of the planets and of the Moon became the paradigmatic applications of the method of analysis offered by Newton's "laws of motion" and his "law of gravity."

Perhaps we need to remind ourselves that the bulk of Newton's work was theological, not scientific, and that he once described space as "God's Sensorium."[9] That's where the trouble came, in the mixing of the theological and the scientific, the God's-eye point of view and the "absolute" with the human. The concrete realities lying behind the apparently "absolute" character of some notions that appear in the sciences, *atoms, fundamental particles, the origin of the Universe*, and so forth gets discussed briefly in chapter 10.

There is a process at work here that we would do well to look at and register, one that is a rich source of confusions and problems, the kind of seeming sense that it is the business of philosophy to untangle and uncover and reveal as empty. Typically, we start with a homely, everyday word such as "simultaneity," a word that gets its sense from its use in the practical contexts of arranging meetings, measuring duration, and so forth. It is then wrenched loose from the context of those practices and given new, Universe-wide work to do without any discussion of how it is to carry out that work. No new practices were devised that would allow a determinate answer to be found for a determinate question in this new expanded arena. In this new environment the word simply traded on its old sense and on the false belief that the old sense could carry over intact into this new area and use. Einstein's stunning achievement was to show that no new practices of measurement *could* be devised that would enable it to do the work now being asked of it.

In chapter 7 I identify that same process of detachment at work emptying sense from the notion of *doubt* in Descartes's would-be action of "hyperbolical doubting" which is the basis of his method. There are actually two troubles here. One is that Descartes deliberately lifts his notion of "doubt" out of the context of actions and the reasons for actions or abstentions from which that notion gets its sense, and enjoins us to doubt but not to "make use of" the doubt for "the conduct of life." That already empties the notion of any sense. The second trouble is that he makes doubting itself into a kind of voluntary action, something we can turn on and off at will and "make use of for the contemplation of truth." Lewis Carroll comes to our rescue here, highlighting the nonsense of that instruction through the White Queen's parallel instruction to Alice (who has said she can't believe that the Queen is one hundred and one, five months and a day): "Try again, draw a long breath, and shut your eyes."

I would like to return to Newton and to a process of thought that offers temptation and has the appearance of giving sense to the move beyond the everyday practices to the absolute and transcendental, to the notions of *absolute* space, and *absolute* time. It is a process and temptation that seem to be implicated in the notion of *progress* and in the improvements that we see in various areas. Since Plato deployed the arguments so powerfully in trying to give sense and flesh to his vision of the Forms that were for him the explanation of so much, there has been a tendency and temptation to think that progress could only be conceived of as "progress toward" something that lay always beyond. The Forms were, of course, that something. The progression we discern among concrete things was meant to point inexorably beyond and to entail the existence of something, an ideal or absolute, toward which they were progressing. These ideals and absolutes were presented as being implicated in our ability to range those concrete things in an order of refinement or improvement. They were to be the final resting place of a restless progression, at the same time defining it as a progression.

I have doubts about the force of that argument and have criticized it in chapter 11, "On Misunderstanding Science." While I would not want to go on record as saying that it could give no sense to the transcendental, I would stick firmly on the point that it can give us no license to mix the transcendental with the secular, as was done with Newton's notions. Actually at that level, the accusation against Newton would not be right, and seeing why not may give us a better grip on one rich and flowing source of nonsense that floods philosophy with problems. A rough description of that source is that it is like the mistaking of the function of certain maps and pictures and asking inappropriate questions of them and drawing inappropriate conclusions.

Newton titled his great work *The Mathematical Principles of Natural Philosophy*, and it is just that – a work of mathematics. In a work of mathematics he is licensed to talk about ideals: straight lines, ellipses, circles, time and space, without having to say how these are to be measured, laid out or determined in practice in whatever sphere we are applying his theorems.[10] The role of his famous definitions of absolute time (which, it is important to note, he calls "mathematical" time) and absolute space is to absolve him from giving those methods of measurement that would connect his mathematical model with actual astronomic and physical practice. He could not base his definition of time on mechanical practice as he saw Euclid could base his definitions and constructions on ruler and compass operations and the practices of carpenters and builders.[11]

The physical measurement of time was something that would not stand still in that way and was rapidly evolving in what can only be described as a "dialectical" manner. Galileo used his pulse to time the pendulum, and then theorized the pendulum in a way that established it as the test of, and more accurate than, his pulse. Later theorizing revealed sources of inaccuracy in the pendulum, say from heat expansion and lengthening that could be compensated by vials of mercury, which by their own expansion would keep the center of mass the same. Air resistance could be reduced by a better aerodynamic shape. Friction of components could be reduced by jeweled bearings, and so forth. Later, theories established my means of these clocks revealed still more accurate ways of measuring time based on other natural periodicities, of crystals, atoms, electrons or light. What should be noticed is that these natural periodicities were discovered, and discovered to be more accurate, ultimately by means of the clocks that they supplanted.

The progress I have described does not appeal to the notion of *approaching a goal*, and the scientists who were carrying out those improvements had, and could have, no use for that notion in their work. They had only the existing clocks which they could analyze in the light of existing theory to look for sources of inaccuracy. The ideal of *absolute time* could have no role for them. That is because, as I argue in chapter 11, the notion of *approaching* a transcendental or an absolute is an incoherent one. The notion of *approach* cannot be defined there. The progress we have been looking at is progress defined as improvement over the previous methods, and it proceeds by identifying flaws and sources of inaccuracy and trying to eliminate them. That progression does not define a limit and does not allow us to talk of "approaching a limit." There are two notions of *progress* here, the one practical, belonging to the realm of scientific and secular human activities and concerns, the other religious and transcendental, with an entirely different and incommensurable role in human life.

If we take the presence of those idealized limiting notions of *time* and *space*, those *absolutes* as a signal that what we have on hand is a mathematical model or a method of analysis,[12] not a physical theory that aims at a truth value, we can see them as having a legitimate role there. Arguments that Henri Poincaré sets out in "The Classical Mechanics" in *Science and Hypothesis* that there is no possibility of bringing Newton's three "Laws of Motion" to an empirical test give us good reason to regard those "laws" as methods of analysis rather than as supreme physical laws. Newton's own view of things seems to have been ambiguous. On the one hand, there are reasons, as I have tried to bring out in chapter 11, to say that Newton was himself offering his "laws" as ways of looking, as methods of analysis. His use of the phrase "If I may so say" to qualify his description of the example illustrating the third law seems to indicate a way of looking and a method of analysis rather than a description of things with a truth value. On the other hand his use of the famous "bucket experiment" seems to be directed at establishing absolute space as a concrete description of things, a description with a truth value.

The later confusions identified by Einstein's analysis came partly from a failure to distinguish between a way of looking and a method of analysis on the one hand and a claim that absolute space was a physical reality on the other. The consequence of this was asking of the mathematical model or a method of analysis questions appropriate only to a physical theory. We are back to the person trying to determine the distance from Earl's Court to High Barnet by measurement on a London Underground map, or to those theoreticians who think that physical sense can be made of the notion of "particles travelling backward in time," simply because it is convenient and simplifying in certain equations to put a minus sign on the time variable.

There is obviously much more to be said about all these things, particularly about the difficulties in introducing the notion of *time* into a mathematical model arising from the fact that we cannot give a *construction* in the way that Euclid does in connection with his spatial notions such as "equal in length," "right angle," "circle," and so forth. But that discussion would be out of place here. What we need here is to make out one way in which a notion or an expression may fail to have sense and why yet it may seem to have sense because of the practices it has left behind and a failure to notice that it *has* left them behind.

Yet we must be careful here. The passage from the concrete, and the sense that comes from practices that have their home there, to the absolute and the transcendental necessarily leaves behind the literal sense that it gets in those home surroundings, but that does not mean that *nothing* is carried forward.

St Thomas Aquinas described the knowledge of God (our model of the transcendent) as "analogical" – one could equally say "metaphorical" – and his method in the *quinque viae* of reaching beyond the literal and the secular is to identify ordered processes that from a secular point of view are endless, but which seem to call for a closure because of a dependent relation between one link and another. He then posits God as the closure, as the first or the final term.

Much confusion and nonsense has been generated by the temptation to import this procedure into the sciences, where it generates ideals that get mistaken for concrete realities. We need to notice that even though we cannot give a concrete and literal sense to Newton's notion of *absolute time* – that is, cannot incorporate it into practices that will give it a literal and physical sense – it is still a *time* variable we are talking about. It may be a place-holder only, but it is a "tagged" placeholder and not just anything can be put into the place it holds. It has a specific place in the mathematical model and method of analysis that Newton has put together, and that place is related somehow, and at a remove, to the practices of measurement and dating that give sense to our ordinary notion of *time*.

The notion of God as "first cause" may be related analogously to our ordinary secular notion of *cause* even though we can make no *literal* sense of the notion of an *absolutely first cause*. That is, our ordinary, secular notion of *cause* allows us always to ask of anything offered as the cause of something, "And what is *its* cause?" (And we can see that those scientists who think that they can reach some final account of "the origin of the Universe" are confounding the secular and literal with the theological and metaphorical notions of *origin*. Whatever account is regarded as the "final" story for a time, for example, the "Big Bang," will, in time, be articulated to the point at which it will be a practical question to ask: "What went 'Bang?'" and the quest will start all over again. That is part of the logic of the scientific enterprise and of the notion of *cause*.)

Properly, I should have some account of the notion of *metaphor* on hand, because the thread that I want to draw out of this whole discussion of transcendent and absolute notions is that the sense that such notions may have is a transferred and metaphorical one derived by projection and analogy from the literal sense. That literal sense cannot be severed from the milieu of practices that give it life and sense, and I want to indicate as one rich source of nonsense the mistaking of the metaphorical for the literal. To make that a really useful claim, I seem to need some sort of account of maps, models, and metaphors as representatives of something other than themselves which lead to nonsense by being mistaken for the thing they represent. The model represents the structure, the map the terrain, and the metaphor the literal sense. Mistaking the representative for the thing represented sets us up for nonsense (though it doesn't guarantee it).

And even where we have not mistaken the representative for the thing we can get nonsense from mistaking the form of representation, the form of projection, as when the fundamental particle physicist tries to make physical sense out of a minus sign in his mathematical model and talks about "particles going backward in time," or the unwary traveler measures distances on the London Underground map.

However, I have not got a general account of modeling or representation to offer, and all I can say here is that we are in line for misleading ourselves and for nonsense when we mistake the use and nature of the representation we are working with. That can cause as much trouble as mistaking the representative for the thing itself.

Now I want to look at two expressions, "infinite whole" and "machine intelligence," that I have analyzed in two of the following chapters, as examples of a different way in which nonsense can arise. In these cases it can arise because of a tension or incompatibility between the parts. In the first this comes about because of a play on two different senses of "whole" that is introduced in the first moves of Cantor's *Contribution to the Founding of the Theory of Transfinite Numbers*. There he defines a "set" as a "collection into a whole of definite and separate objects of our intuition or our thought." The two senses of "whole" are, on the one hand, the unity of a category, a unity which is open-ended and does not bring with it the notion of completion, and on the other hand, a functional or structural unity which *does* imply such a completion. To call "infinite" any collection that is a "whole" in the first sense is to say precisely that it is not "whole" in the second, and *vice versa*. We are being asked in the would-be notion of the *actual infinite* to apply both of these incompatible senses of "whole" to the same thing.

In the case of the expression "machine intelligence," what we need is a careful analysis and attention to the notion of a *machine* (or, for that matter, to the notion of an *artifact*), notions which generally get ignored in all the furious debating about the possibility of creating a mechanical intelligence. If we give that careful attention to the two notions of *artifact* and *machine* we will see an incompatibility with the notion of *intelligence* that comes from the fact that both artifacts and machines already involve the notion of *intelligence* in a way that precludes the kind of further connection that is so vigorously argued about. Roughly, the argument is that both artifacts and machines are identified as the products of another intelligence, not as bearers of their own.

What I want to suggest here is that these expressions "infinite whole" and "machine intelligence" lack sense because of an incompatibility of the parts that they are attempting to join. That view has at least the appearance of coming into conflict with Cora Diamond's exposition of

Wittgenstein that we started with. The point is that she insists on the senselessness arising because of "determinations *not* made" rather than the result of "determinations that *have* been made," whereas the incompatibilities that I have tried to bring out in "Infinity," in "Fool's Intelligence," and in "How to Tell Your Friends from Machines" below require determinateness of sense, of the parts, anyway.

Does that give us "illogical thoughts" or "senseless sense?" I think not, and I suspect also that Cora Diamond would be sympathetic at least in broad terms with the line of argument in all three chapters.

When in the *Tractatus* Wittgenstein describes "the correct method in philosophy," this involves for him *demonstrating* to one who "wanted to say something metaphysical" that they "had failed to give a meaning to certain signs." If we ask how that demonstration is meant to go, I think it can only be in some such manner as we have been trying to bring out in analyzing Einstein's argument, in talking about models, maps, and metaphors and how we can ask the wrong questions of them, and finally, how we can try to put together expressions out of incompatible parts. All these ways of demonstrating a failure of sense depend on "determinations that have been made." And how else could it be?

But there is an ambiguity in that phrase. The individual or sub-group may not have made a determination of sense with the expression "machine intelligence," but the reason for that failure lies precisely in the determinations that have been made within the language. It is certainly true that those who think that there might be artificial or mechanical intelligences have not determined *for themselves* any meaning for "machine" or for "artifact" in that attempted use, but if we are to demonstrate that failure to them, we are going to have to appeal to the sense that is established in the language. The word "machine" is not like "runcible," something into which anything can be put: it has a place and a role in our language, and it is precisely that which we can appeal to in showing that it cannot be used in this way, and that the resulting phrase is without sense.

In *Artificial Intelligence and Natural Man*[13] Margaret Boden made a suggestion that amounted to a proposal to treat "machine" or "artifact" much like "runcible." Echoing Turing, she suggested that by the end of the century (this was back in 1977) "educated opinion" might have accepted the notion of "artificial intelligence" and the language have changed. Would that have changed anything? Would that have given sense to the notion of an "artificial intelligence" and overcome the incompatibility of the two halves? One can doubt Turing's prediction of an accommodating linguistic change on the ground that the word "machine" and the word "intelligent" have too much important work to do in other spheres to allow this metaphor to pass to the status of the literal. That would involve a very small tail wagging a very large dog. And to what end? What would be gained by this change?

The individual does not make an illogical determination, have an "illogical thought," use an expression whose "sense is senseless," but the individual's failure of determination is possible and is a failure precisely because of the background of determinations that exist in the language, because of those practices that are there, external and apart from the individual. And it is only because of those practices and those determinations that we are able to demonstrate that failure. Only where the maps, models, metaphors or pictures have a definite use can they be *mis*used. So there is a sense in which determinations and sense are *required* for senselessness. But the sense and the determinations do not lie where the senselessness does. The one lies with the language, the other with the individual's attempted use of it.

Here, once again, we see the great gulf that is riven between what is possible for the individual (mistakes in practice, solecisms, for example) and what is impossible collectively (the whole of a linguistic community cannot collectively commit a solecism), and what is possible collectively (establishing the practices which define those mistakes) and is not possible for the individual individually. That great logical gulf between the individual and those things that belong to the individual on the one hand and the collective and what belongs to the social on the other is of the same order of importance as the equally great gulf between the social, the human, and the historical on the one side and the natural on the other. Mystification is the result of a failure to have a clear view of those two fundamental divides and a clear view of what belongs on one side and what belongs on the other. One could even say that humanity is that species which, through a social dimension and the practices (as against habits and instincts) which are its expression, has detached itself from the natural development that is seen in the evolution of species, and in pursuing new goals that were not laid down by that evolutionary process, has given itself a history. Humanity has, in effect, created those great divisions between the individual and the collective and between the natural and the social that we often lose sight of, so creating unnecessary mysteries for ourselves.

Perhaps the deepest problem embedded in the following discussions is that of clarifying the notion of a *practice* and making out the essential connection between it and the notion of the *social*, and at the same time making out the essential contrast between those notions and that of the *natural*. Equally important is insisting on the contrast between the *individual* and the *social,* or the *collective,* and perhaps also making out how the individuality of the individual requires and depends on the social and the collective, and is itself a product of history.

Note: since I have used the word "practice" so often and given it such important work to do, I have no doubt at all that someone, maybe a posse, will out herd me into a corral with a view to putting a brand saying "pragmatist" on some suitable part. While that might be a decorative addition, I think that we need to be shown how that label (or any such) advances things at all, rather than the reverse. Such labelling is, of course, a necessary prelude to the pleasant and harmless occupation of choreographing abstractions in a ballet of "isms," but on the whole, the fashion of labelling is a device of the lazy to avoid dealing with someone's concrete arguments, examples, and evidence. Nowhere is that clearer than in the reception of Kuhn's work by those engaged in the "realist"–"anti-realist" debate which I discuss in "On Misunderstanding Science." Many have sought simply to label and in that way to tidy his examples and his analysis away out of sight, sparing themselves the work of meeting analysis with analysis and example with example. That sort of activity, which consists in substituting labelling for argument, analysis, and clarification, is not philosophy.

There is no doubt much that needs saying about the use I have made of the notion of *practice* and much to be made clear. Labels like "pragmatism" cut off that needed discussion before it can clarify anything and give only the impression that something has been said.

2   Following and formalization

"Then Logic would take you by the throat and *force* you to
do it!" Achilles triumphantly replied. "Logic would tell you
'You can't help yourself' "
        (Lewis Carroll, "What the Tortoise Said to Achilles")

With his usual subversive brilliance Lewis Carroll brings out the mystified character of the notion of *logical necessity* in his mischievous little
piece for *Mind* in 1895. Both *logical necessity* and *physical necessity* are
notions that have come in for a share of mystification in the modern
era. I have suggested earlier that this is because the great secularizing
project of the seventeenth century gave them theological work to do.
Our job at the moment is to look at that work and to try to bring those
notions back to earth and to concrete reality. An associated task that
will be left to later will be to understand the circumstances of, the motivations for, and the mechanisms of their original inflation and
projection out of the world to reign as "other-worldly" or "transcendental" forces set over and above human beings, holding humans in
their grip and determining human reason and human actions.
    These tasks are not easy and will require the same sort of earth-
bound doggedness that Lewis Carroll gives to the Tortoise in clipping
Achilles' wings, tangling his feet, and bringing him to earth.
Fortunately we have an ally in Wittgenstein, who shows just that sort of
doggedness in interrogating those who have accepted and tried to
employ that abstracted and transcendentalized notion of *logical necessity.* His project in the *Remarks on the Foundations of Mathematics* is just
that of bringing those notions to earth and looking for the concrete
realities behind the God-like status that they have been given.
    Even with an ally such as Wittgenstein (and later on, Aristotle) the
task is far from easy. Considerable work is involved in understanding
both of them and seeing the help they can offer in that demystification

project. It will take just that doggedness and unwillingness to be bought off with fine phrases that Wittgenstein shows, characteristics which are essential to the essential philosophical tasks of our time.

This chapter[1] is mostly exploratory. It deals with what look at first sight to be abstract problems about logic and mathematics, yet they run deeper and ramify, and I have often felt that whatever I have written since this early piece, on whatever topic, was already implicit in the understanding I got from the struggles recorded here.

What I shall be concerned with is the first section of Wittgenstein's *Remarks on the Foundations of Mathematics*, and what I want to do is to get myself between the guns of Russell and the Mathematical Logicians on the one hand, and Wittgenstein on the other. I should like to examine this no-man's-land a bit to see if from there one can make out more clearly where the lines are actually drawn. It may also be helpful to compare the views of Aristotle on some of the same topics with those of the others.

The problems which the first section of the *Remarks* circles around are: the sense in which the formula determines the values of the unknowns, or the next place in the sequence, and the sense in which there are logical or mathematical "truths," the sense in which logic or mathematics "forces" us to draw some conclusion, or determines in advance what conclusion is to be drawn. Those problems are, in their way, the ones around which the whole of the *Remarks* revolves: the problem of the apparent inexorability of logic and mathematics, and a problem which is in a way the obverse of this, the problem of mathematical existence and mathematical objects. Though one is not so tempted to talk about "logical objects" as about mathematical, the debates about propositions, classes, nominalism, and the like are just this. The particular part of all this that I want to focus on is best indicated by Wittgenstein's description of the view of Russell which he objects to (I, §21): "In his fundamental law Russell seems to be saying of a proposition: 'It already follows – all I have to do is, to infer it.'"

Wittgenstein does not oppose this directly and explicitly by simply contradicting it, although opposition is implicit in almost everything in the section. Instead he connects this view that propositions can follow from others independently of and prior to anyone's inferring them with analogous views of other phenomena of transition, for example, the steps in series or in counting, views which describe the transitions as "being determined in advance." His objection to all these transitions being said to be "determined in advance" is that saying this is "using a picture."

To deflate the metaphor and bring it to earth he gives particular examples of transitions which we might say were determined in advance; that is, he gives particular and very concrete senses to "being determined in advance," none of which accord with what Russell has in mind, or thinks he has, in saying that "the conclusion is determined in advance." We would say, for example, that we could determine in advance the steps someone was to make by making them first and having that person copy them, or by training them till the steps were habitual, or by hypnotizing our subject. The implicit challenge in all this is for Russell to give a sense to his phrase "determined in advance" independently of his asserting that logical and mathematical steps are determined in advance. Otherwise the suspicion will be that this was no assertion at all, but only a loose and useless definition of "determined in advance" disguised as an assertion.

There is, however, an important point about these particular examples of "determination in advance" which might provide an objection. In all Wittgenstein's examples the determination is of what this or that person will do on this or that occasion. Russell might say that he is not at all concerned, nor is logic, nor mathematics, with what particular people do or do not do at any given time. Logic does not determine in advance the conclusion I actually draw – no one ever said it did; logic determines only what actually follows. If you are interested in determining in advance what someone does, do not go about teaching them logic or mathematics; they may slip up or be perverse. The best thing is to buy a pistol or a thumbscrew.

Wittgenstein's most striking reply to this is one which is at the same time a bit unfair. It is his example of the law said to be inexorable and determinate in punishing murderers and of which it is said "even though mere men may let them go, nevertheless the law is inexorable and determines their punishment absolutely."[2] Can any sense be made of saying that the law determines the fate of the criminal but mere men let them off? What sense could be made is not much help to Russell. But, as I said, this reply, though striking, is somewhat unfair. The point about laws concerning murder is that they specify punishments, which are actions to be taken by the appropriate authorities, so that any attempt to divorce these laws from what people do is on the face of it ridiculous. It is not on the face of it ridiculous to divorce the laws of logic, or perhaps less tendentiously, what is logically determined or mathematically determined, from what humans actually do; so that the question still remains open.

And it is, I hope, through this opening that the relevance of the title of this chapter can be seen. For it is just through formalization that the attempt is made to make complete the divorce of logic or mathematics from the ineptitude and variability of what particular people do. Formalization is the attempt, perhaps fully to mechanize the processes of inference, but at least to make the logical machine as precise and determinate as can be and capable of running with as little human interference as possible.

The vision on the horizon of many of these attempts is something like Carnap's "ideal languages," which are meant, so to speak, to run themselves without human help. The logical relations and possible inferences are to be captured, contained, and exhibited clearly through the crystalline clarity of the forms of the ideal language. Inferences will be possible by inspection alone without the interference of problems of interpretation or meaning. These latter only introduce a wide area of uncertainty and possible error into the business of inference and are held to be a measure of the indeterminacy and inexactitude of the natural language.

The ideal language is to be one which is self-interpreting; i.e. any problem which cannot be solved by inspection alone can be solved by a determinate procedure and appeal to semantical and syntactical rules which settle the question finally and definitively by mechanical means that are not subject to human error.

It is against this program and this divorce of language, logic, and mathematics from human activity that Wittgenstein sets his face. He attacks first the self-authenticating aspect of the program. Russell is not content to say: "This is the rule of inference I propose to adopt in what follows;" he has to go on to say: "and it is right" (for example, in Section A of *Principia Mathematica*.) However, it is one thing to say that the rule of detachment and modus ponens are correct rules of inference but another thing to justify saying it, or even to make out what it means to say that they are "correct."

Now, although *Principia Mathematica* casts its rules of inference as primitive propositions, describes them as "premises" (in defiance of Lewis Carroll[3]) and calls them "true," it is clear enough that *preservation of truth* would be Russell's test, and meaning for "validity" or "correctness" in a rule of inference. But if we say that modus ponens is a correct or valid rule because it preserves truth, someone may well ask *what* is being taken as a test of *what*, or how it is discovered that these rules do in fact preserve truth and so merit the title "correct." Or does the assertion that modus ponens is a valid rule at this point amount to anything more than a reiteration of our definition of *implication*? That is, if we take the truth-table definition of implication and count an implication as holding only in those cases where truth is actually preserved, then modus ponens or the rule of detachment tells us nothing that we were not already given in the definition of *implication*. The appearance of evidence or truth of Russell's primitive proposition: "Whatever is implied by a true premise is true" is supplied by the fact that this is simply the definition of "implies" turned round.

The claims of any such program as Russell's to be correct or to proceed from correct principles or true premises, or the claim of any ideal language to represent correctly the logical relations which "in fact" hold between propositions, must rest in the end either on the self-evidence of each premise on its own, or perhaps premise A may be evidence for B, B for C, and C for A, which comes to the same thing. The one is like a man's being called as a character witness for himself, the other like the members of a gang being asked to support each other's testimony simply by each saying how truthful and reliable the others were. What other sort of evidence for correctness could there be? No one is likely to test modus ponens inferences in quantity to see if one someday might not preserve truth.

Though no one at the time seemed to notice, the game was given away by the accounts of self-evidence in terms of "truth apparent on an understanding of the terms." What is this to say but that they are true by definition, i.e. that they are definitions turned round and tricked out as assertions? The introduction of "correctness," "evidence," and "truth" in this context is inappropriate and misleading.

The other great point of attack that Wittgenstein makes on the program of the ideal linguists is on the claim that a system might be made to be self-interpreting, that a hierarchy of rules and meta-rules could be devised in terms of which the interpretation of the language and of the rules themselves would be laid down absolutely and independently of anyone's or everyone's reading of the rules. Any particular reading of the rules could then be said to be correct or incorrect in some absolute sense.

This, one might say, is asking for even more than those who want to maintain the possibility of a "private" language, one which is made determinate and fixed by a single speaker alone legislating by and for themselves outside any social context. The requirement here is that there be a language which is determinate and fixed independently of all speakers, a language which is not only a law unto itself, but a law which, unlike the ordinary law, has no need of judges and arbitrators.

Against this, Wittgenstein takes up a position rather like that of the Tortoise in the Lewis Carroll dialogue, only more radical. Of any rule, not only modus ponens, he would allow Achilles to draw the distinction between a rule and a premise, would agree that a rule was not a premise, and might even agree to adopt the rule in question as his own rule of procedure, making only one small reservation, the right to apply his own rule for its interpretation. This undoes the unfortunate Achilles all over again.

The point here is precisely analogous to the previous one: no rule or interlocking system of rules can provide its own interpretation, any more than it can provide its own evidence. The appearance that the rules of some formal systems have of being independently fixed in their interpretation comes from the fact that there is a wide and sometimes almost universal agreement over the interpretation of a number of symbols and rules. But agreement is got by strict training and drill. Those who don't calculate as the others do are quickly rapped on the knuckles. This agreement is a contingent fact about human behavior and is achieved by training and socialization. It is not a necessary fact about the symbols and rules that imposes itself on helpless humans.

So the attempt to make logic and mathematics independent of what people do seems to fail because on the one hand the apparent evidence, correctness or truth of its premises and principles turns out to be dependent on, or even an expression of, certain resolves, practices engaged in, and definitions adopted. The point complementary to this is that the rules and symbols in terms of which any system is to be laid down and defined can get their particular meaning only from the use humans make of them. There are no symbols whose meaning is fixed by nature and not by humans and no rules[4] whose adoption is not a contingent matter. It may be inconvenient not to adopt them, but not impossible.

At this point I should like to shift attention to the Aristotelian account of the syllogism. In the *Prior Analytics*, Aristotle defines the syllogism as "discourse in which, certain things being laid down or agreed (*tethenton*) something other than that laid down or agreed of necessity follows from the fact that agreements or positings are such." Now, the interesting question is: what is to be made of this in the light of Wittgenstein's argument against Russell and Carnap with their independently existing logical connections holding between timeless entities called "propositions?" When Aristotle says that something is "of necessity" he means that it cannot be otherwise, and its being so must certainly be independent of what men do or say. Several remarks of Wittgenstein's seem at first sight to be directly and explicitly opposed to Aristotle's view, for example, Wittgenstein's saying that logic does not deal with language and thought in the way that science deals with natural phenomena, and his saying "the connection which is not supposed to be a causal, experiential one, but much stricter and harder, so rigid even, that the one somehow already *is* the other – is always a connection in grammar."[5]

Although it is not clear that there may not be more than one kind of connection in grammar, it is remarks of this sort that tend to provoke the fury of mathematicians. If one takes grammatical connections as invariably conventional, then it is possible to read these remarks as expressing a view which might, given some indulgence, be described as "to the left of" Quine's "Truth by Convention," a view which, in the same mood, might be called "Validity by Convention."

It seems to be this reading that David Pole,[6] and, more recently, M. A. E. Dummett[7] have fastened on in describing Wittgenstein's views as "conventionalist." I am not sure that "conventionalism" has a very clear meaning or that if it were given one, the result might not be that everyone would turn out to be a conventionalist or that no one would. In any case, this is the way Wittgenstein has tended to be read, and, given this reading, there seems to be a complete opposition between his view and Aristotle's. Whatever a "conventional connection" might be, it would not be a necessary one. However, it is important to keep in mind that there are two sorts of connection and therefore at least two sorts of necessity at issue in mathematics and logic.

There is the connection between subject and predicate, on the one hand, and the connection between premise and conclusion on the other. The issues involved in saying or denying that there are necessary connections of the first sort, premises or axioms which we must adopt, are quite different from the issues involved in saying or denying that there are conclusions that follow necessarily from given premises or statements we must accept if we accept certain others.

Failure to keep these two questions apart seems to be one source of Dummett's particular interpretation of, and consequent dissatisfaction with, Wittgenstein's account of mathematics. Dummett's discussion in "Wittgenstein's Philosophy of Mathematics" lumps the two sorts of necessity together under the title "logical necessity" with the result that, as I hope to show, he has misinterpreted Wittgenstein in describing him as a "full-blooded conventionalist" who held that "the logical necessity of any statement is the direct expression of a linguistic convention."[8] He reads Wittgenstein as holding that "whenever we accept a proof we are *conferring* a necessity on the connection between premise and conclusion and . . . are making a new decision, and not making explicit a decision we had already made implicitly."[9]

Wittgenstein's meaning is notoriously not written on the face of what he says, and a long list of quotations could be given to support this reading, among them one I have already given and several I shall.

But this reading makes a mystery of some of the most obvious facts about mathematics – for example, the vast agreement about what is or is not proved, the common standards of proof, and elegance. If each acceptance of a proof were a new decision not included in, or bounded by, things accepted, this amount of agreement and uniformity of reaction among mathematicians would be incomprehensible. It would be understandable only among lower animals or automata.

It is true that Wittgenstein talks a great deal in the first section of the *Remarks* about training and practice, but what should at least raise a doubt about this reading of him is that it places the mathematician on a rather lower level than the circus animal. The latter fail to jump through the hoops at least sometimes.

But the main doubt that I want to raise is whether this reading can be squared with other more important views of Wittgenstein's, in particular, his very central distinction between a definition and an assertion, between making up a rule and following one. In Dummett's account the notion of a *rule* has no place; it has no use or even sense. As each decision or act is held to be free in the sense of being *arbitrary*, on Dummett's reading there would be no rules over and above the individual decisions to which they might conform or not. At most a rule would be something analogous to Dirichlet's definition of a *function* – a set of individual and independent decisions. Individual and independent decisions would determine the rule rather than being determined by it. Even if one insisted on keeping such a notion of *rule* despite its near vacuousness, one could not avoid the complete emptying and inapplicability of the notion of *following a rule*.

Dummett makes the point against the view that he takes to be Wittgenstein's that, if it were right, "communication would be in constant danger of breaking down."[10] This is quite true, although perhaps too mild a formulation. Communication could not even get under way. It would be *impossible*, and it would be impossible for just those reasons which Wittgenstein was trying to make clear in what people have labelled the "private language argument."

Before trying to develop this latter point, I should like to return for the moment to the two sorts of necessary connections at issue in logic and mathematics. Perhaps the nature of the compulsion or necessity of adopting certain axioms or even definitions and the nature of the compulsion or necessity of accepting that given conclusions follow from given premises, though distinguishable, need to be treated together in a general discussion of mathematical and logical necessity so that they can illuminate one another.

However, the problem with which we began was that of trying to get a clear view of Wittgenstein's account of the connection between premise and conclusion and his account of inference generally. Although I want to make a general point about the notion of *necessity* and its apparent alternative, *convention*, by means of a brief look at what I take to be Aristotle's view concerning what seems to be a compulsion or necessity of accepting certain axioms, I hope that the point can be made without more than a sketch of support for what will be viewed by many as a radical reading of Aristotle.

The particular text of Aristotle which I should like to examine here is a striking and apparently uncompromising one from chapter 10 of the first book of the *Posterior Analytics*, which argues that there are principles (axioms, in fact) which though not provable are necessarily assumed and in this are distinct from hypotheses and postulates. These latter are both provable assumptions: the first being believed as well as assumed, and the second assumed simply for the sake of argument, though later proved.

That is neither a hypothesis nor a postulate which of itself necessarily is [so] (*o ananke einai di auto*) and is necessarily supposed [or thought] (*kai dokein ananke*) [And there are such things] for syllogism, and therefore demonstration, does not address itself to the words that are spoken but to what is in the soul. For there can always be resistance [or objection] to the particular spoken word (*exo logos*) but not always to thought (*eso logos*).[11]

At first sight this looks as though it is to be read as a statement of a view which is about as opposed to Wittgenstein's as it is possible to be, a view which goes far beyond "necessary truth" to "laws of thought" of an inexorable kind that determine not only the conclusions we draw from given premises but certain premises which we must accept for what appear to be psychological reasons.

But the crucial question is just what sort of necessity is involved here? If the necessity is psychological it is as difficult to see how there could be differences of opinion on Aristotle's view as it would be on Dummett's reading of Wittgenstein to see how there could be agreements. *Necessity* is for Aristotle "what cannot be otherwise," but it was as clear to Aristotle as it is to ourselves that in one sense people can do otherwise than accept any particular axioms. He lists and argues against several who rejected the most basic axioms of all: Protagoras, Cratylus, and the Heracleiteans, who rejected the law of contradiction and the law of the excluded middle.

Argument would be pointless in more ways than one if the acceptance of those axioms were governed by psychological necessity. Not only could one do more than look for physical or psychological causes for the rejection, but the relation of axioms to "the way things are" would have been severed. There would be no point or justification in "correcting" those who rejected the axioms – except perhaps a social point. Such people would be suffering from a psychological aberration which might bring them into conflict with their fellows. Without laboring the point, it seems clear enough that the necessity involved here is not of psychological channels which govern the way our thought must run. However, if the necessity and the laws here are not psychological, that is, if they are not the result of the "constitution of the mind," we are left with the difficulty of making out what Aristotle can mean by the phrase *dokein ananke* and by saying that "it is not always possible to resist or oppose the thought."

The suggestion that the *dokein ananke* is to be read as "appears or is thought necessary" rather than "is necessarily thought" is implausible in view of the function of the second two sentences of the paragraph, which is to support the claim that there are some things which "we cannot help thinking."

There is a simple answer to the problem, perhaps too simple, which is supplied by an earlier passage of the *Posterior Analytics* taken together with the point which is often overlooked in discussions of necessity. The forgotten point is that "necessary" may mean "necessary as a condition of something," "necessary as a consequence of something," or "necessary *simpliciter.*"

In chapter 2 of Book I Aristotle describes axioms as a form of "thesis" and distinguishes them from the other forms (hypothesis and definitions) as being necessary to all progress or learning whatever in the subject. Without a particular definition or a particular hypothesis at least some learning could go on. Without a commitment to the axioms, we can get nowhere.

Though this may look promising, to say that the necessity of axioms is to be explained simply as "being necessary to all learning" leaves unexplained the point of Aristotle's saying that "one cannot always resist or oppose the thought." It would also be well on the way to circularity because scientific or demonstrative knowledge, and therefore learning, is defined by him in terms of derivation from, among other things, axioms.

Aristotle's view of the source and nature of this necessity is, I think, best brought out in his very central and very interesting arguments on behalf of what are for him the axioms *par excellence*: the law of contradiction and the law of the excluded middle. If Aristotle had viewed these as self-evident in the traditional sense one would have expected him simply to explain them and make understood their terms and then wait for universal recognition. If, on the other hand, he thought them necessary in some psychological or constitutional sense he would hardly have wasted time arguing on their behalf. Nor, if the necessity were supposed to be psychological, could he claim that their "necessity" in this sense was any basis for truth.

However, Aristotle does neither of these things but in fact argues on two very interesting lines: (1) to show that the rejection of these two axioms destroys all possibility of talk, and (2) to show that his opponents do in fact really assume them and that this is shown by their demeanor and even by their denial. He does not say that his axioms are "correct" as Wittgenstein takes Frege and Russell by implication to be doing. He says that the rejection of them leads to consequences which no one does or *can* accept. And the sense of that *can* is the subject of that crucial and perhaps at first puzzling part of his argument to which he gives the name *apodeixis elentikos*. We should linger over that name for a moment because the standard translation as "proof by refutation" hardly makes all clear and misses the forensic associations of the word *elentikos*. "Proof by cross-examination" is marginally better, but the essential point of the form of argument that Aristotle is using is that there must be someone before you who is trying to express and communicate to you a denial of that law. The argument then goes to work on that attempted expression of a view, showing that the attempt at expression is in conflict with the thing that is to be expressed.

If, like Cratylus, someone does seem to be willing to accept the consequences of rejecting those axioms, namely, the destruction of language, the possibility of talk and even of making judgments, and seems to show their acceptance is real by saying no more, Aristotle cannot, and does not try to, demonstrate that their position is incoherent or false. (How could one show such a person anything?) He shifts here to an interestingly different sort of argument. "Such a man," he says (*Metaphysics* 1006a15), "is no better than a vegetable." This is not simply to call him names but is offered as the measure of the dislocation of what Wittgenstein would call "his way of life" involved in the genuine denial of the law. He will appear to have given up his rationality; he would be, by Aristotle's equation of *humanity* with *rationality*, no longer human.[12]

Aristotle's argument (for example, at 1008b13) is not that we *must* in some psychological sense accept the axioms, for Cratylus' case is enough to establish that it is possible not to; his argument is rather that we *do* accept them and that our acceptance is bound up with, and contained implicitly in, everything we do – talking, acting, inferring, deciding, thinking (1006b9). Aristotle's most explicit rejection of the notion that we are in any absolute sense *forced* to accept the axioms comes perhaps in his remark *à propos* of acceptance of the axioms (1011a15) that "those who seek to be compelled by the force (*ten bian*) of words alone ask for the impossible." In talking and acting we are implicitly accepting axioms even though we may not recognize them as our own when they are formulated. However, formulating an axiom we accept implicitly, and getting this formulation accepted is a different matter from getting a rule or axiom itself accepted as a rule of procedure, as a way of acting.

At the outset of his argument Aristotle is quite self-conscious about this difference in his discussion (1006a10 *et seq.*) of the difference between direct proof and "proof by refutation." The latter involves showing that in the argument itself, or in their life, the opponent is already committed to your view. The necessity of certain of our beliefs lies in their being necessarily involved in activities of ours which we have no intention of giving up, activities or ways of life which in some absolute sense we are "free" to give up together with the assumptions on which they are based but which, as a practical matter, no one could in fact give up. Cratylus may have succeeded in eliminating one activity which would have committed him to the law of contradiction, but Aristotle's point is that you must do more than simply talking and making assertions if you are to avoid commitment to the law of contradiction: you must stop making any discriminations at all, even in acting. You must, in fact give up being rational.

He says that the man who walks to Megara and avoids walking into a well *shows* that he does not view these actions as equally "good and not good" (1008b14). And this raises an important point about the *eso* and *exo logos* of the passage from the *Posterior Analytics*, and about the whole question of commitment and the recognition of the things we are committed to. It is clear that, as Aristotle was using the phrase, the man's *eso logos* on the subject of falling down wells is shown by avoidance. But it seems equally clear that to have such an *eso logos* he need not have said or thought to himself "Falling down wells is not a good thing, therefore . . . ." He simply avoids the well, and in doing so he shows his views not only about falling down wells but also about whether the same object can at the same time have contrary qualities.[13]

Part of the point of this excursion into Aristotle's views on necessity is to throw light from another direction on the role and importance of Wittgenstein's central concept of a "way of life" and to suggest that when he says that "all that is given are the forms of life," he is giving expression to a position which seems to be implicit in the whole form of the argument with which Aristotle defends the law of contradiction and the law of the excluded middle. The differences between Wittgenstein and Aristotle here can be seen as differences of emphasis and perspective and can be traced to the fact that Aristotle was arguing against "relativists" like Protagoras who made all truth relative to, and dependent on, the individual. Wittgenstein was arguing against those like Frege and Russell who seemed to take the diametrically opposite view: making some truths independent of what humans do or say and forced on humanity "from above," as it were.[14]

What is essential to recognize here is that although such pairs of tags as "conventionalism" and "realism," or for that matter, "relativism" and "absolutism," can be used for the purpose of vague indication, they become mind-traps when any weight is put on them. Without breaking their grip and recognizing the uselessness of the usual philosophical games that are played with them as counters, we shall make no real sense either of Wittgenstein or of Aristotle. By trying to bring these two into a common focus in order to point out some of the common ground between, I hope to have shown some of the obscuring function of such tags as they have generally been used.

For one thing, Wittgenstein's key concept here is the *way of life* or the form *of life*, but ways of life are not conventions and are not adopted by a convention. In fact, they are not *adopted* at all. "Adoption" implies intentional action or even a recognition of alternatives. Overwhelmingly, ways of life are something people simply grow up into.

However, though mistaken and obscuring, the charge of "conventionalism" against Wittgenstein is not an irresponsible one and does not come out of thin air, but rather from a failure to put certain of his recurring themes into a proper perspective.

Because he wants to emphasize the fundamental difference between a *practice* or *rule* and a *cause* and the very great difference this makes to a description of human activities and creations, Wittgenstein continually insists on the essential point about rules and practices that they are *followed* or *engaged in* by people and not forced on them by nature, by logic or by anything else. There is always freedom, though by no means always a practically exercisable freedom, to reject any given rule or even any given way of life.[15] It is this assertion of freedom which seems to the logician and the mathematician to be incapable of doing justice to their subjects, in which they do not feel a bit free to reject any rule. It is this assertion which gives rise to the charge of "conventionalism."

Though at first sight there seems to be unresolvable opposition between Wittgenstein's emphasis on the freedom which distinguishes what is rule-governed from what is causally determined and Aristotle's argument for the existence of principles which are necessary, this opposition largely disappears as soon as we recognize two things: (1) that the *freedom* that Wittgenstein emphasizes is not the sort that brings moral responsibility in its wake – it is no more than an absence of causal determination, a logical freedom – and (2) that the *necessity* on which Aristotle insists is hardly one of causal, or somehow *external*, determination but rather of what is necessarily involved in (and maybe constitutive of) beliefs or activities which we are already involved in or committed to.

However, an account of the necessity of certain principal axioms which fixes it in their being necessarily involved in running practices or ways of life throws much greater weight onto the problem with which we started – that of the necessity of the connection between premises and conclusion, or necessity in inferences in general. The account simply eliminates the one sort of necessity in favor of the other, and if the second sort is itself based on, or referred to, practice and ways of life, it will have to be connected with them in a different, more direct way which makes no appeal to the notion of *necessary involvement*, since the notion of *necessary involvement* can only be based on inferential necessity. But if inferential necessity is to be referred to *practices* and *ways of life* at all, it would seem that it could only be identified with them. It seems that if you take this view, unless you are willing to say that what people do they do necessarily, the notion of *necessity* drops out of the account entirely.

The real difficulty is that, as I hope to show, the notion of *correct* or *incorrect* inference would also drop out of the account together with the notion of *following*, or *failing to follow*, a rule, leaving us with the anarchic situation which Dummett takes to be Wittgenstein's view of things. There is an important passage in the last section of the *Remarks* (p. 184) which seems to support very strongly Dummett's view of Wittgenstein as holding that the necessity of any logical connection or inference "is the direct expression of a linguistic convention" or decision.

> "If you accept this rule, you must do this." – this may mean: the rule doesn't leave two paths open to you here. (A mathematical proposition.) But I mean: the rule conducts you like a gangway with rigid walls. But against this one can surely object that the rule could be interpreted in all sorts of ways. Here is the rule, like an order! And like an order too in its effect.[16]

The point of this passage seems to be that no matter what rule you accept or adopt you are not bound in any absolute way either to follow a particular path or else to reject the rule; you can always bring your own interpretation to the rule. This seems to be the point of comparing the rule to an order. An order does not carry itself out; it needs to be interpreted by the person who has accepted the task of carrying it out, and they are not bound in any absolute way to any particular interpretation. The person may fail to carry the order out as it was intended, but whatever they do, a rule of interpretation can be devised in terms of which the action can be made out to be in accord with the order. Wittgenstein's remark that "the rule does not do work" seems to be to exactly the same effect, namely, that rules must be applied and interpreted by people and can have only that force which is given them by the way they are acted on.

A further and different illustration of this point would seem to lie in S. E. Toulmin's suggestion that the paradigm of the analysis of logical argument and inference should be the legal argument. When the lawyers are not trying to establish facts, they are concerned with interpreting the rules of statute law or with trying to discover and extend the rules implicit in the decisions of common law. The rules of statute law are laid down for us like orders and we may accept them; but what this means in practice and what exactly we must or must not do, having accepted them, is not immediately clear or settled just like that. The acceptance of the law, the order or the rule does not in itself bind us absolutely to a given course of action. We must interpret it or apply it in this given case, must discuss the intention of Parliament or "the spirit of the times."[17]

But are the premises, the things laid down, accepted or adopted in logic and mathematics to be compared to the law in this respect? That is, is logic really, or need it be, concerned in an essential way with rule and interpretation? I think that it need not be concerned essentially and that, though for Toulmin pressing the legal analogy may be part of an attack on the Russellian-Carnapian view of logic as a preexisting system handed down to us "from on high," the legal analogy is unfortunate precisely because, as used by him, it at bottom accepts and fosters the Russellian-Carnapian view as the only one.

Drawing an analogy with the institution of the law could very well be used effectively in giving an account of the *force* of logic and of logical laws, but in an analysis of the *workings* of logic and of inference, the analogy with the working of the law tends to support the view that the premises we accept and the rules we adopt are borne in on us from outside like the rules, decisions and statutes of law, and so always stand in need of interpretation in the way law does.

There is a problem of interpretation in the case of the statute law because those who frame it and those who apply it to individual actions or situations are generally different people or different bodies, so that the latter are always faced with the task of discovering the intentions of the former in relation to a particular case. But fortunately not every rule, premise or decision stands in need of interpretation, or is even *open* to interpretation. If they were, adopting a rule would itself mean nothing, and nothing definite would ever have been decided, as any interpretation would be subject to reinterpretation.

However, when I decide to do something or even to do something always, or in general, there is no question of interpreting my decision to myself. I know what I mean and just go ahead and do it. I could not apply any rule of interpretation to my decision, save that by some intellectual dishonesty I might apply some interpretation rule to the *words* of an expressed intention. If there were any real question of interpreting my decision to myself, one would say that there had not been any clear decision. I cannot decide to become a vegetarian and then be perplexed about what to eat and what is forbidden. If I have no notion of what counts as a vegetable and what does not, or even how to go about telling, or if I am quite vague about what counts as eating something, then I have made no real decision. I may have said some words over to myself, but that is about all. The words expressed no intention, or even, had no *meaning* here.

Of course, there can be more or less vague decisions and vague intentions, and situations which the seemingly clearest decisions did not envisage, but *something* must be excluded from my range of action if I am to be said to have decided anything at all.

By now this argument can be recognized as a pillar of the "private language argument." However, the point is not to convict Wittgenstein out of his own mouth but to raise the question whether there may not be two sorts of rule at work here – one, the rule in a formal context, the rule that has been made external and independent by being made part of a formal system, whether of law or of logic; and the other, the rule of the sort that is embodied in the decision or intention of the individual, for example, to give up sweets for Lent. The former is tied to the words involved in a way the latter is not, and is subject to interpretation in a way the latter is not. The distinction can be seen as corresponding to Aristotle's between the *exo* and *eso logos*.

Despite the apparent drift of the passage quoted above from the *Remarks*, it does not seem that Wittgenstein ever held that of every rule whatever there was a question of interpretation. To say this would, among other things, demolish language. If the rule I adopt does not bind me until it is interpreted, it is no rule at all, only the empty form of a rule – a hollow shell. Similarly, with the interpretation rule I may apply to the first rule, and so back and back. Unless there is a rule standing at the head of this column which does not need, and is not open to, interpretation, a rule whose adoption binds me on its own, then the whole system of rules and interpretation rules will remain an empty shell into which anything whatever can be fitted. (*Principia Mathematica* could be read as a musical score with the right interpretation rule.) If I am not bound to anything by the rule I adopt and there is nothing it excludes, then there is no question of violating it or making a mistake, or of deciding or saying anything either.

This again is not an argument that can very well be brought against Wittgenstein in the way that Dummett wants; it is too much Wittgenstein's own, and it also shows why one must go beyond saying that communication would be "in constant danger of breaking down" in the situation described by Dummett. Wittgenstein's point is that if inference and action involved nothing but new decisions and were not a matter of making explicit things already accepted – were not a matter of engaging in practices and following rules implicit in them – then communication could never get started.

This is of a piece with his opposition to extensionalism as pretending to give a final account of mathematics. And it is of a piece with his criticisms of Cantor.

There is a point which is easily missed and which, if missed, leaves Wittgenstein looking like an extreme nominalist or extensionalist. The point is that he is in fact trying to give an account of the ultimates which we do in practice accept and make explicit in particular inferences, acceptances of proofs, calculations, or in the applications of words. (Not what we *must* accept – in some indefinable sense of "must.") What he does say, and what can lead to misunderstanding, is that these "rock-bottom" acceptances where "my spade is turned" are not like assenting to a proposition, but are to be assimilated more to acquiring the ability to calculate after drill in the times table.

The application, the making explicit of these rules, must be automatic (though not infallible) and there must be no room for *new decisions* about their application – at least in their normal range – no room for interpretation in the way there would be in the case of assent to a proposition (where this is taken to be like Aristotle's *exo logos*).

Wittgenstein can in fact be looked on as being centrally concerned with giving an account of what is involved in the relation between the implicit and the explicit. In trying to give an account of what a *mistake* might be in the application of a concept or following of a rule in which there is no question of interpretation, he is led to fix what is given and what is accepted, that is, the rule, in the collective practices of a society or culture, in what he calls the "forms of life."

But this is meant to be an account of, not a denial of, the notion and the fact of making explicit what is implicit – what goes on in the application of concepts to particulars, or in the acceptance of particular proofs. What causes confusion here and introduces the appearance of extreme nominalism is the failure to take seriously or to keep in mind Wittgenstein's arguments about what is *collectively* possible but not possible to individuals: the "private language argument," which holds that without dependence on collectively made rules and collective practices, no individual could make a rule or body of rules in pre-social isolation, in which there could even *be* such a thing as a mistake, much less a question of finding out when a mistake had been made. Rules or principles which are not open to further interpretation cannot be identified simply with the dispositions of individuals to act in certain ways. Nor can they be identified with the pattern of their past actions. For either identification would again rule out giving sense to the notion of a *mistake*.

The account of the *implicit* and of its relation to the *explicit* are crucial here because this relation is for Wittgenstein the heart of inference if not the whole of it. And the connection between the *implicit* and the *explicit*, between practice and formulated rule, can certainly be described as a necessary one; not causally necessary, but "logically necessary" in the sense outlined, one which leaves the possibility of mistakes.

There may remain a difference between Wittgenstein and Aristotle over the second part of Aristotle's definition of the syllogism, which claims that the conclusion is "something other than" what is laid down in the premises. However, though I am not going to pursue this question here, I think that in the end there is no disagreement and that remarks such as that "a mathematical proof molds our language" and the insistence on proofs creating new paradigms are to be read as expressing Wittgenstein's view on the novelty of the conclusion of a proof rather than as expressing an extreme extensionalism or nominalism which, from his own point of view, would be very nearly self-contradictory or self-destructive.

We shall return several times to this theme of rule and application and to the important notion of a *practice*, emphasizing its essential social character and its consequent profound difference from the notions of *habit* or *instinct* in relation to regularities of behavior. Though later chapters will, I hope, not be so taxing as this one, many will have the same form – that of trying to bring to earth and interrogate various phrases and concepts that have been given more work to do than they can honestly undertake.

The first of these to be examined is the notion of *infinity*, particularly its role in the phrase "the actual infinite," a phrase that seems to designate some sort of entity which, because it is described as "actual," would have to be in some mysterious sense "complete" and "rounded off." This topic follows on immediately from the present discussion of rules and logical necessity because it is just that "logical necessity" that has seemed to project infinitely beyond the immediate.

3 Infinity

Though at first sight it looks like a problem that concerns cosmologists and mathematicians chiefly, the notion of *infinity* has a central and almost emblematic importance for philosophy as an example of a notion that seems constantly to be pulling away from its roots in everyday practices and techniques to take on a kind of transcendental significance and status. Examining that process can tell us a lot and will provide us with an example that can help illuminate other problems too.

At a conference in the fifties Professor J. N. Findlay made a plea that the topic of infinity be rescued from "the grip of the experts." Since it seems fair to assume that this was not simply another area in which the cult of the amateur was making itself felt, we can take it that the experts in question were mathematicians and that the plea that was being addressed to the philosophical world at large was that someone should extract the general philosophical issues concerning infinity from the welter of technical discussions about the law of the excluded middle and the law of double negation, the axiom of choice, arbitrary sets, free choice sequences, impredicative definitions, inaccessible cardinals, hyperarithmetic sets or quantifier-free notation.

By and large, there must be a great deal of sympathy with this plea and the point of view from which it springs. There seems to be all too much to support the view that what was once a perfectly good philosophical concept and complex of problems have been dragged onto mathematical ground, where they have immediately taken on characteristics that combine those of Proteus and the Holy Grail and have led everyone a chase over a constantly changing landscape whose only uniform feature is its thorniness.

Certainly philosophers did once talk fairly freely about infinity and certainly they are now rather inhibited from doing so, or at least when they do it is with a nervous look over their shoulder. What is particularly striking about the situation is that despite the general sympathy with the plea and the number of philosophers with mathematical interests and the number of mathematicians with philosophical interests, no one has come forward to attempt the liberation, for all that the main business of philosophy is often claimed to be the seeking out and making explicit of the often unformulated assumptions of other subjects.

I am not going to take on the task of a general deliverance of the concept of *infinity* or of the traditionally central problem, the problem of the "actual infinite," from the technical issues of set theory in which they are supposed to have become embedded. On the contrary, the question I want to raise is whether there is any philosophical problem about the infinite that has become enmeshed in, or otherwise hangs on, the problems or issues of set theory or the foundations of mathematics. In tackling this question, however, I am not going to make the wide survey of technical problems that this way of putting the question might suggest.

In fact the question will be dealt with through one not very technically treated example, though the problem chosen can fairly be described as a central or crucial one. It is Cantor's claim that the transfinite arithmetic must be regarded as defining "actual" infinities. I want to raise questions first about the meaning of this claim, and also about its relation, if any, to philosophical issues. And finally, in part, and by implication, I want to raise questions about the relation between philosophical problems and mathematical ones.

However, before trying to assess the Cantorian claim to have produced an "actual" infinity, or trying to see whether the traditional philosophical problem of the actual infinite has been swallowed up by mathematics, it is necessary to give some account, even if partial and idiosyncratic, of what that problem was traditionally taken to be. Like many other philosophical problems that have shown a remarkable hardiness down the centuries, the problem of the "actual infinite" was first explicitly formulated by Aristotle.

Certainly the roots of the problem go further back – to Anaximander and the Pythagoreans, who offered the *apeiron*, the unlimited, as an ultimate constituent in things or an ultimate explanatory principle. Typically, the word *apeiron* has the sort of deep ambiguity that one almost expects in the key concepts of Greek philosophy. It can mean either "unlimited in extent," in the sense we should now render as "infinite," or "indefinite" in the sense of "unformed," "undefined," "featureless," or "characterless," and a certain amount of the difficulty about the notion of *infinity*, even down to the nineteenth century, seems to have arisen out of the interplay and occasional confusion of these two distinguishable concepts. It is not even certain to what extent Aristotle in his attack on the idea of a separately or actually existing *apeiron* clearly made this distinction, so that, though he is usually read as attacking the idea that infinity is a kind of actuality – the view that to call something infinite is to give its actual size, rather than to say something about its capabilities – many of his arguments can also be read as directed against any conception of an independently and actually existing, though completely featureless, something. That "featureless something" might be either the void, claimed as an actual something, or some ultimate, "prime," matter. These two concepts are difficult to distinguish when pressed hard and can be seen as well to be blood relatives of the notion of *space* as it is often treated nowadays. Space has come to be regarded often as a kind of separate existent, a something with its own properties, something that can be altered and even manipulated rather than a mere field of possibilities.

What *can* be said is that the explicit definition of *apeiron* which Aristotle finally adopts seems to have been directed to the first sense, answering to that of infinite as limitless in potential size. His definition is in terms of *potentiality* and describes the infinite as "that of which one can always take a part beyond what has already been taken." He rejected, as did Bolzano after him, the conception of the infinite as an absolute limit either as "that beyond which there is nothing" or "that which is incapable of being added to." These phrases, he points out, more properly describe the concept of a *whole*. Something which is whole is precisely what you cannot add on to, what lacks nothing. This concept is so far from being equivalent to the concept of *infinity* that it is actually incompatible with it. The infinite is precisely what is *never* finished, completed, rounded off, whole, or in so far as it implies all these things, *actual*.

Aristotle is, of course, by no means denying that anything actually has the character of being infinite, but is only saying something about what that character is. He is saying that infinitude is not a way of being finished off or completed and is, rather, a special fact about the potentialities of whatever is described as infinite. I shall take Aristotle's argument and his view as defining the philosophical problem of the "actual infinite," and this in the sense that he has given definitions of *actuality* and *infinitude* in virtue of which the two notions are incompatible and has thereby made it incumbent on anyone wanting to talk about an "actual infinite" to challenge either his definitions or his argument.

Historically one of the first challenges was made, surprisingly enough, by Aquinas. Aquinas was put into great difficulties in his enterprise of adapting Aristotle to Christian use by this view of Aristotle's because Aquinas felt bound to say of God that He was both fully actual and fully infinite, in fact, that He was the most infinite and most actual of all beings. Aquinas broke through the dilemma by challenging the definition of "infinity." He rejected Aristotle's definition in favor of a conception that seems rather more akin to the Pythagorean concept of the "unlimited," though by no means identifiable with it. Aquinas allows himself to describe as "infinite" both *form* that has not been particularized by *matter* and *matter* that has not been specified or delimited by *form*. However, Aquinas does not give an explicit definition of infinity in this new sense, and it is hard to see what one would be like.

The problem of trying to decide whether it is possible to find an explicit definition of "infinity" that will fit Aquinas' usage, though perhaps interesting in itself, is here irrelevant, and I should like to pass on to a challenge to the Aristotelian position which does involve an alternative definition of "infinity" – and is the focus of this chapter. The challenge was issued by Bolzano[1] and developed by Cantor.[2] This break with the Aristotelian view is one which has been at the center of a great deal of mathematical development, has been one of the key factors in the founding of foundations studies in mathematics. At the same time it has led to the situation which Professor Findlay deplored, the apparent transformation of philosophical problems about infinity into technical issues of set theory, proof theory, or foundations studies.

The Bolzano definition of "infinity" is one which is in direct competition with Aristotle's in the sense that it is a rival formulation of what seems essentially the same concept involving the same usages, rather than a suggested new concept, such as Aquinas offered. This is the famous definition of the infinite as "what is capable of being put into one–one correspondence with a proper part of itself." Properly speaking, though the concept of a "one–one correspondence with a proper part of itself" is due to Bolzano, it is first used as a *definition* by Cantor (and then only negatively to define finite classes). Bolzano in fact defines an infinite set as a sum of all finite sets, having defined finite sets as sets accessible or exhaustible by counting or addition of units. "Being equal to a proper part" is then claimed to be a *property* of infinite sets defined in this way. However, in support of this claim, Bolzano simply offers the example of two particular infinite sets for which the property can be shown to hold.[3] History seems charitably to have averted its eyes and credited him not only with the concept but with having used it as a definition.

Cantor set out armed with a definition of infinitude based ultimately on Bolzano's conception of a one–one correspondence with a proper part and armed with a set of generalizations and redefinitions of ordinary arithmetical operations and relations to cover infinite sets. Above all, he armed himself with the "diagonal argument" which he put forward as showing that one had to make distinctions among infinite sets and that the extended concept of *size* he had introduced in the transfinite arithmetic did not apply simply vacuously to infinite sets. Cantor claimed as a result to have produced objects that must be described as "actual infinities."

Such a claim, if borne out, would appear to settle the philosophical problem of the actual infinite once and for all. I have said "would appear" because it is precisely the nature and meaning of this claim that I want to discuss and not the paradoxes of set theory or whether the diagonal argument is an "impredicative" procedure. I want to try to see whether any philosophical issues hang on the consistency, or otherwise, of set theory or the transfinite arithmetic that Cantor developed.

We have here what seems at least a *prima facie* conflict between a philosophical view and a mathematical development, and it is the nature and genuineness of this conflict which is to be our primary problem. Though quite obviously these problems can only be dealt with by talking about the views that are being said to conflict. And the first problem is to see just what Cantor meant in describing the transfinite numbers as "actual infinities."

What Cantor meant by calling them "infinite" is clear enough and is given by the Bolzano definition. But what he meant by calling them "actual" is not at all clear, even though he seeks to spell out his meaning somewhat by describing the transfinite numbers as "absolutely determined as limits"[4] toward which the numbers of the preceding number class tended. He also wanted to describe the sets of which the *alephs* are the numbers as "wholes."

Though the use of these phrases would seem to make the conflict sharp enough between Cantor and the Aristotelian view, one has still to see what is meant in applying those phrases to the transfinite numbers, since it is clear that the use of "whole," "limit," and "determined" has been extended, and the sense of those phases at the same time correspondingly attenuated. It is not at the same time clear just how far.

A series whose "limit" was ω and had the number *aleph nought* would not in the ordinary way of speaking be said to have a limit at all. And one could call *alephs* "absolutely determined" only in a sense that was very much more attenuated than the sense in which one could apply "determined" or "definite" to, say, the number of primes between 100 and 1000. And above all, it is not clear what it is that is being said about the transfinite numbers in describing them as "actual infinities."

But if one stops for a moment and reflects on it one can see what a surprising thing it would be if a genuinely philosophical view were to be upset by a mathematical discovery. One must look very carefully to see how such an impression could arise. One has to ask especially how it might be that a mathematical calculus and the objects defined by it could take on a special philosophical significance, a significance that reached beyond their definitions and their homely mathematical uses without so much as a by-your-leave. One would say that they could achieve this new philosophical status only by honest work in philosophy, that is by being *given* a genuine philosophical use. (They don't come into the world with that use attached like a label round their necks.) Then and only then would they be in a position to be offered as counter-evidence for any philosophical theory. Of course, the same holds true in the opposite direction, and one would be amazed to find a mathematician giving up an otherwise consistent calculus because of a conflict with however deep a philosophical principle. (The conflict between Berkeley and Newton over "infinitesimals" is a good example here. Newton and his successors were quite rightly not prepared to give up the calculus on the ground of Berkeley's criticisms. And, it should be added, Berkeley did not mean them to.[5])

In trying to see just how it is that the transfinite numbers came to be regarded as a mathematical discovery that is at the same time philosophically significant, it is necessary to make some distinctions among the expressions applied to those transfinite numbers in making philosophical claims. We shall have to divide the expressions into those which have a meaning defined within and by the transfinite arithmetic itself and those which are not given any special meaning within the transfinite arithmetic and therefore, if they have a sufficiently defined meaning in general currency, and are applicable, can be used to say something about the transfinite arithmetic as a whole and to place it with greater or lesser exactness in some wider sphere, whether mathematical or philosophical.

An illustration here would be the concept of "limit." This is given a special use by Cantor inside his calculus and therefore, although he does try to use it to make general *philosophical* remarks about his alephs and transfinite ordinals, it is not available for that purpose, and to use it in that way is to trade illegitimately on its ordinary use outside the transfinite arithmetic. That is, to describe his *alephs* or his *omegas* as "limits" is either false or vacuous according to which sense of "limit" you apply.

The ordinary analysis of the concept of *limit* involves, as Cantor himself points out, not only that it is the smallest number of the succeeding number class but that one can choose members of the class of which it is said to be the limit, which are "as close as one pleases" to the claimed limit. In fact, in the ordinary use of "limit" it is the latter property which is the essential one, and the former belongs properly only to those limits which are at the same time *upper bounds*. But it is only the former, inessential property which is shared by the transfinite ordinals and which provides the special meaning of "limit" in transfinite arithmetic.

If, therefore, without giving due notice that a special sense is involved, one describes the transfinite numbers as "limits" in the course of a general philosophical argument about their status, one can at most succeed in deceiving one's hearers and probably oneself. One cannot use the word to say something about the transfinite arithmetic itself and its wider philosophical or mathematical significance. For a word to succeed in doing that it must hold itself open to the ordinary philosophical or mathematical tests of applicability. It cannot come into this new arena only pretending to obey the rules prevailing there, while secretly playing some quite different, or deceptively similar, game.

Now, all this is quite unfair to Cantor as a mathematician and as a man, and although I suspect that some will be taking me to be enjoying a kind of philosopher's revenge, I am not at all trying to get at Cantor or to impugn his honesty. What I am trying to do is to get at the logic of the situation in a way in which Cantor was understandably unable to do. Above all, I am trying to see as clearly as possible how, if at all, a mathematical calculus or other mathematical discovery could come to have philosophical significance. Where this seems to have happened, as in the case of the transfinite arithmetic, I want to try to make out the details of the process if I can.

By looking at some of the accounts of infinity that were extant in Cantor's day, and against which he felt he had to battle, it is possible to see how it was that he was not in a position to be clear about the relations between the transfinite arithmetic and philosophical views about infinity. Above all, one can come to see what Cantor meant in applying to the transfinite numbers that set of expressions "absolutely determined," "definite," "actual infinities," and "wholes." These expressions are not given a special meaning in the formal structure of the transfinite arithmetic itself, though it may be that they are given special meanings in being applied to it or, more properly, to the objects defined by it or within it.

If they *are* given special meanings in that application, then we must ask how they have earned these new meanings. What other work have the words been given to do in this line? They cannot derive the new meanings simply from this one new application alone without rendering vacuous Cantor's assertions which try to use them where the old meanings won't work and the new meanings have yet to be defined or assigned.

A conception or definition of "infinity" which has always been a common one and seems to have been no less common in the nineteenth century was the view that infinity was, in Cantor's phrase, "a variable finite." This was the view that infinity was a "variable quantity" or a "quantity which grows beyond all limits," and this view had at some time or other collected the name the "potential infinite." Cantor described the infinite defined by these phrases as "the improper infinite," and regarded it as the chief rival or obstacle against which his transfinite numbers had to struggle, and from which they must be clearly distinguished. And he so distinguished them by calling them "actual" as against "potential," "determinate" as against "variable," "limits" as against "unlimited." He took his conception of infinity ("the proper infinite") embodied in the transfinite arithmetic as clearly contradicting this view of the infinite, and it might be thought that here was a way to philosophical significance for the transfinite arithmetic and a way in which the words Cantor wants to use to say something about his calculus and the objects it defines can acquire an honest sense. For if the transfinite arithmetic can be used to overthrow a significant philosophical doctrine (as it seems to have done in the case of the now more or less defunct view that infinity is a variable, or a "variable quantity that grows beyond any pre-assigned limit"), it has gained, to that extent, philosophical significance. The denial of a philosophically significant proposition is also philosophically significant.

There are two snares here. One is making sure that the proposition is in fact denied, and the second is making sure that the proposition denied is neither a tautology nor nonsense. Unfortunately, however, the view that an infinite quantity is one that "varies or grows beyond all limits" is, in fact, nonsense. It is simply incoherent and, while denying it, in the sense of pointing out this incoherence, may be a useful thing to do, a proposition or a theory which is its formal contradictory does not by that fact gain any significance.

Those who tried to define infinity in this way, as a species of variable or "growing" quantity, noticed the obvious fact that infinity has to do with number or quantity, although quite clearly it is not a number like other numbers. One cannot significantly ask the same questions about it or perform the same operations with it with the same kind of results. A variable, one might say, also has to do with number, although equally clearly it is not a number like other numbers and one cannot significantly ask the same questions about a variable or operate with one with the same sort of results that one would get operating with particular numbers. Nothing would seem more natural, then, than to describe infinity as some species of variable, especially since its peculiar characteristic is to run away beyond our grasp.

Unfortunately, however, infinity is not *any* species of variable, and to think so was only possible in the nineteenth century, not only when the concept of a variable was not well understood but when there was a positive barrier to a proper understanding of it in so far as the assumption was made that a valid analysis ought to come up with a notional concept describing some kind of object, however bizarre. It was not thought sufficient to describe the functioning of some word or sign and let it go at that. *Negation* is another example of a concept which this assumption made it impossible to give a coherent account of.

Bolzano had already pointed out that what the earlier mathematicians called a "variable quantity" is not properly a quantity at all, but went on to say that it was only "the idea and notion of a quantity." In this he was moving in the right direction, though stopped short by the above assumption. What we should now say is that not only is a variable not properly a quantity, but it is not improperly one either, nor is it the "idea" or yet the "notion" of a quantity. It is not a kind of quantity of any sort, not even a radically ill-defined quantity, which, I suppose is what one might mean by "the idea and notion of a quantity."

A variable is in fact a referential device of mathematical grammar analogous to a pronoun in ordinary grammar. (Although, with the advent of quantification, the variables of logic and mathematics have become much more finely articulated and selective devices than the pronouns of ordinary English.) A variable is no more an "indefinite" quantity than a personal pronoun is a person of no fixed character (whose proper name, I suppose, would have to be "Someone").

The concept of *variable* is grammatically unfitted to the job of providing a definition of infinity. Infinity is no species of referential device, no matter *how* qualified. Infinity or infinitude is an attribute of that to which quantity or number apply, and not a way of referring to number in general or to any particular number. A variable is a way of referring to number and not an attribute of number. No number is variable. No number 6 or even 6.99 is going to metamorphose subtly into 7. The two concepts variable and infinity can no more be made to meet than the 6 can be made to meet the 7.

The work of Frege and Wittgenstein, very largely, has earned us freedom from the traditional assumption that the analysis of a word necessarily consists in providing a notion or concept which governs the use of that word. And Wittgenstein has helped us to free ourselves from the assumption that for a word to have meaning there must be something to which it refers. It is therefore possible for us to understand and give an account of variables in a way which was not open to anyone who set themselves the impossible task of finding something over and above a set of rules or practices governing the use of variables, the task of finding and describing something *in virtue of which* they had the use or function they did, a unitary ultimate source of the rules themselves. As a result of this new understanding, we can see, in a way which would have been difficult if not impossible in the nineteenth century, that the attempt to define infinity as a kind of variable or variable quantity, the view which was called the "potential infinite," was void *ab initio*.

In so far as Cantor's use of the words "actual," "determined," and "whole" to describe the transfinite numbers was intended to dissociate himself and his theory from this point of view, one can only sympathize and approve. But one must add that this intention and this employment are not sufficient to give philosophical sense to his use of the words. Nor is it sufficient to bestow a philosophical significance on the transfinite arithmetic. It is not because of the success of the transfinite arithmetic that the theory of the "potential infinite" has to be discarded. It has to be discarded because it is a nonsense and internally incoherent. It does not say anything, so that its contradictory does not say anything either.

Hausdorff saw that the word "whole" had no special function within the transfinite arithmetic and described the preliminary definitions of "set" in terms of it as "explaining the unknown by the unknown." Making use once again of the point of view that Frege and Wittgenstein have won for us, one might say that while Cantor's definition of a set as a "collection into a whole of definite and distinct objects of our intuition or our thought" might be a useful prop in setting up or working through set theory, the meaning of "set" ultimately rests on, and is defined by, the set theory that emerges. And once the theory has been set out or understood, the prop becomes superfluous.

For the benefit of those who are made to feel comfortable by jargon, one could say that in the definition the word "whole" had a *heuristic* function only. What Cantor's use of the word "whole," or, for that matter, the words "determined" and "actual," do *not* succeed in doing is defining a relation between the transfinite arithmetic and some wider philosophical context in which these words are used in an unspecialized sense and according to rules which, like the case of "limit," differ in important respects from their use in the transfinite arithmetic, even though there may be a measure of overlap with their application to the transfinite arithmetic.

There is a feeling of anomaly, mystification and, in extreme cases, vertigo that usually attends those discussions of the transfinite arithmetic that attempt to place it in such a wider setting. The source of this feeling lies precisely in the intersecting of two differing though similar sets of rules governing the same words. It comes from the attempt to play two different games at the same time with the same words. The sense of thrilling, vibrant mystification comes from trying to combine two incompatible viewpoints or two incompatible usages. Philosophical reality, on the other hand, one might say, is plain – very plain.

Aristotle's remarks in the *Physics* about the concept of "whole" seem in general very just. In one ordinary way if we describe something as "whole" we mean that it is "complete," "made up," "finished off," "lacking nothing." And if it were an ordered collection of things that was in question we could not count it as "whole" till the last member was accounted for or put in place. "I haven't got the whole collection" means that some have eluded me. But if the things I was collecting turned out to be infinite in number, one would naturally say that there was not a "whole collection" that I could aim at having, or that the words "whole collection" had not any sense here.

There is, however, as Aristotle points out, another perfectly good sense of "whole" in which one can apply the word to all the things answering to a given description, things forming a unity of a different sort, a *class*. Of wholes in this latter sense, the same questions cannot be asked significantly, and the same conclusions cannot be drawn about the parts or members of such wholes. For one thing, there is no implication about members of wholes in this latter sense that they are all actual or existent. Deceptions past, present, predictable, likely or only possible form this kind of unity or whole. These are two quite different senses of "whole," and the only thing common to the two of them is that whatever is said to be a whole in either sense must form a *unity*. But as there are different kinds of unity, so there are different senses of "whole" answering to them. One kind of unity is made by sticking things together with glue or combining them to serve a single function, as the bits of my watch form a unity. And certain things must be true of anything said to form a whole or unity of this sort.

The new mainspring which I have just ordered does not yet form a unity with my watch, and my watch is not whole without it. There is, however, a sense of "unity" which is so different from this that it seems almost an equivocation to use the same word. This is the unity of *sameness*, the unity of things belonging to the same class, the unity of the class to which they belong. The criteria that things must satisfy to qualify for this sort of unity and the conclusions that one can draw from their "unity" in this sense are utterly different from those of the other sort of "unity." Even the mainspring that has only just been ordered can enter into unities or wholes of this classificatory kind even though, for the moment, it exists only in the mind of the watchmaker. It is nevertheless a *mainspring* that I have ordered and not something else. It belongs in that class.

It does not make sense to raise questions about "last members" of unities or wholes of this latter, classificatory sort, even where the things forming the unity are naturally ordered. Nor can one say that they are any less unities or any less wholes in this sense because there is no "last member." There is no last member because the concept of *last member* is not defined for this kind of whole. One must not say that wholes of this latter definitional or formal sort "lack a last term or last member," as though they ought really to have one but have somehow missed out. Something can only lack what it makes conceptual sense for it to have.

Much of the mystification about the transfinite has had its source in the interplay between these two radically different senses of the word "whole." There are probably enough philosophical problems raised by both concepts of *whole* to occupy more than one symposium paper. But despite this, it is clear enough to common observation that there are at least two senses, and that the two senses that have just been described are in fact incompatible.

For an object or collection to be called a "whole" in the first sense (the "physical" or "functional" wholes), not only must a last part or member be defined, where there is an ordering, but this last part or member must actually be present for the object or collection to merit the title "whole." By contrast, things said to "form a whole" in the second, conceptual or definitional sense, by being members of a single class, do so precisely in virtue of some relation of similarity among them. Generally, what they share, what brings them into the unity, can be shared by other things without numerical limit, so that the concept of a *last* has no application. There is also no implication that the members of such a classificatory whole are all present-and-accounted-for or actual.

If, having made these distinctions, we ask in which sense the aggregates bearing the transfinite numbers are "wholes," then it seems quite clear that it is in the second, definitional, sense. They are certainly not wholes in the first sense, to which "unfinished" or "incomplete" is the proper opposite. There is no danger of such aggregates being unfinished or incomplete. There is no sense in which they could be "finished" or "complete" either, or "whole" in that sense outlined above, which involves these.

But if this is the case, we should not be surprised or mystified by the fact that there are ordered aggregates which are wholes and yet have no last term. This is simply a normal feature of classificatory wholes and is no more mysterious than they are in the first place. What one must not say is that such classificatory aggregates are (or are not) "complete." To describe them as "complete though lacking a last term" is mystery-mongering without much scruple. One might as well make a mystery out of the fact that virtue is weightless or numbers invisible.

Collections or wholes of this sort are just not the right kind of thing either to have or lack a last term, or to be "complete" in any ordinary sense of that word. The transfinite arithmetic and the remarks about it do not succeed in setting before us or defining any extraordinary sense of this word, or of the words "actual" or "whole" either. And even . if the transfinite arithmetic were to set before us some new extended and attenuated meanings of them, this would not produce any philosophical surprises. We should still have to ask what, if any, was the relation between these new senses of the words and their ordinary, untechnical, senses.

What would produce pretty well impenetrable mystery here would be the assumption that there must be an ultimately single and unequivocal sense underlying both uses of the word "whole" from which they are both derived and in terms of which they can both be defined, a kind of *ur-wholeness*. This archetypal wholeness would have to combine contradictory properties on a heroic scale.

I have so far not said anything explicit about that traditional centerpiece of discussions of the transfinite arithmetic, the diagonal argument. I have contented myself so far with looking in some detail at the meaning of the words "actual," "whole," "complete," and "limit," whose application to the transfinite numbers has given the transfinite arithmetic an air of philosophical significance, and I hope that what I have had to say has gone some way to showing that this air of philosophical significance is falsely come by, and the atmosphere of thrilling paradox is manufactured and unnecessary.

However, it could be said that it is precisely the diagonal argument that is the source of the philosophical significance of the transfinite arithmetic, and that while it might not be sufficient to give a sense to, or license, the application of the above set of words to the transfinite numbers, it does at least show that in some sense, however attenuated, the transfinite numbers must be regarded as "definite and determinate." Otherwise it might seem they could not have the feature demonstrated by the argument: that one can be "larger" than another.

This argument, however, must face the same basic dilemma that met the other claims that sought to impose a philosophical significance on the transfinite numbers by force, as it were, or by stealth. We are being asked here to accept that the diagonal argument proves something not only in the transfinite arithmetic but in philosophy as well. And we are not only entitled, but obliged, to ask searching questions both about what is supposed to have been proved and about just how this new meaning is meant to have been established. One must have the same sensitivity and alertness here that Hume suggested that we should exercise in observing the passage from an "is" to an "ought." This is not to deny that the thing is possible, but only to press the question how it is to be done.

For an argument to establish a philosophical conclusion it must first establish itself as a philosophical argument, and to do this it must start from premises that are both philosophically significant and acceptable. And what, again, must be guarded against here is that whatever words, such as "definite" or "determinate," are chosen to express the putative philosophical significance of the transfinite numbers are not having their application justified according to one set of rules and then having their claim to philosophical significance made out according to another set.

If the transfinite numbers are shown to be "definite" and "determinate" by the diagonal argument, then the kind of definiteness and determinateness they have is also shown by the diagonal argument and is limited to that. One could say that, in its widest application in set theory, the diagonal argument shows that of any pair of sets of which one is defined in terms of, or generated from, the other in a special way (i.e. is its power set) any function or relation which can be used to pair off systematically the members of the given set with the members of its power set can also be used to define or pick out a member of the power set which that particular function will fail to pair with any member of the original set. This is not the usual way of describing the diagonal argument in discussions about its philosophical implications, but I think that something like this is the way in which it must be described if the description is to avoid what is, from a philosophical point of view, an objectionable play on two separate senses of the words "whole," "complete," or "exhaustive" (words that sometimes hide behind the expressions "a mapping" or "a 1–1 correspondence").

However, describing the diagonal argument in this neutral way causes a great deal of its supposed philosophical significance to evaporate, and with it most of the sense of surprise and mystery. It seems neither very surprising, mysterious, nor philosophically significant that there are classes so defined in terms of one another that any pairing rule can be used to select or describe a member of the one class which is inaccessible to the given pairing rule simply because it is systematically defined out of reach. It is, nevertheless, no mean achievement to have proven this, especially in the full generality of Cantor's proof, which lays no restrictions on the means allowed in the attempt to produce a correlation between the two classes.

Now we need to ask: what philosophical conclusions are licensed by this discovery about the impossibility of pairing exhaustively the members of two inter-defined infinite classes, and what special uses of the words "definite" or "determinate" are so licensed? Can these be used to draw philosophical conclusions? The answer is by no means easy. And this is because the question is by no means definite. If one asks specifically whether the argument is sufficient to license a denial of the Aristotelian doctrine that to describe a class as infinite is to say something about its potentialities rather than its achievements, to say something exact about what can or cannot be done with it rather than something obscure and inexact about its size, then I think that the answer must be that it does not.

It seems quite possible to accommodate the results of the diagonal argument to the style of talk that Aristotle recommends and say that it shows that there are definite, describable relations even among potentialities. And this fact would not be philosophically very startling or very new. It is, of course, quite possible to question the value of applying philosophical language of this sort to mathematical results, but one must observe that this objection cuts both ways and amounts also to a denial of philosophical significance to the diagonal argument or the mathematical results.

One important disclaimer that I must make here is that I have not been trying to show that a mathematical result can never have philosophical significance, but rather to ask just *how* it can come by such an extension to its ordinary mathematical uses. I want to deny that any mathematical system or theorem springs into existence fully armed with philosophical significance and bristling with philosophical relations. Whatever philosophical significance a piece of mathematics may get it has to be given by being put to philosophical uses, by being assimilated, together with other phenomena, into a single picture into which further things can be shown to fit. It cannot by itself seize philosophical significance by force and thereby force some philosophical issue to a conclusion.

What I have tried to do is to chart the natural history of one such attempt at seizure of power by a well-known bit of mathematics and to show that the transfinite numbers based a false claim to philosophical significance on the ground that they showed new and surprising facts about "wholes" or "complete" collections. I have tried to demonstrate that in fact this claim was vitiated by a failure to distinguish two separate senses of "whole" and cognates, and by the resulting attempt to run with the hare and hunt with the hounds simultaneously.

The "experts" have not got their grip on any philosophical problem, though it may be a philosophical problem to show that they have not.

4 Miracles

The concept of a *miracle* is sometimes thought of as marking a border between science and religion, that is, between the phenomena that belong to science and are subject to scientific understanding and scientific explanation and those which belong to religion and are subject to religious explanation and understanding only. As such, it is a concept whose analysis can be extremely useful in getting clear about the nature of both types of understanding, even if it is only to show, as I hope to, that there is no common frontier between the two and that there are no phenomena that are in the ambiguous, even contradictory, position in which the traditional popular view of miracles places them. This ambiguous position consists in their being considered to be phenomena which seem at first sight to belong to the scientific sphere, that is, are of the right *type* to get a scientific explanation, but are somehow such that they "obviously" never will or can get such an explanation. That is what is supposed to be so striking and challenging about them. They are meant to challenge the run of scientific law and lawfulness itself.

First we have to notice that there are many places where that law doesn't run, things that we understand in ways other than scientific. Our understanding of the aptness or the wittiness of a remark does not involve scientific theorizing, nor does that scientific understanding come into our grasping the reason for the mood of a person or actions of some group, the suicidal depression, for example, that overtakes whole tribes of Amazonian Indians as a result of the encroachments of the type of "civilization" that the West has introduced there. Nor would we look for a scientific theory to "explain" the outrage we may feel at some injustice.

There are also coincidences. These also don't get scientific, causal explanations, even though each of the separate events or occurrences that make them up might get such an explanation. What any explanations will miss out is precisely the *connection* between the coincidental occurrences that is somehow remarkable, striking, or shattering even. There may be a perfectly good scientific causal or secular historical account of the happening of each, but their happening *together* is just what escapes understanding in those terms and is often handed over to a religious account. My finding a five-pound note or the coming of rain just after I have prayed for such a thing will certainly escape a scientific account. There will no doubt be a perfectly good secular story to explain the presence of the five-pound note just where I found it and no difficulty in understanding my praying in my extremity, if I am a person of a certain sort, but these are two different stories, neither (nor both) of which explain the running together of their outcomes.

But coincidences, though a religious person may well regard some of them as miraculous, do not present the challenge to science that is supposed to be thrown down by the kind of phenomena that the popular notion of *miracle* points to: the prodigies, the outrageous, the "inexplicable" that are offered as setting some kind of limit on science and its pretensions.

To deny the existence of phenomena in the contested position popularly assigned to miraculous events is not to deny the existence of miracles or the existence of things which are to be understood only from within a body of religious beliefs or from a religious standpoint and attitude to the world, or at least to the events in question.

I am not religious myself in a way that would allow me to use the notion of a *miracle* in my account or understanding of any event, but I would certainly not deny, and in fact do not doubt, that there are many for whom that notion does have a use and a sense and a legitimate place in their understanding of things. That understanding is itself a religious understanding, and my argument is that it is only within that religious context and from those surroundings that the concept of a *miracle* can draw life and strength and have a legitimate application. What I want to argue is that the notion can't *force* an entry into the scientific sphere and make a home for itself there.

People have tried to lay onto the concept of *the miraculous* tasks it could not bear. They have thought there might be events that would present themselves to every observer in such a way as to be open to one form of explanation only, events that could challenge and break the grip of the scientific world-view and convert the heathen scientist by force, as it were. They have sought to defeat the scientists on their own ground and thereby force them to recognize and employ religious conceptions in dealing with the world.

This conception of *the miraculous* involves misconceptions of both scientific or secular understanding and religious understanding and the religious point of view, deep misunderstandings. And I want to try to bring this out – chiefly by looking at how the working scientist works and looks at things. We shall at the same time have to keep a critical eye on the notion of *evidence*, because events do not come before us with a label attached that certifies them as evidence for or against this or that. Observations and agreed descriptions of events are *used* as evidence; *being evidence* is not one of their natural properties.

We need also to keep in mind that *events* and *descriptions of events* are things of quite a different order and must be kept separate and not confused. A failure of care here has infected many current discussions. Miss Anscombe,[1] for example, talks of a lump of phosphorous "turning into" a bird without, it seems, being alive to the many assumptions that are buried in the phrase "turning into." The best we, as careful observers of the event, could probably say was that where there had been a lump of phosphorous there was subsequently a bird. We would have to be able to ask a lot of questions and do a lot of careful investigating and even theorizing before we would really be justified in saying that the one thing had "turned into" the other. The expression "turned into" has sense only within, and gets its sense from, a whole setof practices and perceived regularities. The milk "turns" sour or is "turned into" cheese by the cheese maker. It is those practices and those regularities that allow us to distinguish between transformation of one thing into another on the one hand and replacement of one thing by another on the other hand.

The concept of *the miraculous* that I wish to reject has been used in an attempt to stake out in secular terms an area which is appropriate to secular understanding or explanation but is at the same time obviously or *demonstrably* inaccessible to secular or scientific explanation. By contrast, I want to go some way toward showing that *the miraculous* is a religious notion, which, far from *forcing* a religious point of view on us, requires such a point of view to give it sense and application.

Religious understanding and explanation, on the one hand, and scientific understanding and explanation, on the other, are radically different enterprises and not in competition for the same phenomena. The miraculousness of an occurrence, that is, its religious significance, is a feature of it in which scientists have no stake and no status. They may be called in, like the doctors at Lourdes, to give an accurate description in scientific terms of what happened, but it is not for them *qua* scientists to say that the event has religious significance, or even that it has not. But these are positions that must be argued for.

Before what is commonly called the "scientific era" there was a competition and a conflict between religious explanation and what can be called loosely "scientific explanation" in that people were then more ready to see the hand of God or gods in what happened, and, having set this down as the cause, were not inclined to look for any other. The religious explanation was taken as sufficient in itself, and as excluding any other. Describing a phenomenon like thunder as the work of God or the anger of the gods removed it from the natural order and assigned it to the supernatural.

In our own day, even among those who are more than nominally religious, the position is reversed and it is usually assumed that where an event has a scientific explanation it can have no religious significance. The reversal can also be seen in the attempt to define "the miraculous" in purely secular terms – that is, as "the not scientifically explicable." This definition, which I hope to show is a misguided and unusable one, I shall refer to as that of a "secular miracle." Of course, as R. F. Holland has pointed out,[2] such a definition is too wide and would include acts of devilry as well as divine miracles. Since I am only concerned to show that it won't do as a definition at all, I am not bothered by this and will continue to refer to this putative class of the scientifically inexplicable as "secular miracles" without, I hope, causing too much confusion.

The fundamental difficulty with the notion of a "secular miracle" and its implied view of the relation between science and religion is that it is based on a view of science as an alternative, quasi-theological system defining a world-view that is in genuine competition with other religions (Christianity, say) and disputing the same territory. This view seems to be shared by some philosophers commenting on the sciences; but it gets no support from the actual secular work of the practising scientists. This view of things has also been taken up from the other side by the "creationist" branch of fundamentalist Christianity, who aim to promote the Bible as an account of the origin of species that is in competition with Darwin. The damage that this has the potential to wreak on scientific education in the US is nothing compared to the damage that it can inflict on religious consciousness and any sense of the Bible's depths. Perhaps one should say that it grows out of (though at the same time it spreads) a superficiality of religious feeling and understanding that is trying to compensate for this radical lack of depth by intensity and stridency.

Of course, like everyone else in our era, working scientists have been subject to the seductions of the world-view generated from scientific practice and variously called "scientism," "mechanism" or "naturalism." But, I want to say, this world-view is the product of, and remains within, the scientists' non-scientific activity and needs, and has no legitimate place in the work of their working day. This "mechanical world-view" is the converse of creationism. It is the product, if you like, of a felt human need for a larger context than their scientific work can legitimately provide. What I mean by this and the nature of the difficulties and incoherences in the attempt to forge a complete world-view out of the sciences will have to be made out. At the moment I shall only indicate the area of difficulty by saying that it is at the bottom of the determinist and reductionist fantasies that have been ghosts at the scientific feast of the modern era.

What these attempts at a science-based world-view have in common is that they present the sciences as a potentially complete system of explanation, and then, following a familiar theological impulse, they want to go on to talk about conditions at the limit. Only from that quasi or would-be theological mountaintop could one talk about the "absolutely inexplicable." One could say that those theological aspirations of scientism or the mechanistic world-view have set themselves up for the kind of counterattack posed by what I have called "secular" miracles.

Down here amongst the working scientists one could only talk about what was inexplicable at a given moment, or relative to a given theory. But notice, anything that is inexplicable in terms of a given theory and lies within its claimed range would be counted in the balance against that theory and would motivate the search for a better and more inclusive one.

If we keep to this workaday world of the working scientist, we have no way of distinguishing between "secular miracles" and "unsolved scientific problems." The problem posed by the secular miracle has got to be an unsolvable one – not just unsolved – and unsolvable without any restriction laid on the means to be used in solving it, either on the concepts or on the theories, except that the means and the resolution must be "scientific" rather than religious.

I have put scare quotes around "scientific" because I think it is pretty clear that a burden is being laid on that word which it can hardly be bolstered up to bear. That is, to make the concept of a "secular miracle" viable, one would have to give a definition of the concept of *scientific* which set sufficient restriction on the theories and concepts counted as scientific to be able to show that there could be an event which no theory calling itself "scientific" would be capable of explaining.

And here one has the outlines of the crux on which I hope to break the concept of a "secular miracle," because it is not any sort of happening that is a candidate for miraclehood: it is only those occurrences and those properties which are of the right type for a scientific explanation whose permanent and necessary failure to get one would constitute a miracle in this "secular" sense.

Only the hardest-bitten reductionist or determinist would claim that everything whatever was subject to scientific explanation. (And one suspects that even the hard-bitten manage this only by tacitly erecting scientific explicability into a test of reality, making it into a demand, so that they can conveniently dismiss the claims of awkward counterexamples.) If we don't follow the reductionist into this tautological position, the concept of "being of the right type for scientific explanation" remains a concept with content, that is, it makes a selection from among the things it is possible to talk sense about, and not everything comes under it.

It may be by no means clear what qualifies something for potential scientific explicability, but it is at least clear that this will be some conceptual rather than a contingent feature of it. But if, on the other hand, one described a "secular miracle" as something permanently excluded from scientific explicability, one would presumably be happy only in ascribing permanence to this exclusion if it were necessary and conceptual.[3] Secular miracles will then have to be both included in and excluded from the scientifically explicable on conceptual grounds. Roy Holland may be prepared to talk about "contradictions in our experience" as he does in describing what I have been calling "secular miracles," but here I think one can see the contradiction runs deeper than that, into the conception of a "secular miracle" itself, requiring it to be at the same time the right type and the wrong type for scientific explanation to apply.

Uniqueness is, of course, a central feature of the miraculous. If water were to start turning into wine fairly regularly this would soon cease to be considered a miracle. It would just be the way things were, a natural fact about water and wine. This requirement of uniqueness can be made the basis of an argument which has rather too short a way with secular miracles. One of the characteristics a phenomenon must have in order to secure the scientist's attention and to be considered by them to be in need of explanation is repeatability. What is not repeatable does not concern the scientist. They can't get a grip on it to study it. Results or phenomena that cannot be reproduced by any reasonably competent practitioner with the right equipment are simply rejected by the scientific community as inaccurately observed or described, or else ignored as of no scientific interest.

The term "freak result" is a term of scientific dismissal. Science no more concerns itself with the unique or the individual than it does with the accidental. There is by definition no scientific explanation of the uniqueness of the unique, or to put it in the Aristotelian way, there is no explanation of the unique *qua* unique or the unique in so far as it is unique, but only of an occurrence in so far as it comes under some general heading. Something offers itself for scientific study only in so far as it is not unique but has characteristics in common with other things or events. But if a miracle is essentially and necessarily unique, it is by that fact alone not a candidate for scientific explanation. It simply joins the unremarkable ranks of those things like accidents, coincidences, the significance of speech or the appropriateness of a melody to the sentiments expressed in a song, things which are of the wrong sort to get a scientific explanation.

There is something important in this argument, but it nevertheless has too short a way with the concept of a *secular miracle.* One can see this as soon as one notices that the problem we are dealing with here is essentially the same as the classic problem of "the uniformity of nature." The difference between the two lies largely in the conclusions one is meant to draw from the discovery of the supposedly recalcitrant event. In its role as "secular miracle" it is taken as evidence for the interference of God in an otherwise orderly Universe. As counter-evidence for *uniformity* it is supposed to show that the Universe was not orderly to begin with and only led us up the garden path to that belief by a short-term and accidental appearance of uniformity.

But it is clearly too easy a way to let scientists turn their back on any alleged un-uniformity saying simply that science concerns itself only with regularities, and that it was a conceptual mistake to look for a scientific understanding of the irregular and unique. This would give science security at the cost of usefulness. One could never count on its applicability.

The sciences can only tell us about "the world" (in practice, what to expect and how to operate) if they can as well tell us something wrong and something whose wrongness is not a subjective matter of decision but has external and public criteria.

Though it may be true that science has "by definition," one might say, nothing to do with the irregular or the singular, this cannot justify the scientist in dismissing any particular occurrence as for that reason permanently outside the concern of science, as our argument seemed to suggest they could.

The trouble would be that not only would science as an enterprise be made secure from upset, but the particular theories held at a given moment would be made secure from criticism or modification. Scientific development would either be stopped or else made completely capricious. There would always be a free, unfettered (and unguided) choice whether to take the event or observation as miraculous or as counter-evidence for the theory or regularity that it was violating. The area of science in which one was working could not provide a criterion which would eliminate this arbitrariness because it is precisely that area which was under investigation. It could hardly at the same time be the *tested* and the *test* in relation to the same experiment.

It can happen, of course, that an individual scientist or the scientific community as a whole may at some period hover between treating a given theory as a test or as the tested. And a particular theory, instrument or even experiment may at different periods be given different places in the hierarchy of beliefs, theories and practices that make up that confederation of enterprises gathered together under the title "science." Any given theory or instrument (the mercury thermometer, for example) might be given the role of test at one time and at another may become the tested. (The history of the methods and standards of measurement abounds with examples of that change of status.) What cannot happen is that the one thing is both test and tested at the same time.

The concept of a *miracle* or, for that matter, an "irregularity" in nature can therefore have no criterion of application drawn from within the sciences themselves. It is, and will remain, from the point of view of the sciences an empty and unusable concept. It has no role within the sciences and can be given no role there.

There are certainly a great many things that happen both outside laboratories and inside them which should not happen according to current conceptions and current theories. Sometimes the body of scientists accept them and treat these happenings as evidence of the inadequacy of the reigning theory, seeking to modify or enlarge that theory to take account of the recalcitrant results.

They need not. They can stick to the theory as adequate and dismiss the occurrences in one of several ways. If the results are repeatable occurrences, that is, a phenomenon that can actually be studied, the scientists can apply the useful term "anomaly" to them and put them to one side. This itself can mean several things. It can mean that they have confidence that the theory can in the end be shown to cope with the phenomenon, even though for the moment it does not seem to. It can also mean that, while they have an open mind on the question of the adequacy of the theory to the phenomenon, they have not yet got the materials together for a significant enlargement of that theory and are going to go on using it meanwhile. Or it may amount to a judgment that the phenomenon is not important or significant enough to warrant the effort of a major readjustment of an otherwise useful theory.

The crucial thing here is that calling some repeatable phenomenon "an anomaly" is not to assign some permanent or absolute property to it but rather to assign it a temporary place in relation to the state of the art. In using the term "anomaly" the scientists are not doing what would undermine their whole enterprise, namely, making a final judgment on the awkward phenomenon as lying outside the scope of the sciences.

The same is true of the scientist's way of dismissing particular observations or results that go against accepted theory. A claim like the Russian one to have observed volcanic activity on the Moon was quite rightly treated with a great deal of skepticism so long as it was made at one observatory only. Though a certain amount of attention was immediately focussed on the area where it was said to have been observed, majority opinion was that probably something else had been seen and misdescribed or misinterpreted. The view that the Moon was volcanically inert remained generally unshaken. So long as there was no confirmation from any other source, the claim was not dismissed entirely, but it was given a very low order of probability. Misobservation was the general opinion.

Had it been an observation for which there was in the nature of the case no hope for further confirmation or disconfirmation in the not too distant future, it would rightly have been ignored completely and might have remained for some future historian of science to dig up after theories had been revised, as an example of prescience or perhaps injustice. "Misobservation" is, however, not a final and irreversible dismissal. And the same is also true of "freak result." Applying this term to an apparently unrepeatable occurrence in dismissing it is, for the scientist, to say that there is, as yet, not even the beginning of a theory about it. Describing it as "freak" is to say that for the moment it can only be seen as isolated, and not as one of a class of events (which is the precondition of its receiving a theoretical explanation).

But to say this would certainly not be to say that it can never or will never be seen as a member of some class of events. No scientist could ever justify saying that. The scientists can't pronounce the event to be "unique" and thereby dismiss it finally and absolutely. What kind of evidence could they have? It is probable that most freak results will never in fact receive an explanation, but this will be because they have simply been forgotten, not because they have received some scientifically final and absolute dismissal.

There could not be a class of events in the ambiguous position of being the right sort to receive a scientific explanation and yet being miraculous, because to be the latter they would have to be unique, and if unique they would be rejected as not candidates for scientific explanation. What the subsequent argument showed is that the scientist would never be justified in rejecting an occurrence as unique in a final or absolute way because uniqueness is not a scientifically determinable property of anything. However, it may still look as though the scientists, by successfully fitting an occurrence into a theoretical system or bringing it under some general classification, may be establishing that it is not unique and thereby eliminating it as a candidate for miraclehood, so that they might at least have this negative function with respect to miracles.

This is a mistake which is fundamental to the whole notion of a *secular miracle*, and to see what it consists in one needs to specify more closely the crux posed in the first section of this chapter. To say that explaining something is to show it is not unique is once again to try to define the "unique" and thereby the "secular miracle" in terms of scientific explicability, in particular as the complement, or part of it, of the class of the *scientifically explicable*, that is, as part of the class of the "not scientifically explicable."

However, the concept of *scientific explicability* does not define a class which is of the right sort to have a complement class; there is no class of the not-explicable. To have a complement, a class must either have a finite extension or else it must have a criterion that unambiguously settles its membership or the application of the class concept.

But the class of *the scientifically explicable* satisfies neither of these conditions. There is no criterion that settles whether something is explicable or not, only whether it is explained. The most that one can imagine is that it might be possible to produce a proof (perhaps even a non-constructive one) that some type of phenomenon was explicable or not explicable by a particular axiomatized theory. But apart from this latter rather special case, there is in general no way of deciding that a particular event or phenomenon is explicable or not.

Also, a contradiction could be produced from the assumption that the class of the scientifically explicable was finite. The class of the scientifically explicable where no restriction is laid on means, either on the theories or the concepts, is a class which is neither extensionally nor conceptually well defined, and therefore the idea of its complement is an empty one and cannot be used to say anything about anything.

The situation here is in some ways similar to those in which the intuitionist mathematicians want to withhold the use of the law of the excluded middle, i.e. where the characterization in question neither corresponds to a finite class nor is effectively or constructively defined. Here again, one might say, the question of a complement does not arise and therefore the law of the excluded middle has no point of application.

Both of a putative pair of complements cannot be defined solely in terms of one another, the "unique" as the not explicable or assimilable to theory, and the "explicable" as the not unique. If one wants to operate with the concept of the *unique* in the absolute sense in which it is used in relation to the concept of the *miraculous*, it must be supplied with a definition from somewhere else. And if it does get such a definition in terms other than that of *scientific explicability*, there will be no *a priori* reason why its being unique and miraculous would be incompatible with its receiving scientific explanation. Its uniqueness would be a different sort of fact about it like the uniqueness of Jesus or the Bible for Christians, which is not a would-be scientific uniqueness.

One could perhaps describe my argument as trying to show that a limit to science is not to be drawn from within science. As such it is likely to be accepted or even regarded as a truism by many. However, I want to go beyond this to say that a limit is not to be defined from outside either (if one can talk for the moment in these rather large terms). In particular I have been trying to show that religion, religious phenomena and religious concepts do not serve to define such a limit.

If one is religious and recognizes religious phenomena, they will do as examples of things lying outside the scope of science, but this would be neither new nor noteworthy, and it would not be to define a limit. Science and religion have no common frontier and no disputed territory.

I have described as "quasi-theological" the conception of science which is common to the determinist, the reductionist, and the attempt to define miracles or the supernatural in terms of scientific explicability. A suspicion that something like this may be the case is aroused as soon as one notices that we have here what seems to be an attempt to define a religious concept in terms of non-religious ones. Without claiming that there is any more of a logical barrier to such a definition than there is to the derivation of an "ought" from an "is," I would say with Hume that we should at least treat such a transition with a great deal of skepticism and caution. One may at least suspect that the conception of *science* and *scientific explicability* which is the starting point is as religious as the concept of *miracle* or the *supernatural* which is supposed to be got from it.

What can be meant by this claim is perhaps best seen in the comparison between the concept of *nature* and *the natural* which is implied in the expression (which I have carefully avoided) "the laws of nature" and the concept of *nature* and *the natural* which is used by Aristotle. The Aristotelian concept of the natural is of that which "tends to happen," "happens generally" or "for the most part." For Aristotle, nature may be a source of change and movement, but it has not got an antecedent necessity; it is not a sufficient condition for what happens. The most important and striking difference, however, is that for Aristotle nature is not an abstract notion and especially not something standing outside, "over and above" the things of this world, directing their behavior. In Aristotle's conception, nature is firmly attached to individuals, but, one should add, attached only to individuals that belong to a species or type of stuff or at least a definite category, and the nature that is attributed to those individuals is attributed through and because of that belonging and is part of their identification as that sort of thing. It is only individuals that have natures and not the Universe as a whole; "nature" does not get a capital "n."

As a result, when Aristotle talks about the *para physin*, the unnatural, as he does at *Physics* 197b35, this is not an example of the supernatural. It is only a violation of the nature of one particular thing or process that he has in mind, presumably by something else natural. It is not "nature as a whole" which has been violated from outside, as must presumably be supposed to be the case where there is talk about interference or interruptions in "the laws of nature" or "the natural order." If the concept "the natural order" or "the order of nature" is to be given any sense at all in Aristotelian terms, it can only signify the aggregate of particular natures belonging to particular individuals. With such a concept of *nature* and the *natural*, if one were to talk about "violations of the law of nature" (which one would tend not to do anyway), this would amount to saying that what generally happens with this sort of creature, or this sort of particle or what-have-you, did not happen on this occasion, and one would presume that this was because something had interfered with it.

The Aristotelian concept of the *natural* has not got the *supernatural* as its contrasted term. It has two terms contrasted with it: on the one hand there is the artificial, that is, the deliberate, conventional or purposive; things that have not come to be naturally but by contrivance and skill embodied in a rational agent external to the thing. The contrast is between an internal and an external source or principle of change. The other contrasting notion is the *accidental*, which includes coincidences and good and bad luck, things of the sort that might have been deliberately contrived by a well-wisher or an ill-wisher, but weren't. The accidental gets *no* explanation, either internal or external. To say that I met a friend at the market "accidentally" is to say that while there may be an explanation for my being there at that time and another explanation for her being there at that time, these explanations are unconnected and there is no one explanation for our both being there at once.

Obviously, neither of these contrasts to the natural are subject to what we should call "scientific" explanation, since by this we mean explanation by "natural" science. The latter, i.e. the coincidental or accidental, is not subject to any sort of explanation at all. But something which is "para physical" or unnatural in Aristotelian terms is not thereby inexplicable. Calling it "unnatural" is just to signal that the explanation will have to involve some external disturbing factor, a factor which by contrast will be acting quite properly according to its own nature in violating the natural development or behavior of the other. Prodigies, freaks, and sports of nature can all be investigated and explanations sought. In fact we look for explanations for those deviations from the natural and normal forms and development. By contrast, "it's normal" or "it's natural" puts our inquiry to rest even though it is not an explanation. (The fact that this does not amount to an explanation gets discussed in chapter 12.)

The Aristotelian concept of *nature* is such that we could give no sense to talk about "the nature of the Universe as a whole" in the way which is necessary to formulate the problem of the uniformity of nature or to define secular miracles.

Only particular things have natures, and only those particular things have natures which, when compared together, are seen to have characteristics in common and to behave similarly. This excludes the unique. By definition it can't take part in such a pattern shared with others. As I have said above, to have a "nature" in Aristotle's way of using the term, a thing must belong to a "type of thing." It is precisely by observing those things that we have drawn together into a type or a species that we can form expectations of how the thing will develop or act on its own. The Aristotelian notion of *nature* comprises just what the thing *of this sort* can be expected to do without interference, or at least without the kind of drastic interference that changes it utterly.

But the Universe has no fellow and nothing to be compared with. Its very notion implies that it is solitary and unique and doesn't share a pattern with anything else. The obvious move of trying to find a pattern by talking about "comparing it with itself at different periods" is tempting only so long as one does not raise in any detail questions about whether the dating and time measurement involved are to be made by reference to events and processes within the Universe or not.

Talk about the Universe itself changing or changing "as a whole" would require an "absolute time" external to the happenings in the Universe and therefore capable of measuring them.[4] Through Einstein's work we now know that notion to be incoherent and without sense.

Also, one should notice that the concept of the *Universe* is such that it is not the sort of thing to which the concepts of *action, movement, development,* or *change* apply, and therefore neither does the concept of *nature* as the principle of change. Particular things within the Universe develop and change, are created and destroyed, but these verbs are not to be extended to the Universe as the aggregate of the particular changing things. It would make as much sense to describe the class of automobiles as having become lighter or more powerful than it was on the ground that automobiles were these days lighter and more powerful than they were. So long as the Universe is taken to be just the aggregate of everything there is, it is of the wrong logical type to change, to have a nature or to have its nature violated from outside. Aggregates can only get bigger or smaller. But even those notions wouldn't make much sense as applied to the Universe.

By now it is perhaps a bit clearer what is meant by describing as "quasi-theological" those concepts and views which assume that "Nature" can be used as a proper name and thus warrants the capital "N," concepts like "the laws of Nature," "the order of Nature," "the uniformity of Nature," or even Galileo's "Book of Nature." I suspect that they all derive ultimately from concepts such as "God's Plan" and that the physical determinist is only the theological determinist with "Nature" written in for "God." But the important point about these notions is not their historical genesis, but rather the concept of *nature* they all involve.

If one holds on tight at this point and presses the concept hard, there seem to be two possible accounts of that implied concept of *nature*, both of which end up in theological notions. If one uses "nature" in the Aristotelian sense, it will be necessary in these uses to consider the Universe as a single determinate entity with characteristics belonging properly to it itself and not just to the entities which make it up.

This can be done in theology all right, where one can talk about the Universe as a whole having a relation to God, being God's creation and the like. But the theological concept of *creation* is logically quite different from that of the *Universe*. It is something over and above a simple aggregate, and subject to properties or characteristics in its own right precisely because it is, unlike the Universe, defined in relation to something outside. Creation might have a single nature owing to this relation to God, but the concept of the *Universe* as the simple aggregate of everything there is cannot have characteristics as a whole or act or change as a whole because it is not in a proper sense a "whole" at all.

Something is a "whole" in a proper sense only if it makes logical sense to talk about it "not being whole" – i.e. if it makes sense to talk about it lacking a part.[5] But there is nothing in the Universe which is essential to it in this way, nothing whose removal would force us logically (and not just cause us sentimentally) to say, "the Universe is not complete."

So, if our use of the concept of *nature* is such that it must be tied to some entity which is then described as having some determinate nature, we must, if we are to talk about some all-embracing Nature which could be upset, interrupted or violated, found this all-embracing Nature on the concept of "creation" rather than that of *the Universe*. The alternative is to skip the Aristotelian requirement that nature as a principle of change and movement inheres in some particular object. Then at least we would not have to appeal to the concept of "creation" to provide the appropriate sort of object for this "Nature" to inhere in.

However, if we are not made dizzy by the grandiose concepts we are dealing with, it becomes apparent that the cost of this move is much greater than the gain, and one ends up with a conception which is quite mystical. Taken seriously, as it has to be in the would-be problem of "the uniformity of Nature," the concept of an all-embracing *Nature* which is inherent in nothing, "Nature" which rates a capital "N" as a proper name, is quite a mystical concept indeed. Describing the "laws of Nature" as the causes of anything, either of some particular event or of those particular regularities that one finds, is either deeply mystical or else just a logical joke. So long as this Nature is not inherent in any physical thing it is quite clearly a conception that scientists in their scientific capacity could neither make sense of nor use. Such an immaterial notion could never be the subject of scientific investigation, nor could it ever be legitimately appealed to by scientists in explaining anything. It is scientifically idle. (See chapter 10.)

And this is not surprising since it arises out of questions about the Universe as a whole and the attempt to treat the Universe as a whole and not just as an aggregate, which makes sense from a religious but not from a scientific point of view. The problem of secular miracles and the problem of the uniformity of nature turn into the question of whether the Universe as a whole or nature as a whole could be interfered with or could alter spontaneously. This question could only be given a religious and not a scientific sense.

There can be no border disputes between the sciences and religion because, properly understood, they can be seen to have no border.

5 How to tell your friends from machines

When a problem has been around as long as has the problem of minds and machines (or, for that matter, its twin – the problem of "other minds") without either being very productive or being laid to rest, it is perhaps time to look beyond simple conceptual muddles and unclarities to deeper sources in philosophical practice and assumptions that enter there undiscussed. To get the proper measure of the problem it may even be necessary to go beyond the stricter bounds of philosophy itself to look at the sources and the role of certain philosophical views and problems in a wider context, to provide what might be called a "social pathology" of the problem.

Though this may provide some understanding of the longevity of certain muddles, it raises, in its turn, questions about the nature of philosophical problems and how they come to present themselves to us, questions that I do not see my way clear to tackling at the moment (though I have a go at them in chapters 1 and 12). I shall confine myself to trying to bring out the basic muddle in the notion of "machine intelligence," that is, the contradictions lying between conditions of application of its two parts, the notion of a *machine* and the notion of *an intelligence*. I hope this discussion will throw light on the slightly different, but related, muddle lying similarly at the center of the notion of "artificial intelligence" which gets discussed in chapter 8. I shall also make some suggestions about the social roots.

Other extra-philosophical analyses have recently been offered. Geach has turned to the notion of religious deviance in characterizing the belief in machine intelligence as "idolatry."[1] It is not clear whether he intends this characterization as a contribution to our understanding of the attraction the notion seems to have for some people, or whether it is meant simply as a piece of what might be called "dissuasive description" – or, more baldly, "name-calling." I do not share Geach's religious convictions, and perhaps because of that, the characterization does not seem to me to be effective in either role. Without some pretty large assumptions about humanity's need to worship *something-or-other*, it hardly helps us to understand or explain the belief in intelligent machines. As name-calling it would be least likely to sting just those people on whose heads it was being rained down.

One justification (though not the only one) for bringing in the medical term "pathology" to describe the kind of account needed here is that a serious belief in the intelligence of any machine would be as much a manifestation of schizophrenia or paranoid schizophrenia as would a real doubt about the existence of other minds.

Some years ago the Duty Officer of one of the television companies took a call from a woman who told him that her television set was watching *her*. "It's trying to get something out of me, but I won't let it," she added, without saying what it was she was keeping from the set. Our reaction to this is immediate and unequivocal. We have no doubts about how to assess the situation. We do not ask what it was about the set that led her to this conclusion so that we could weigh up the evidence to see whether her belief was well founded. Nor do we feel a dawning suspicion as we look at our next television set. Though I suppose someone who was imaginative and suggestible might feel a slight shudder going past a shop window full of television sets changing their pictures in unison and presenting a common front. This reaction, however, would be on a par with a child's imagining that its dolls or stuffed toys "come alive" at night, or even in the daytime can share secrets, sympathize, join in play, or feel. But imaginative play is one thing, and a seriously held belief on which important decisions, policies, and styles of behavior are uniformly to be based is quite another. Play and imagination are "bracketed" activities, held apart – perhaps excessively and too rigidly these days, but held apart nevertheless – from everyday prosaic life.

Sincere, non-imaginative confusion between animate and inanimate in what we should call "central" cases can be excused only in a child or a primitive from a non-scientific culture where the distinction is not yet drawn in the way we draw it or things seen and understood in the way we see and understand them. The primitive may well seek to propitiate the spirit of some machine he has only recently encountered for the first time, but if our next-door neighbor is found sacrificing a guinea-pig because his car has been giving him trouble, we take steps.

And our society's reaction to behavior that manifests a genuine belief in the intelligence of machines is quick and extreme. We classify such people as psychologically severely disturbed and almost invariably put them away from us in an institution as schizophrenics, paranoids or paranoid schizophrenics. They range from those who think they are being persecuted by machines, through those who think they are being controlled by machines, to those who think that they are *themselves* machines, and are said to be subject to what is described as "severe depersonalization."

The severity of our society's reaction to these aberrations is itself interesting. It could be that those unfortunates express in a concrete metaphor unpalatable truths about the condition of most of us in the modern world, in developed industrial societies particularly – that our actions and our lives are conditioned and determined by forces felt as external. Political, economic, social forces bear on us, and our actions seem to be shaped to serve purposes that are not our own – almost as machines are made to serve purposes. It is also true that for most industrial workers one or more machines stand astride their working lives like a dominating master demanding to be serviced, or to be fed with raw materials, and in some cases completely determining the movement of the worker's limbs and rhythm of work. And there is also the work of Frederick Winslow Taylor and his followers, who initiated the process of "de-skilling" of work and aimed to reduce the worker to the level of a machine by specifying jobs in terms of the movement of the worker's limbs and body.

It may be that the view the "depersonalized" schizophrenics have of themselves is just too close to home. At the moment this is by the way and we shall have to come back to this point later.

The problem of machine intelligence is not a real problem for us in the sense that nothing hangs on its solution. There are no legal, moral, social or diagnostic decisions that will be determined by the answer that is given. None of the individuals who find themselves arguing on one side or the other of the question are really puzzled about how to conduct themselves in relation to machines of any kind. No one really wonders whether to treat machines as moral agents, or whether to look on a mistake in a calculation as malice or as malfunctioning. It is a problem that springs from, and remains within the province of, imaginative play.

In this it is of a piece with, and set with the same traps as, its twin problem, the problem of "other minds." Once we are seduced by Descartes's method of doubt into pretending to doubt, what we cannot really doubt without abdicating our humanity and giving up our whole human life; we are dragged onto false ground where we can find no bearings or settle any standards of argument. If we are asked to doubt in play or imaginatively whether the person next to us in the queue, or the newsagent, or our parents, are really human beings and to imagine that they may be only automata, we may, with a strong imaginative effort be able to pretend this briefly. To believe it *really* and to live out that belief would be to be mad. We are then asked to believe, not pretend this time, that it is an intelligible and even a necessary enterprise to set about trying to give reasons why that doubt is unreasonable which we have just with such difficulty summoned up.

But how does one resolve an imaginary doubt? Would imaginary reasons do? The enterprise is a game. Descartes keeps his doubt in his study, firmly away from reality – and his life. The trouble is that we do not quite know the rules.[2]

If, stepping outside this artificial game situation, we ask ourselves genuinely what it is that keeps this doubt from getting a grip on us, the only honest answer we can give is: "our whole human life with others." What does keep us from going mad, after all? Not reasonings, anyway.

The problem of machine intelligence is exactly parallel to this in its nature. We can, imaginatively, and with some effort in a prosaic age, see inanimate objects as animate, sentient, or even intelligent and purposive. We can see caryatids as bowed and groaning under the weight of the porches they support, or, fearing some telephone call, see the telephone as aggressive, black, and menacing. The unconscious poetic and metaphorical relations between people and cars is much believed in, and exploited by, design, marketing, and advertizing executives in the motor industry. Helped by drugs such as peyote, LSD or even cannabis, people spontaneously and without conscious effort seem able to see almost any sort of object as animated and capable of feeling, or of motivated, intentional intelligent action. But the central point about these situations is precisely their being "bracketed," set aside from, and even a reaction to, the normal, prosaic course of life. No architect could use the animistic picture in calculating the load-bearing role of the caryatids. And if you complained to a telephone engineer that your phone was menacing, he would be nonplussed or else would report you as "malfunctioning."

If one is asked to conceive as intelligent some large and complex machine, a computer one has just played chess with, or that one has just been shown controlling an automatic factory, a production line of workers, or arranging introductions or marriages, one can reply: "Yes, perhaps I can if I try, but so what?" What we really need to know is whether we are being asked to do more than engage in a piece of artistic or imaginative play. Are we being asked to take the pretended belief out of the brackets that insulate it from life and conduct, and turn it into a genuine belief with consequences for action? If this is the case, the argument about the intelligence of computers or other machines would in effect be a moral argument: "You ought to be more careful in your conduct toward computers. They are sensitive and intelligent, and it is no good swearing at them or giving them peremptory orders or setting them insultingly simple or boring tasks. You must engage their sympathy and cooperation and treat them as equals. Get them to see your point of view and your problems. You cannot bribe or threaten them, you know. They are fearless and incorruptible."

If suggestions of this general kind, even if not just these, are not at issue and nothing practical really hangs on what we say about machines and intelligence, then perhaps it doesn't matter *what* we say. Excepting that the two words "mechanical" and "intelligent" have traditionally been used to mark an important distinction, and if these two are made incapable of marking that distinction any longer, other words will have to be brought in to do that job. My own view is that less confusion would be created by letting the original two go on doing it.

The nature of this distinction is best brought out by considering what is meant by a "machine" – something to which very little attention is given in the usual discussions of the question whether machines might think or be intelligent. Unless it is clear what is meant by "machine" or "mechanical" in this context, all the daring and alarming claims and predictions made by proponents of machine intelligence don't really amount to much. They will contain no usable information or testable assertion.

Perhaps one should start with what a machine is *not*. The nature of the material it is composed of is completely irrelevant to the question of whether a given object is a machine or not. It is of no account that some clocks or computers, for example, Pascal's, have been made of wood, bone, ivory and gut – all of them organic materials. One could perhaps make a machine out of living tissues or organisms, though it would obviously be impractical and worth doing only to prove a point. A computer with live flip-flops might be pretty unreliable, but it is possible.

Equally, being made wholly or in part of glass, wire, transistors, or anything else normally counted as inorganic, presents no conceptual bar to a thing's being counted as animate or intelligent. Given a glass eye, a plastic kneecap or an artificial arm I become no more mechanical or machinelike than I was. The arm is a mechanism, to be sure, and its articulation has to be understood mechanically, in terms of electric or pneumatic or hydraulic forces. But if I use it to make a rude gesture, to sign a check or to strike someone, these things do not get explained mechanically.

From the descriptions of its behavior, one accepts Fred Hoyle's Black Cloud, from the novel of that name, as an intelligent being in spite of its radical departure from known organic patterns. If something like that were actually to appear on the scene, the result would be an upset of biological theories and a redrawing of the somewhat hazy line between organic and inorganic materials or patterns.

Not only are the materials of which something is made irrelevant to its being a machine or not, but even their form and arrangement are irrelevant. This is shown by the genre of junkyard sculpture, which can consist in recognizably mechanical bits – gears, levers, wheels, pulleys acting together in recognizably mechanical ways without their constituting a machine. More than this is needed. We can understand what is needed if we notice that someone might well see that some piece of sculpture of that sort could be used to perform some mechanical task they had in mind and might buy it for that purpose and put it to use. It will then have changed its status – become *declassé*, if you like, and turned into a machine. Those who torture themselves with the problem "what is it really?" are chasing a rather metaphysical question, in the bad sense, which there are no agreed procedures for settling. Sometimes we allow the purpose for which the thing was made to take precedence; sometimes the purpose for which it is currently being used determines what we call it. The hammer used as a paper-weight is still a hammer, but the bottle used as a lamp base is, I suppose, a lamp base. Since generally nothing much hangs on the question, no clear lines have been laid down. If anything did, the situation would be different.

Two things emerge from this. One is that whether or not something is a machine has to do with its function or purpose, either the purpose for which it was made or the purpose for which it is being used. The second is that despite its apparent simplicity and straightforwardness the question whether something is "really" a machine or not might in certain circumstances be a somewhat pointless or unanswerable one.

Usually there is no difficulty because the uses to which machines are put tend to coincide with the purposes for which they were built, and no conflict arises. However, if a crackpot inventor builds a completely useless contraption or builds something for a completely impossible use (for example, a time machine), then we might be hard put to it to say whether the thing was to be counted as a machine or not. The question might also be rather pointless in the case of our utilized piece of sculpture, or in the opposite case, where someone like Marcel Duchamp seizes on something that started off life as a perfectly operational piece of machinery and, without any modification at all, puts it on a pedestal in an exhibition and offers it as a work of art. If one shares or accepts Duchamp's artistic view, one will be prepared to call it a work of art; if not, one might insist on calling it a piece of machinery out of place.

But these are admittedly marginal cases, and I don't want to dwell on them. The point of bringing them in here is to show that the concept of a *machine* and the problem of deciding whether an object is a machine or not are not always as simple as they seem. But I hardly want to claim that we do not know what we mean when we use the word "machine" – only that there are some cases which our normally sure, intuitive use of the word does not decide in advance. There are some objects and some situations about which our normal use is no guide, and we may be left to make up our own minds or to define a new usage there.

What I do want to claim is that any object which gives rise to a question of ascribing intelligence or rationality would by that fact alone be a marginal case and our normally simple *prima facie* tests of what the thing was made of (for example, metal, gears, levers, wire, glass, semiconductors, etc.) or what context it was found in (for example, a factory) would not be sufficient to settle the question whether the thing was to be counted as a machine or not.

It is just here in these marginal cases that we would have to look more deeply into the intuitions which guide our use of the word. What I want to try to show is that when we have looked into them we shall see that precisely those observations that might make us want to describe something as "rational" or "intelligent" would make us not want to describe it as a "machine." The *Oxford English Dictionary* gives a hint of this in noting a transferred use of the word "machine" to describe "a person who acts without intelligence."

Roughly speaking, a machine is a useful artifact. We might refine this to deal with the case of the junkyard sculpture by saying that it is manufactured to serve some useful purpose or else is pressed into useful service, whatever its reason for manufacture. That is, its function can be given to it either by its manufacturer or by its user. This definition has the disadvantage that it covers tools of all sorts and perhaps even medicines. One could cope with this, by adding the requirement that it be mechanically articulated or, nowadays, electrically.

However, I am not at all concerned to produce a completely

adequate definition of the ordinary meaning of "machine." All I want to notice here is, first of all, the essential role of the concepts of *purpose* or *function* in qualifying an object to be called a "machine," and secondly the way in which an artifact gets a purpose or function. It is just here in the phrase "having a purpose" that there is an ambiguity deep enough to count as a play on words. It is play on this ambiguity, or else failure to notice it, that is at the root of most of the muddles and arguments over the possibility of "thinking" machines or "artificial intelligences."

Simply put, the muddle starts from the fact that, on the one hand, it is one of the distinguishing marks of a machine that it is built for, or made to serve, some useful function or purpose. This condition is quite fairly described in perfectly good idiomatic English by saying that a machine "has a purpose." However, it is also one of the distinguishing marks of intelligent, rational or intentional actions that they are purposeful, i.e. that they have or serve a purpose. This, again, can be quite aptly and fairly described by saying that the individual "has a purpose" in doing the action. English idiom seems hardly to mark any difference here. Both humans and machines are said to have purposes, and the performance of humans when related to their purposes is called "intelligent," so why not extend the same description to the performances of machines when they are related to the machine's purpose? Only the oversubtle, it might be said, could see a difference between "having a purpose *in* doing something," on the one hand, and "having a purpose *and* doing something" on the other.

One thing that may raise suspicions about this argument, however, is that it proves too much. If one were really to accept it, one would have to regard all machine performance, without distinction, as intelligent. Though it might at first sight seem plausible to describe the performance of an automatic factory or an advanced computer as exhibiting intelligence in its operations, it would become obvious that something had gone wrong with the criteria by which we apply the word "intelligent" if we found that we had to apply it to the performance of simple room thermostats, ballcock valves in lavatory cisterns, and perhaps even Australian boomerangs. All machines have purposes, and unless they are being misused or are failing to function properly, their performance will be related to the purpose in question, that is, they will tend to serve the purpose for which they were built. But a concept of intelligent behavior that has to be applied to all properly functioning machines is no longer our ordinary concept, and, what is more, it can no longer be used to say anything interesting or startling about machines. With *this* concept of *intelligent behavior*, to say of a machine that it is "behaving intelligently" will be to say merely that it is functioning properly and no more. The verbal currency will have been devalued to that point.

What has gone wrong here is that there has been a failure to notice the two radically different ways in which something may have a purpose – a primary way and a derived or parasitic way – and a failure to notice further that anything which has a purpose derivatively gets it from or is given it by something having purpose in a primary way.

My toothbrush has a purpose, viz. to clean teeth, but it gets that purpose from *me*, from the use I make of it. If I were to use it in some other way, for example, to clean my typewriter keys (this was first written on one), then it would have another and different purpose. If people found some new way of cleaning teeth that didn't involve toothbrushes and could not find a new way of using their now redundant toothbrushes, these would have lost their purpose. Government surplus stores are filled with objects whose original purpose is often very difficult to guess, but which have certainly lost whatever purpose they once had and are waiting to be given another. "Make a lovely ink stand, sir" – or hat rack, or fish tank.

What purpose such inanimate objects have they get by being used for a purpose or by there being a practice or tradition of using them in some way. Without this they are useless, without point, purpose or function. To try to picture them having purposes in splendid isolation from any actual or possible human uses is idle metaphysical romancing. Excepting, I suppose, in a religious context someone might claim that some humanly useless object had a purpose as the instrument of God's will.

There are, then, two entirely different senses in which something can be said to "have a purpose." One is by being *used* for a purpose. The other is by being capable of *using something else* for a purpose that belongs in the first instance and primarily to the user and devolves from there onto the thing used. The thing used has an *imposed* purpose, a purpose that is given to or imposed on it, and otherwise would not have that purpose. The other sort of purpose is not imposed but belongs in a primary way to the user, the purposive agent.

Though the paper which was the basis of this chapter was originally written because of a commitment to speak to an undergraduate society, my purposes in writing it were my own even though they fitted in with, and were occasioned by, the purposes of the secretary of the society who got me to agree to speak. The purposes would still have been mine in a primary and not an imposed sense even if he had used threats of blackmail or violence to get me to speak. That is, the purposes I had would be particularizations of general purposes I already had before, in this case the avoidance of exposure or violence. If I had not got these already, if I were not afraid of exposure or were just spoiling for a fight, then he would not have been able to move me in that way.

So in one fairly clear sense he was not imposing a purpose on me. But this sense must not be got out of perspective or the argument taken as proving that no one can ever be imposed on or used. In the face of the obvious fact that people are exploited and used all the time, this would turn into an empty logical or verbal point which would be of no interest except to interested parties. *They* might want to use it to pretend that exploitation did not exist. I shall come back to this point.

At the moment I *am* concerned only with a conceptual question about the ways in which people and things "have" purposes and am starting with a large and perhaps crude distinction between having-by-being-given, as a man might be given a scar, a cold or a suit of clothes, and the way in which a man may "have" two eyes or red hair, not by being given them in any recognizable sense. No doubt much more needs saying here, and finer distinctions drawing, but I hope this is a gesture in the right direction.

Now it is, of course, true that, just like an inanimate object, I can have a purpose imposed on me, can be used, in a pretty hard and literal sense, for a purpose which is not my own, i.e. does not belong to me in a primary way. This is usually done to people by misleading them about what it is they are doing.

To the extent to which the crews who dropped the atomic bomb on Hiroshima were not told or were not clear about what they were carrying, they were being used as a piece of machinery might be. It seems also that innocent people are sometimes tricked into becoming espionage contacts or smugglers by being misled about just what it was they are doing or what it is they are carrying. History and mythology are filled with stories of people being used to do something which it was not their purpose to do, to kill, destroy, or betray, simply by being misled or deceived about what it was, in effect, that they were doing.

Hypnosis is another way in which people may be used for, i.e. given, purposes which are not their own purposes in any "primary" sense. However, it seems likely that a hypnotist accomplishes this by preventing the person from seeing or knowing just what it is that he is doing. The person's suggestible condition is used to deceive him about his state, status or circumstances.

Now, what I hope I have brought out in all this are the radically different ways in which the notion of *purpose* is attributed. In the "primary" way it is attributed to someone who is capable of *using* something, making it an instrument, giving it a purpose that comes from the user. It is attributed in the second way to the thing which is *used*, the instrument, tool or machine. The pair "user–used" is a member of a large and familiar class of paired concepts such as "producer–product," "aggressor–victim," and "tester–tested," concepts that relate to two sides of a transaction. But these pairs are such that they cannot both, for logical reasons, be made to relate to the same feature or aspect of the same thing. The father who is also a son must be a father in relation to one transaction and son in relation to another.

My claim is that intelligence and machines are related as *user* and *used*. An intelligent being is precisely one that is capable having a purpose in that "primary" way and of turning something into an instrument, and it doesn't matter whether the thing used is a paleolith or a sophisticated weapons system. A *machine* is precisely what stands on the other side of this relationship as something that has been contrived for, or given, a use.

So there turns out, after all, to be an intimate connection between the two conceptions *intelligence* and *machine*, though not perhaps the one usually argued for. We may rightly be reluctant to admit something made exclusively of glass, wires, and plastic into the community of intelligent, purposive, tool-using beings, but if we were to, we would have to stop calling it a "machine."

At this stage of the argument I am usually faced with objections that seem to call for a further chapter with the title: "Is There Intelligent Life on Earth?" The objectors grant the fundamental opposition I have tried to bring out between "intelligent" and "mechanical" but deny that there is any way of showing that there are in fact any intelligent beings that make or use things or have purposes in what I have called a "primary" way. After all, I have not provided any criteria for identifying "primary purposiveness;" so how can we tell that there is such a thing?

I would like to make two points in reply to this. One is to remark that if there were no intelligences, there would be no machines either, given the way the two concepts are connected. Objectors of this kind are in some danger of falling for the Argument from Design and being landed with a celestial architect if they still insist on seeing machines and mechanisms about them. But my central reply is a blatantly *ad hominem* argument. It is to refer back to the first section of this chapter and to say that if the objection is based on a serious difficulty or doubt whether there are any intelligent beings on Earth, then it is not argument but treatment that the objector needs. If, on the other hand, the objector can recognize some intelligent beings and can already make use of the distinction "intelligent–mechanical" in their everyday life, then there is no point to this demand, and just because it has no point and is really idle, there is no way of meeting it. It also springs from a mistaken conception of concepts as mere registers of perceived characteristics.

There may, of course, arise some genuinely difficult cases (though so far these are only fictional), such as zombies or androids. One of the latter in Fred Hoyle's *A for Andromeda* would, if actual, provide a really difficult case, since the android makes the transition from being the mere instrument of an extra-galactically controlled computer to being a fully purposive, intelligent human being.

Just as it would be difficult for us to spot the original deception,[3] it would be difficult to spot the change; though my contention is that we wouldn't and couldn't do this by the application of definitions and criteria which were given in advance in behavioral terms. In any case, if we were to be so mechanical ourselves in our techniques of android detection, we would only give weapons to the android manufacturers in their efforts to deceive us. This is precisely what A. M. Turing was trying to get us to do in inviting us to play his "imitation game." According to his rules for that game we are to specify in overt behavioral terms what we mean by various human characteristics up to and including "thinking" or "being intelligent." That is, he requires us to become behaviorists in order to play his game.

But "intelligent" is not a concept like that, one that can be defined in behavioral terms as Turing requires. To decide that something is intelligent is not simply to record that it has passed certain behavioral tests or exhibited certain features, whether behavioral or physical. It is, rather, to define one's whole human relation to it. It is to say in effect what sort of behavior and attitudes are appropriate or even necessary in relation to that being.

So much for mechanical intelligence. The slightly more vogue term "artificial intelligence" involves similar incoherences that can be brought out by looking carefully at the notion of "artifice" or "making." The intelligence lies with the maker, not the thing made. The product, the artifact, at best embodies and exhibits the intelligence of the producer. There is also incoherence in the idea of *causing* or *forcing* something to have its "own" purposes. Short of that "causing" or "forcing," how are we to claim the intelligence as our "artifact?" (We'll come back to that in chapter 8.)

What seems most objectionable about the usual treatments of the notions of *machine* or *artificial intelligence* is that there is a deep and important point lying buried in the muddle which those discussions almost wilfully obscure and turn to ridicule.

While it may be true that machines are, by definition, made and controlled to serve human purposes, it would be superficial and in bad faith, as well as bad logic, to stop the analysis there with the pretense that there is only one sort or relation between "humanity" and "machines." "Humanity" is an abstraction and stands in no concrete relation to any machine. When one comes to particular human beings and particular machines it is immediately obvious that they stand to one another in all sorts of ways.

My relation to my car, typewriter or power-drill is one thing. The relation of the drop-forge operator to his machine is quite another. The man said to be "in charge of" several looms, knitting machines or spinning machines might as well, or better, be described as "in the machines' charge." His actions are dictated by their needs, not *vice versa*. When they run low on raw material he fetches, when they tangle he runs, and when they need oiling or adjusting he does that too, unless it is a union shop, in which case he calls someone else to do it.

It would therefore be deeply false not to supplement the conceptual argument about the notions of *machine* and *intelligence* with an analysis, of the kind that Sartre and Simone Weil have given, of the ways in which machines can shape and dominate the life and work of human beings and "determine" their purposes in a sense not literal enough to cut across the conceptual points we have been trying to clarify, but very real nevertheless. Of course, machines do create new possibilities and enable humans to have new aims, like flying, and understanding gene structure. Some machines do that all right, but others assign tasks, fix schedules or necessitate shift-work which disrupts social and family life.

In perhaps most industrial situations, and especially the more mechanized, the worker works for the machine and not the machine for the worker. The worker's actions while at work and even the hours of work, rest and leisure are determined by the machine requirements.

René Clair had a brilliant vision of this in his beautiful, prophetic film of the early 1930s, *A Nous la Liberté*. In that film there is a deadly comparison between conditions of life in a prison and on the prison production line and conditions in a factory "outside" with its dormitories for workers, and on the factory production line. The regimentation is indistinguishable.

But Clair's film is a comedy, and in the tradition of film comedy human freedom, in the form of human irrationality, wins out (for the hero at least) – bringing the production line to a halt in a complete tangle, allowing him to escape to resume his life as a tramp. This option is not open to most people. They must learn to suppress their human wants and instincts and shape them to the requirements of the factory and the machine.[4]

Here it would be easy to misuse my argument about the user and the used to insist that machines are by definition what gets used and cannot use, even if the use to which they are put is the exploitation and use of one human being by another. Of themselves, it could be said, inanimate machines cannot impose purposes or aims on intelligent beings. "Yes," one wants to say, "true in a sense," but it is rather like insisting on the conceptual incoherence of determinism in the face of political, economic, social, and legal constraints, the constraints of ignorance and poverty. "Humanity" may in some abstract and not very helpful sense be "free" and the individual not. Certainly not if the individual happens to be an Arab worker in the Paris "Bidonville" or his Indian equivalent outside Quito or Caracas.

If we come down from our conceptual pinnacle, where we can talk happily and comfortingly about the relations between abstractions such as "humanity" or "intelligences" on the one hand and "machines" or "tools" on the other, and actually look at the situation of real people now, it is not so clear where these abstract relations are to be found exemplified. Who makes the machine nowadays? And who puts it to use? "Management" is an abstraction that at best stands for a committee, a board of directors. Can we really suppose that they feel free to introduce or not introduce the machines that require shift-working and the disruption of family life, machines that subject workers to unnatural rhythms and destructively mindless tasks or even exposure to radiation or hazardous chemicals? On the contrary, they are themselves part of an economic structure by which they feel completely constrained. As soon as the machine comes into existence they feel compelled to introduce it into their factory almost whatever the consequences for their workers. As directors and managers their job is to maximize profits.

What about the inventors and designers? As soon as we look at *them* concretely and not in abstract conceptual terms it is apparent that even they are not in a position to dictate purpose or function. "The designer" or "the inventor" is probably a team or even a complex of teams each with a specified task set them from higher up in the organization. The overall task, of which they may be assigned only a part, will probably include specifications as to price, function, ease of manufacture, and maintenance. Even for the managers responsible, these specifications will in turn be dictated by external factors out of their control: the position of competitors, the state of technology, the financial and manufacturing resources of their own company.

Wherever we look the purposes seem to come from somewhere else and the purposiveness slips through our fingers and disappears.

These are the realities that the otherwise idle and empty talk about "intelligent machines" or "artificial intelligences" might refer to if it did not wilfully obscure them, as though its real job were to protect us from a painful recognition of our situation by making it impossible to think clearly about it.

A worse motive is suggested by Simone Weil's remark that "Automatic machines seem to the model for the intelligent, faithful, docile and conscientious worker."[5] If machines and people can be made to look not so different in kind, it may come to seem perhaps not so shocking that people are treated like machines.

Perhaps Hobbes should have the last word on the arguments for machine intelligence: "When men write whole volumes of such stuff, are they not mad, or intend to make others so?"[6] They are certainly distracting us from the real issues, the real problems that are bearing on humanity, on real men and women, out of whose lives point and purpose are slipping, to be replaced by "storefront religion" and the equally cheap attractions of the shopping mall.

6 Nature and necessity

Determinism is a specter that has haunted our scientifically oriented culture from the beginning. I happen to think that it is literally a "specter," a trick of the vision, an appearance with an internal cause only, and is no more than the ghost of our own conceptual determinations projected outward into a world in which it has no place and no proper being.

From one point of view it is no more than an alienated fantasy involving a number of incoherent assumptions. Of these, one of the most important, and one of the most deeply eroded by much contemporary work, is the assumption that science and scientific understanding is a potentially completable system, the assumption that lies hidden in the innocent phrase "a complete scientific explanation," which slips so easily into the discussion of many topics. From another point of view, however, the deterministic picture can appear to be an inevitable product of scientific activity.

But there is an element in the deterministic picture which raises the problem I want to look at, namely, the way in which "laws," natural or scientific, are supposed to bear on individuals, and generally the relation between laws and individuals, either individual things or individual happenings. For there is an interesting contradiction in our views here. At one moment, when we are observing or experimenting, we are perfectly clear that laws lag behind the doings of those individual things we are observing; but at another moment, when we set about using those laws predictively or manipulatively, we can hardly help seeing them as having a prior, determining existence, and the individual happening or the individual thing as being "subject" to them, the happening determined by them and the thing in their grip.

These apparently contradictory points of view are complementary and perhaps necessary to the enterprise of science. The first gives it its procedure, and the second gives it its point. Resolving the dilemma and accommodating both views is no doubt the center of the problem of determinism.

But it is no use looking for a complete treatment of that problem here. For the moment I only want to make a beginning by looking at the notions of *necessity* and of the *individual,* and particularly the notion of a *concrete individual* in order to see whether the two can be brought into relation to each other. This will involve criticism of some of the recent attempts (by David Lewis, for example, and Alvin Plantinga) to revive the notion of *de re* necessity. All these attempts, in purporting to attach necessities to bare individuals, in the end only destroy the notions of the *individual* and the *concrete,* and I want to try to go some way toward bringing this out.

Far and away the most interesting recent work in relation to the notion of the individual and its relation to modal notions is that done by Kripke since coming to the philosophical realization that the notion of a "possible world," that favorite of the modal logicians (his former self included), is more problematic and obscure than those notions it was meant to help clarify. (I have in mind here chiefly his long piece "Naming and Necessity" in the collection by Gilbert Harman and Donald Davidson, *The Semantics of Natural Language.*) However, Kripke's interest there, and his methodology, turn around the problem of *reference* to individuals and whether this act requires us to be in possession of a unique conceptual counterpart (whatever that might be) of the individual referred to. This question has a close relation to my problem of whether the notions of *necessity* and of *the individual* can be brought together without mutual annihilation, though my methodology and approach will be different and more unapologetically metaphysical. But we need to pause here for a moment over the problem of methodology.

In one sense there are no new philosophical problems. And around any important problem the ground will, over time, have been ploughed and reploughed, trodden, and churned by the academic professionals until landmarks are nearly obliterated and firm footing hard to find. Even the ear for the English language (or whatever vernacular) gets debased by the coinages and the neologisms that are introduced, supposedly to clarify. Generally, whatever clarity these coinages manage to get is drawn from a prior unsophisticated understanding. Rather than adding to it mostly they just obscure, or nearly destroy the prior intuitive clarity they feed on.

Nowhere is this more true than in the area we want to look at, that of necessity in nature, *de re* necessities, the bearing of laws on individuals, or, if you like, the relation of universal to particular. And this poses big methodological problems. Where can we start? With what ideas can we begin to work in any process of clarification?

Well, I want to start from the notion of the individual and the concrete individual, and that choice may look like needing some defense in the first instance. (In the end, of course, it will have to defend itself.)

Despite the amount of philosophical puzzlement there may be about the nature of the *individual* and the *concrete individual*, in an ordinary, working, everyday sense we understand these notions quite well. We have no ordinary puzzlement about them, and that is good enough. The philosophical account can come later.

One way of putting it is to say that I want to take the notion as a starting point, but not as a *foundation* for the discussion that follows, a point of departure only, and one that may have to be modified and clarified in the subsequent discussion. That is to say, it is relatively clear, but not absolutely clear. Or, perhaps better: it is clear in one way but not in another.

The contrast I have in mind can perhaps be brought out by noticing the way in which the older empiricist tradition took the notion of *experience* as not only clear enough for ordinary everyday purposes, but philosophically unproblematic as well, capable, that is, of bearing the weight of a whole philosophical system. Of course it can't, and these days many have come to see that.[1]

Now, in one way it is as clear as anything can be that we live in a world of concrete individuals, objects that move and change and act on one another. Our whole way of talking and thinking and acting is built around this point. Of course, we may be tempted by Hume into his study and, thinking abstractly in that artificial context, be persuaded briefly to look at our world as composed of, or created out of, experiences sewn together somehow. But when we come out into the light of day and actually engage with the world and with others, make a cup of coffee or play darts in the pub, we can't sustain that viewpoint for a minute (as Hume himself admits). But Hume draws the wrong conclusion from this fact. He takes it to show that our ordinary ways of talking, thinking, and acting are somehow deficient and faulty, the result of "carelessness and inattention." They show, rather, that his account is faulty, that it has some wrong assumptions, and a wrong goal.

But to take the notion of the *individual* or the *concrete individual* as a starting point is not at all to say that that notion is in every way clear and can serve as some sort of foundation for the explication for every-

thing else. Specifically, it may be that the notion of the *concrete individual* needs to be philosophically clarified and determined precisely in
the discussion of its relations to our modal concepts of *necessity* and *possibility*. And it may also happen that these notions are clarified in that
same discussion. This may sound a bit like two blokes agreeing to lift
each other off the ground at the same time, but it is not really. It is in
this way that philosophical clarification often works. I shall leave it at
that so as not to turn this into an essay on philosophical methodology.

Very roughly, my strategy will be to argue for an identity between the
world of nature and the collection of concrete individuals and then
raise the question of the anchorage of the modalities of *necessity* and
possibility in nature as a question about the relation of those modalities
to concrete individuals. No doubt this identification of the world of
nature with the collection of concrete individuals can do with more
examination than I am going to give it here, though the notion gets
discussed in a number of other places in this book, viz. chapters 4, 10,
11, and 12. Perhaps the use I want to make of it will help make clear
just what further examination or strengthening it may need, or
whether it can be accepted at all.

Having said a fair amount about the methodology, I had better start
talking about the problem itself; though I should perhaps add that the
chief aim of the chapter is to define and clarify and resite the problem
rather than propose a solution of any dramatic or definitive kind.
Defining it will need a number of attempts. (Maybe a lot more than
will be made here.)

I'll begin by trying to see how it has appeared at various times and
to various people, and then try to identify its sources, and criticize
some of the discussions and existing conceptual tool-stock to see if
something helpful may emerge from all that.

One place from which we can start is a remark in Aristotle's *Posterior
Analytics* (87b38): "Sense (*aesthesis*) is necessarily of the particular
(*hekaston*), whereas science (*episteme*) is of the universal." A great deal
can be got from exploring the apparent paradox there. And all the
problems of model and interpretation, theory and practice, are
already embedded in those two facts already remarked on, namely,
that in the experiment, the experience is of the individual and it is in
the driving seat and determines the law, whereas in the application,
the law, that is, the universal, is in the ascendant and supposed to
determine the behavior of the individual.

How can we know (or can we *know?*) which way the individual thing
will jump? We can't know it by *aesthesis* (something like Russell's
acquaintance), as that doesn't put us in touch with the thing's past or

with its future or with any connection between them (a point with analogies to Hume's subversive analysis of the notion of *cause*). Nor does *aesthesis* put us in touch with causes or reasons. Aristotle's example in the *Posterior Analytics* (I.33) is an eclipse. Sense tells us *that* the moon is darkening, not *why*. And it is the *why* that is transferable from one case to the next and puts us ahead of the event. Science or *episteme*, on the other hand, doesn't tell us about *this* individual, only about things of this *sort*. So the problem comes up, what kind of knowledge do we have connecting this particular individual to some particular sort? If we really have what can be called "knowledge" here, it seems it can't be got through either *aesthesis* or *episteme* for obvious reasons: it has to span the relation between the objects of the one kind of knowledge and the objects of the other, the relation between the particular and the universal.

That is the problem in its epistemological clothing, and though there may be faults in the way it is posed, it seems at first sight a good puzzle. But I'll leave the unraveling of it to others, for I want to take up the same problem in a metaphysical form and discuss it in a metaphysical setting. Oddly enough, a way through to that is via Hume, even though in the end I hardly want to talk about the problem from his perspective or in his terms. Apart from anything else, for historical reasons, Hume seems to have a right to be consulted in any discussion of necessity in nature.

When Hume asks in the *Enquiry*: "Are there necessities in nature?," he seems at first to have made the question into what could roughly be called a semantic one: has our idea of necessity an internal, or has it an external, anchorage and reference? But for Hume the origin and the reference of an idea are necessarily coincident, so that the semantic question can hardly be distinguished from an epistemological one. That is the result of his assimilation of the *reference* relation to the relation of *copying*. An *idea* is an "idea of an experience," and unless the experience is of something external, the idea will have no external reference either. This is a key stage in reaching his conclusion that "the necessity of any action . . . is not a quality in the agent, but in any thinking or intelligent being that may consider the action."[2]

Hume's motives for trying to base the referring relation on the copying relation are the individualistic ones common to empiricism. Human beings are thought of as essentially and at the outset isolated from one another, and it is only through the common focus of experience, ideas, and ultimately of language that they can be brought together in communication and community. The relation of copying is thought by Hume to be an "objective" one, one that is capable of projecting and preserving a common focus of experience into the realm of ideas and thereby into language. It is supposed to guarantee that we are talking of the same things when we talk, and thinking of the same things when we think.

This underlying individualistic conception of humans as at first isolated and then only later joined to others through experience, language, and Social Contract has been attacked in different ways by both Marx and Wittgenstein. For them, men are first of all social beings, and it is only later that they succeed in detaching themselves and come to see themselves as individuals. (This is the central question at issue in chapter 12.)

For those of us who have taken this message, language and the community of ideas are the expression of, the embodiment of, the common life of human groups and not its cause or precondition.

But (though I am not going to pursue the point) one should remark here that Wittgenstein, like Hume, refuses to separate off questions about the reference of expressions from questions about the way we come to grasp the sense or use of those expressions. Of course, Wittgenstein's conception of this latter process is totally different from Hume's. For Wittgenstein it is a teaching–learning, social process and not something that can be carried out by individuals on their own in the privacy of their study, cave or head. Kripke's account of *naming* moves in this direction too, and it seems that any successful attack on these problems will have to take place in this area, appealing to what is possible in concert but not individually.

But first, we are trying simply to get the measure of the problems themselves. For the moment, with the above criticisms in mind, let us go along with Hume, because his insistence on the question of the anchorage of the modal notions of *necessity* and *possibility* is an important one even though, as I would like to say, his way of posing it gets distorted by the assumption that an account of that anchorage must be given in terms of the origins of those ideas in the individual histories of the individual men and women who have achieved those notions for and by themselves. These histories would for Hume have to be spelled out in experiential terms.

It seems to Hume clear that the ideas of *necessity* or *possibility* are not to be found in an individual experience. When we first meet a thing, stuff or situation, we can't tell how it may or must act or develop, what we can or cannot do with it. But if those ideas are not in the first experience by itself, they cannot be in the second, or the third, etc., since each of these, taken by itself, must be qualitatively identical to the first. And so, by a line of reasoning reminiscent of the paradox of the unexpected examination, if we take experiences to be individual and self-contained entities (as Hume does), it seems that the modal ideas cannot have their origin there in experience. They have no proper grounding in experience but have their origin only in "habit" (and to that extent are not really grounded).

"But," one is tempted to ask at this point, "how is Hume to get the crucial notion of habit off the ground?" For, by parity of reasoning, if our first experience of A and B together has the power to create only a small degree of expectation, the second experience will have no greater, and ought only to confirm that minute expectancy rather than increase it. After all, our successive experiences of the blue of the sky hardly darken our idea of its color.

However, picking holes of that size in Hume is a waste of time, and what I really want to do is to change the whole perspective of the discussion – though I have thought it helpful to see what the perspective is changed from.

Let's return to Hume's question of anchorage in a different way and ask: do the modalities of necessity and possibility attach to individuals or only to our classifications of them? Can we make sense of saying that *this* concrete individual must be or must do something or other? (Notice that this is a different question from asking whether we can have a sound basis for claiming such a thing. Though the questions are obviously connected, the nature of that connection is in no way obvious, and hasn't been made so, even by Wittgenstein's notion of *criteria*, which I think no one would claim to be perspicuous.)

To define the question a little more sharply, let's make use of the distinction between *de re* and *de dicto* modalities as it is drawn by Hintikka. The distinction itself has had a varied history, but Hintikka marks it in a clear way that is useful here.[3] For him a *de re* modality is one that applies or is attached to a definite individual (in its own right, so to speak), whereas a *de dicto* modality is one that applies to whatever fulfils some condition, or "whoever meets some description," simply on the ground of its meeting that description. In an older idiom one would have said that the *de dicto* necessity applies to a thing *qua* member of some class or sort, in virtue, that is, of having some property or other. By contrast the *de re* necessity applies to the individual thing in its own right, just as this *particular* thing.

Our question then becomes "are there *de re* modalities or only *de dicto*?" If the latter turns out to be the case, determinism seems to lose its grip. Necessities become conditional, not categorical, and unless the conditions are themselves fulfilled with categorical necessity, the whole thing gets no send-off.

Look at the problem in another way, which connects it more clearly with our original question about necessities in nature. If we take nature to be the world of things that act and move and change, it seems clear that this is, as I have said, primarily the world of individual things. Roughly, what I mean by that is that it is only particulars that have strong enough and flexible enough criteria of identity for the concept of *change* to get a grip in any central and unproblematic sense.

Of course, it is possible to talk, and we do talk, about change and development in non-concrete things – the sonata form, the institution of marriage, the conception of romantic love, the techniques of transplant surgery. But these are cases that are puzzling and difficult and need understanding, not clear, paradigmatic, and capable of giving it. It would be as silly and wrong-headed to base a discussion on, and to give an account of, a concept of *change* by means of such examples as it would be to take the identification of gods and goddesses between Greek and Egyptian mythology as a central example in a discussion of the concept of *identity*. What we can in any case say is that the conception of change among those things is dependent on, and derivative from, what happens on the concrete individual level. This might involve several removes of abstraction. Nevertheless if there were no change at the concrete level there could be no change or conception of change at the other, abstract levels either.

If the primary arena of change and action is the world of individuals, it would seem that necessity will have to catch hold there if it is to have a toehold in the world of nature. (I'm only partly convinced by this argument, but let's start from there and see where it gets us.) It puts the weight heavily on the notion of *de re* necessity: must this concrete individual thing necessarily act or react in some particular way? Or does the necessity that seems to attach to it lie really in the ways we classify, identify or describe it? And what about possibilities and potentialities? Do they attach only to the type or can they attach to the individual *sans phrase*?

Making out the sense of those questions is one of the chief objects of this chapter, but *prima facie* at least it seems that almost all philosophers line up against such an idea. Kneale, for example, says:

> If what I said is right, it is clear that there can be no ordinary properties of which it is proper to say that they belong with absolute necessity regardless of the way in which those individuals are selected for attention. But there may be, and obviously are, some extraordinary properties, such as being a natural number, and a number of truistic properties, such as being prime-or-not-prime.[4]

Of the two exceptions Kneale allows here, the first doesn't apply to our case since Kneale is talking about the wider class of individuals (*sans phrase*), in which he includes numbers, and we are concerned only with concrete individuals. (Though perhaps some "extraordinary" properties can be found even for them. Maybe the mediaeval "transcendentals" would do.) And the notion of a "truistic" property seems to me an empty one, internally contradicting the notion of *property*. To belong to all is to belong to none. The notion of *belonging* has evaporated.

In *Naming and Necessity*, where Kripke gives these topics an extended and important treatment, he seems to lay it even more clearly on the line at one point: "whether a particular necessarily or contingently has a certain property depends on the way it is described."[5] Now, Kripke and Kneale are here only talking about the necessary attachment of properties to individuals and not explicitly about the necessity of an individual acting or developing in some way or of responding in some definite way to something done to it. However, it seems fair to assume that under the heading of "properties" they would include dispositional properties and others like "magnetic" or "heavy" or "hot" with definite implications for action and reaction, and so they would both seem to be taking a stand on our problem.

However, some of the things that Kripke says later in "Naming and Necessity" seem to reopen the possibility of the direct attachment of modalities to individuals unmediated by a particular description or means of identification. For example, at first sight it looks as though his concept of a "rigid designator" might be put to such a use, and it will be helpful to look more closely at that notion.

When one looks in history for supporters of *de re* necessities, they turn out to be difficult to find, though there has been some press-ganging. Popper, with his passion for organizing philosophers into parties, planted a standard with the word "essentialism" on it and tried to frog-march Aristotle, among others, into its shadow. Essentialism is supposed to be characterized by the view "that in every single thing there is an essence, an inherent nature or principle which necessarily causes it to be what it is and thus to act as it does."[6] Now, that is a clear statement of a *de re* view together with a supporting metaphysic. What we need to see is whether anything in Aristotle corresponds with it.

What Popper seems to have in mind here is the Aristotelian concept of *physis*, described by him as "an internal principle of movement and change" and usually translated as "nature." Now what we have to look at is the relation between the *physis* and the thing that has it. Is it causal or constitutive? Popper describes the essence as "causing" the thing to be what it is and to act as it does. But of course Aristotle doesn't operate with Popper's concept of *causation*. And if Aristotle were asked which of his four types of "cause" to range *physis* under, there is no doubt whatever that it would have to come under his heading of "formal cause." *Physis* is a kind of temporally articulated formal cause and therefore constitutive rather than "causal" in our modern sense. One cannot separate Aristotle's formal cause (or his "material cause," for that matter) from the thing itself. We haven't got a case of something acting and something being acted on. There just isn't a separate something to be acted on, and the Aristotelian conception of *cause* does not aim to pick out something separate in the way that the modern conception of *cause* does.

If, for example, one said "being bounded by three straight lines causes the thing to be a triangle" (a paradigm of a formal cause), the obvious question raised by the modern use of "cause" would be: "causes *what* thing to be triangle?" And one couldn't answer "the plane figure." For we would then need to know what the plane figure was doing before it was a triangle, what it was apart from being a triangle.

The usual paradigm of the Aristotelian *physis* is the acorn growing up into an oak. The *physis* is described by Aristotle as "the internal principle" of that particular development. What he means by that is that there isn't something *outside* the acorn that is forcing it to follow that path and no other. Nor, of course, is there anything *inside* either, a sort of seed within the seed, with the obvious opportunities for regress that that would offer. No, "internal principle" does not mean "something inside." "Internal" has to be taken as in "internal relations," a conceptual relationship. The fact that it is or could be growing up into an oak is just what constitutes the thing an acorn. If it were to leave off that activity (through genetic manipulation, say) or lose that potential and adopt some other direction of development (it was eaten by a pig), it would stop being an acorn by that very fact. Its sortal identity and trajectory are one. Its individuality and individual identity is something else and comes from its material and accident-prone aspect.

It is precisely here that one sees the beginnings of the Leibnizian conception of the "individual notion" or "notion of an individual substance." Leibniz is extending to particulars and concrete individuals something like the conception of *physis*, which Aristotle had reserved to species and sorts. (Or rather, as we said earlier, Aristotle reserves the notion to individuals *as belonging* to sorts or species.) One consequence of Leibniz' giving each individual an individual nature that belongs to it (and identifies it) as *this particular individual* is a determinism against which Leibniz is always fighting a desperate rearguard action. This problem doesn't face the Aristotelian ways of talking.

Aristotle's *physis* involves only a general direction of the thing's development, a direction which identifies it merely as a member of a particular species or sort (of material, say). What gives the thing individuality is the matter it is composed of, and matter as the accident-prone aspect of the thing opens up the possibility of different lines of development for our acorn. It only has to keep within the loose bounds set by its becoming an oak. And what would happen if the thing strayed beyond those bounds and started bearing pears? That would simply call into question our earlier identification of it as an acorn, or else would make us look around for some genetic manipulator who had slipped in when we weren't looking.

Leibniz cuts out the accident-prone matter and therefore has to make his individual keep strictly to an utterly detailed scenario. For Leibniz it is just this detailed scenario written for it and somehow incorporated in it that constitutes it *this* individual. If anyone is an essentialist, it looks as if it has got to be Leibniz. A definitional necessity not only attaches to but for him actually *constitutes* the individual as *this* individual.

David Lewis has tried to ease the deterministic situation within a general Leibnizian perspective by introducing his notion of "counterparts" in other "possible worlds," which looks like bringing back a certain amount of slack into the system and opening up some alternative possibilities to the individual. And it could be argued that the roots of this idea are already in Leibniz himself – in so far as he allows himself to talk of "an infinity of possible Adams" of which God has chosen only one. This talk of an array of Adams seems to force a distinction between traits which are essential, defining or identifying and those which are accidental. (However, Benson Mates in his chapter "Leibniz on Possible Worlds" has wanted to deny that Leibniz made any such distinction.)[7] This and the notion of *counterpart* seem to make Adam into a class of creatures of which God might have chosen several, either successively or simultaneously (putting them on different planets if necessary).

For Leibniz the individual is saved from expanding into a class only by agreeing to stick strictly to the script God has given him. Possibility gets detached from individuals and applied only to worlds as wholes on this sort of account. But the idea of free-floating possibilities inherent in nothing actual seems to me unintelligible, but we shall have to come back to that when we tackle Quine's "possible fat men."

However, we are getting ahead of ourselves here. Let's return briefly to Aristotle in order to reemphasize one important point before going on to look at the source of some of the attractiveness and difficulties of the "possible worlds" analysis of the modal notions such as *possibility* and *necessity*, and the possibility that it seems to offer of a direct attachment of those modal relations to individuals, particularly the modality of *necessity*. We tried to show that neither the Aristotelian concept of *essence* nor its diachronic extension in the concept of *physis* committed Aristotle to Popper's essentialism or to *de re* necessity.

The reason for this was that neither *essence* nor *physis* is something separate that can be connected to, or attributable to, or had by, anything separate from it. The subject is *constituted by*, and not *connected to*, those things. The word Aristotle uses to designate that relation (which he calls an atomic (*atomos*) or *per se* (*kath' hauto*) relation) is *hyparchein*. This gets translated misleadingly as "belongs to." That is probably as good a translation as one can get, but it does give the mistaken impression that Aristotle is talking about a relation between two things which are separate or separable. He is not. His rejection of such a separability is best seen in his arguments against "separable" forms.

This point is enough to seize on here, even though any adequate treatment of these matters would have to come to terms with Aristotle in some detail and be backed up with a thorough treatment on the scale of and with the care shown by Hintikka's very useful book *Time and Necessity*.[8] Aristotle's was the first, and, with Leibniz', the most powerful and impressive attack on the problems of change, time, and necessity, but in an analysis as rough and schematic as this, he is going to get pretty crude treatment. Aristotle is being used only to lay down some bracketing fire on the problem I am chasing: the problem of the attachment of the modality of necessity to the concrete individuals that make up the world of change and development within which we live and operate.

Let's turn now to the attractiveness and the limitations of the Leibnizian "possible worlds" analysis of modals. To see the attractiveness, let's start with the classical reduction of modals to temporal notions by a young contemporary of Aristotle's, Diodorus Cronus. Diodorus translated those notions according to the neat schema: "X is necessarily Y" reduces to "X was *and* will be Y;" while "X is possibly Y" comes out as "X was *or* is *or* will be Y." The odd, and at first sight paradoxical, thing about this reduction of modals to temporals is that it works all right for the atemporal and abstract – classes, universals, and numbers (perhaps also propositions), but if we try to apply it to time-bound particulars, to historical situations or events, to concrete particulars that come to be and cease to be, we get straight into trouble. *Necessity* will apply to none, and *possibility* rather vacuously and artificially in most cases.

But this is not at all surprising when we reflect that the equation read in the other direction would equally allow the inference to temporally unrestricted modal assertions about changing individuals from incidents in their history. From the fact that I did once run a mile in a certain time, it does not follow that that possibility can simply and without restriction be attributed to me. I'm afraid that possibility was itself already all too time-bound and to that extent not available for further translation into temporal terms. (And here we see a limitation that has to be put on the old scholastic tag: *ab esse ad posse valet consequentia.* The inference from existence to possibility is not valid for the concrete, time-bound individual or situation unless we curtail the possibility to that concrete instance and moment, in which case we haven't got much of an inference.)

No doubt with a good deal of ingenuity and fancy footwork, difficulties generated by Diodorus' translations can be staved off, but I'm afraid the cost will be great, and the difficulties will only reappear somewhere else. Hence the attractiveness of the "possible worlds" analysis if one is attempting to apply modalities to concrete individuals. What is interesting to see, and important to keep an eye on, is just what happens to the notion of an *individual*, or a *concrete individual*, under that "possible worlds" analysis of modals.

If we are to try to apply modal notions directly to individuals, we are going to have to modify slightly the classic definition of necessity and possibility in terms of "truth in all" and "truth in some possible worlds." If we want to talk about some individual necessarily being, having or doing something, we shall have to say that it is, has or does that thing in all "possible worlds;" and with *possibility* we would have to say that the individual "is, has or does" the thing in *some* "possible world."

And here we come right up against the problem of what has been called "transworld identification:" what gives us the right to talk about "the same individual" in these various "possible worlds" we are imagining? As usual, the abstract and the universal present no problem; their whole point is to be transferable and to apply to many. But the concrete individual lands us right in it. How are we to talk about the "same" concrete individual appearing in several different "possible worlds" without making him, her or it sound like a member of a touring rep company?

But one enters this Leibnizian "enchanted world" at one's peril. Bearings and even one's ear for the English language are soon lost. Plantinga, for example, in his curious book *The Nature of Necessity*[9] seems almost determined to confuse himself and his readers by indulging himself with expressions like "existing in a proposition" and going on to describe the philosopher Quine as "existing in the proposition" "Quine is America's foremost rock-climber." If Plantinga means the chap Quine who once taught me logic, I wonder how he likes it there in that proposition? Perhaps we should send him a food parcel or alert Amnesty International to try to get him out. What else can one say?

If Quine the man is described as "existing in a proposition," then clearly he will be able to "exist" in an infinite number of them, and will, I guess, have to be described as "existing" timelessly. He will have stopped being a locatable, datable chap and become a universal "existing" no particular when and no particular where. It is hard to see the point of that sort of coinage or even what it is meant to achieve.

What it does achieve is an obliteration of the distinction between the concrete particular and the universal, the individual and the general. Nothing could compensate us for that loss, and Plantinga's usage seems unlikely to catch on, even among philosophers, who have fallen for some pretty queer ways of talking before now.

Once he has confused himself to that extent, it is not surprising to find that Plantinga can't understand what problem there may be about "transworld identification" (p. 98) and, more importantly, one realizes that when he claims to have defended the notion of *de re* modality, it can't be the notion of *de re* modality we have been exploring, because he cannot be talking about the concrete, time-bound, locatable individuals we are interested in.

Another would-be defender of *de re* modality, David Lewis,[10] has similar enchantments for anyone who is enticed into his world of "possible worlds," only *his* aim seems to be to undermine if not destroy the distinction between the actual and the possible.

He does this in two ways. On the one hand he tries to drive a distinction between *being* and *existing*, saying "there are more things than actually exist." (Cp. 86). This is meant to accommodate "unactualized possibles" and in particular "possible worlds" by allowing them to "be" without necessarily "existing."

But I'm afraid I just don't understand what that means. If I say that there *is* some sort of thing, what I say is true if and only if that thing actually *exists*. The terms are convertible. Of course, what I am claiming exists (or is) may itself be a possibility. But again, for my claim to be correct, there must actually *be* such a possibility. Ordinary English idiom would allow us to say just as well that the possibility "actually exists." But when I say that there is a possibility of snow, I mean only that the clouds and temperature are right, not that there is some "unactualized snow" waiting in the wings, "lacking only the quality of existence to perfect it." The possibility of snow isn't a special sort of snow, "possible snow" stuck in a waiting-room full of hopefuls and rejects from the world of existence.[11] It's just a set of meteorological conditions.

Here, one can have all sympathy and support for Quine balking at "possible fat men" in the doorway while feeling both that he has misidentified what is objectionable about them and that his own solutions are just as objectionable, and for similar reasons.[12] The trouble comes with the move from talking about the possibility of a fat man in that doorway – meaning just that the door is wide enough and the sill strong enough – to talking about a queer entity, not really known to the English language, "the possible fat man." Once we have one of these on our hands we don't know how to deal with him, or how to apply the phrase.

I suppose, for example, that I could describe a friend as a "possible fat man," meaning by this that he is saved from seventeen stone only by his wife's execrable cooking. But I don't think that he would fill Quine's bill. We don't know how to answer the question: "How many "possible fat men' can dance on the point of a pin?" even though we can make some kind of sense of the question: "How many fat men can possibly dance on the point of a pin?" Now, it may be that this is a possibility which has never been actualized, and no fat man has ever tried to dance on the point of a pin. But one feels no conceptual or metaphysical difficulty is created by the failure of the world's fat men to take up the challenge. The question really has to do with the point of a pin as a locus for dancing and the room it might or might not afford for any fat man who cared to present himself along with some friends.

No, it is the "possible fat men" in themselves who create the difficulty, together with the would-be process of their "actualization." One wants to say that there can be no such process, conceived (as it is here) as an absolute coming-to-be, because there is nothing to take part in it or nothing for it to happen to.

When Aristotle talks about the "actualization of the potential" (as he does in his account of movement or change) he is talking about the actualization of the potentiality in, or of, something that exists already under another description. The man becomes fat, or the egg becomes an embryo, then a man and then a fat man. If there is a "potential fat man" it is in the man or the genetic structure of the egg that the possibility lies, not in thin air, or the imagination. We can also talk about

what an *actual* fat man could possibly do or could not possibly do –
stand in this doorway or dance on this pin.

But Quine's own solution to some of the difficulties in this area suf-
fers from exactly the same faults. Quine's complaint that allowing talk
about "unactualized possibilities" peoples the world with "untidy" and
"inelegant" and unnecessary elements shows an attitude toward the
relation between linguistic forms and conceptual schemata that needs
to be applied to his own suggested canonical language. In that new
language he proposes to reparse names as general terms, or rather to
split the proper name into two parts, a referential and a descriptive.
"Quine exists" becomes "There is something that Quines." If we take
this seriously, we have to ask what it is that is supposed to engage in
that supposedly idiosyncratic activity of "Quining" or "being Quine" or
"being identical with Quine." We can't break Quine into a bare reference point or a bare existent which is somehow fleshed out by the
activity of "Quining" any more than we could find such a thing as "a
possible fat man" who could be brought into existence by being the
subject of some process of actualization. (It is no wonder that the
Ontological Argument is becoming popular again. Quantificational
logic seems an absolute set-up for it.)

David Lewis's second move subversive of the actual – possible distinction consists in maintaining what he calls an "indexical theory of
actuality." This "theory" involves, and may be equivalent to, the thesis
that the word "actual" behaves like "I," "here" and "now" in that "it
depends for its reference on the circumstances of utterance, to wit: the
'world where the utterance is located'" (p. 86). One could spend quite
a time on that single proposition. For one thing it is not at all clear that
the word "actual" has a referring function like the words "I," "here"
and "now," any more than the word "dagger" which has in Macbeth's
"Is this a dagger I see before me?" The referring function is there carried by the "this" and the "which I see before me," and what Macbeth
is wondering about is how to describe what has already been referred
to: is it real or actual? Can he grab it? Can he kill with it? (Also, one
cannot help opening one's eyes rather wide when Lewis describes as
"less controversial" the analogous thesis that "Our present time is only
one time among others," and called "present" because "it is the time
we inhabit.") One would be tempted to send him a copy of the *Critique
of Pure Reason* but for the presumption that he must have one already.

Except as a misleading description of some parts of special relativity
theory, that "doctrine" is not so much controversial as unintelligible
and therefore not a very useful measure of problematicality. However
that may be, Lewis' "indexical theory of actuality" is meant to license

him to say: "The inhabitants of other worlds may truly call their own worlds actual." But that claim, if allowed, would not simply relativize the actual – possible distinction. It would subvert and destroy it. I could write a novel (which is, after all, a kind of "possible world"). This novel happens to be about a novelist who is himself writing a novel. The curious thing about this novel-in-my-novel is that it is about me writing my novel. In my novel I shall have my character say of me and my story that they are "possible worlds" and of himself and his life and activities that they are actual.[13] Now, on Lewis' account, what my novelist says about himself and me will be true within the "possible world" which he inhabits, and relative to that world, just as true as what I say "within my world" is of him. Lewis' theory seems to allow for no hierarchy and no ultimate choice between us. That is what the "index-ical theory" is all about. No matter that he is my creature or that his "possible world" has its origins in my imagination and my writing. It is a "possible world," nevertheless, and his word, suitably relativized, is taken to be as good as mine by Lewis' theory.

This problem does not arise for Leibniz, the father of all this talk. His system has a monotheistic theological setting (a fact that is usually overlooked by logicians who think they can loot it for useful devices), and this enables Leibniz to maintain an absolute distinction between actual and possible. Leibniz can say that, for reasons best known to Himself, God has chosen *me* to do the writing in reality and my novel-ist character is not *actually* writing but only writing *in my novel.*

One could say a lot more about the Lewis theory, but it would take us out of our way. Though it may be just worth pointing out that by making *actuality* indexical, Lewis will be making truth indexical as well, since the two are correlatives. The result of this is that he will in the end be unable even to talk about his "possible worlds" and to say anything about them that is either true or false. His sayings will not be sayings within those "worlds" and therefore not true *in* them either. Can they be true *of* those "worlds?" Only if those sayings can achieve their truth within his own "world." And that would require the possible world he is talking about to have some existence or "being" there in his own world.

Of course, he might try the obvious dodge of talking about what one of the other-worlders could or could not truly say about his own "world." But even that trick won't get Lewis past the gates. For Lewis' propositions to be true, there must be something actually the case in his own world which his proposition refers to. And what is that? Neither the other-worlder's utterance nor the actuality that makes it true in *his* world are facts or actualities of Lewis' world; so there is nothing for Lewis to talk about and nothing to make his pronouncements true or false.

This is the inevitable result of cutting away the theological base on which Leibniz built his fantastic edifice of "possible worlds." The ordinary notion of *possibility* has its origin in the capacities of types of things – to nourish, to be broken, to bear weight, to hold water – and has to be attributed to those things. By extension, possibilities can be attributed to situations and complexes of things. But still, the (dangerous, volatile, auspicious) possibilities inherent in those situations derive ultimately from the potentialities of those concrete things which are the elements of the situation.

Leibniz' "possible worlds" are an adaptation of the scholastic device of trying to delineate conceptual boundaries by saying what God could or could not create. The possibility of Leibniz' "possible worlds" is inherent in God. It is God's power that is supposed to underpin the possibility of those "worlds." Since none of us has any inside knowledge of those powers, it's hard to see what all this can accomplish apart from providing a single focus for the conceptions of possibilities that we have from other sources, namely, our experience of how things work. It is still worse when God is dropped out of the picture and the possibility of these "possible worlds" is left hanging in the air, underpinned by nothing at all. Then we really do have something not only "inelegant" but mysterious for Quine to complain about.

The seventeenth-century philosophers and scientists sought to go behind the Aristotelian individual substances to find deeper explanations of why those individual things or types of things had the potentialities they did. Because the philosophers were then looking for ultimate foundations, those who were not materialists could find no stopping point short of God. But for Leibniz, God was not just the ultimate cause or source of those potentialities or capacities, but in a way their ultimate subject as well. The possibility of a "possible world" lay in God's power, God's *actual* power. The materialists, for their part, created an abstracted and mystified conception of "Nature" that was projected out of the world and turned into something transcendental.

But those who in these days try to operate the Leibnizian scheme without God don't seem to notice that there is no subject for the possibility of their "possible worlds" actually to inhere in. A "possible world" is like a "possible fat man," and the objections to them are much the same. One might as well ask "how many possible worlds can rotate on the point of a pin?" Unless they can be given some kind of anchorage in the actual world, there is no way of discussing those "possible worlds" or settling any arguments about them.

That is perhaps why Kripke, whose important work in modal logic centered on "possible worlds," in his recent move into philosophy proper, has at the same time retreated rapidly from them to something more like an Aristotelian position that starts from concrete individuals rather than stories or scenarios (which is what "possible worlds" are).

In *Naming and Necessity* he apologizes for his past misconduct, though he does give an explicit definition of his concept of a "rigid designator" that seems to appeal to "possible worlds" (a rigid designator is one that "designates the same object in any possible world"). At the same time he makes it clear that his own view is that the "problem of transworld identity" is pretty well a pseudo-problem and that our whole talk about possible worlds is parasitic on our talk about concrete individuals (his favored example is Nixon), and on our ability to talk about what Nixon might or might not do in different circumstances. Since he wants to claim that these abilities of Nixon's are not based on the association of any set of descriptive terms with the rigid designator, in this case the proper name "Nixon," it looks at first sight as though we might have here a means of designating an individual that would allow us to attribute necessary features to it, in its own right, features that in this case could not be found wrapped up already in our means of designation. Might Nixon have been a frog, or might he become one? Or can we say that he must necessarily be a human being? Is there at least *this* necessity attached to the individual, Nixon? To answer this question, to make sense of it even, I think we have to go right back to the Aristotelian insights into the difference between change and development on the one hand and destruction and replacement on the other.

By and large, we would say that Nixon couldn't be a frog, or couldn't become a frog. If one moment we had Nixon in front of us and then suddenly a frog, knowing the sorts of things that happen on stages, we might suspect that he had been spirited away in some extremely clever way and rightly refuse to make the identification. Even if we witnessed a continuous deformation from man into frog, we might still not know what to say and would probably want to withhold judgment until biologists and physiologists had a chance to study the case (assuming they had been on hand with a suitable array of instruments.)

And there would be a great many things we would want to know. For example, unless Nixon turned into a very large frog, we would want to discover what had happened to the excess material. Without answers to these questions, we might still suspect some very clever trick or illusion and would withhold judgment and would probably not want to make the identification.

On the other hand, if as in Ionesco's play *Rhinoceros* people started doing that sort of thing all over the place and turning into rhinoceroses with unsettling regularity, we might want to think again. We might then come to recognize it as a stage in human development, like senility, or like metamorphosis in insects, and be happy to say: "yes, it is Nixon, all right. He's just having one of his froggy spells."

What's the lesson of all this? Well, without having room to argue it out or to bring out all the points that very much need making here, I can only come to the platitudinous conclusion that our ways of making identifications have to do with regularities we find in form and in development and therefore follow, rather than precede, experience. The illusion we sometimes have of *a priori* necessities in this area comes from the fact that our classifications sum up past experience and can, for a time, and within limits, blinker future experience. The necessity of certain behaviors or developments is one that we have *conferred* on them by our classification of them as something of *this kind*. We can, of course, withdraw that classification too. On the one hand, if the thing doesn't behave properly, we may reclassify it. Or we might even find that a particular way of dividing things up was not as useful as we thought and propose a better classification.

What is the upshot of this torturous journey? It is, I suppose, that the specter of determinism is no more than a specter, a trick of the vision. We have mistaken our own ways of looking, thinking, and talking. By projecting them outward, we have come to regard as something external things that are in fact human creations. And those projected creations in their turn have come back to haunt us. That wouldn't be the first time in human history.

7   Skepticism about skepticism

Is there any content to the doubt that Descartes enjoins as the basis for his philosophical method? Is there anything we are actually being asked to *do* in attempting to carry it out? If not, what is going on here? Christopher Cherry has attempted to bring the Wittgensteinian dictum that "the inner process stands in need of outer criteria" to bear on the would-be skeptical position of general doubt in order to raise doubts about the intelligibility of that doubt and the possibility of any such position.[1] That characterization is not entirely certain because of his tendency in that discussion to keep out of sight behind some puppets called "the modernist" and "the traditionalist" together with various sub-species and fellows-at-arms whose fate can hardly be of great interest to us.

What is more certain is that if that is the project he has started on, he has made some serious slips in carrying it out. These seem to be made while he is speaking on his own behalf and not on behalf of his various puppets, and the slips tend to strand him in a standard behaviorist position that not only does not advance things, but actually subverts the possibility of making out the emptiness and incoherence of the skeptical position. The fact that I have a general sympathy with both his project and his method may give to my remarks a disappointed asperity that conceals much common ground.

The chief slip comes with a familiar hardening of the notion of *criteria*. This brings Cherry to talk about some things called "D-behavior" and "D-specification" which appear to be a class or characterization of behavior that stands to the skeptic's doubting as providing a "logically adequate basis for the ascription of such doubt." Later in the same paragraph, he describes "D-behavior" as "requisite" (presumably to the ascription). So we seem to have our familiar friends "necessary and sufficient conditions for ascription": a far cry from criteria. More importantly: that there is or could be no such class is a feature not of the incoherence of skepticism but of the incoherence of behaviorism generally. So it provides no specific argument against skepticism.

Another by-product of this hardening is Cherry's uncritical acceptance and use of that curiosity of behaviorist theory, the notion of "linguistic behavior." Finally, there is his apparent belief that "a mad doubt is still a doubt." But as this seems to me to be false and to go to the heart of the matter, I shall come to it again. First, something about criteria and behaviorism.

Much blame must be laid on the Wittgensteinian dictum itself. The word "criteria" has a seductively hard ring. It seems to carry with it the suggestion of both the possibility and the need, of specifying, delimiting or describing something called "behavior" (the "outer") which can stand in some relation to a separate thing, "the inner process," in a way which allows us to discuss the nature of the linkage. We can easily get the impression that these are two generically detachable items about whose generic connection we can talk sensibly. We cannot. But in the face of the still common notion that we can, it is worth dropping a hint about how we come to think so.

It all comes, as many philosophical muddles do, from an unnoticed and illegitimate passage over the great gulf that is riven between the individual and the general. We can talk about a split between the "inner" and the "outer" in the case of a particular individual all right. The individual has a definite story and is placed in definite circumstances that will give us a context within which to work out their feelings, principles or beliefs, and we can as a result talk about a disparity between their feelings or principles and their actions. This fools us. We think that this disparity can be lifted out of those particular circumstances and generalized, and that we can go on to talk sensibly about the relation between the "inner" and the "outer" as such. And this we cannot do. As soon as we try to make the dissociation generic – to abstract it from those concrete circumstances – the categories disappear and we no longer have the "inner" feelings to talk about. We can't get a handle on them. Nor do we any longer have the concept of "behavior" to work with. Behavior is, after all, not mere physical movement – as has been pointed out often enough. Behavior is, precisely, informed and directed movement, or abstention. It needs the "inner" to be counted as *behavior* at all.

Though this is a piece on skepticism and not behaviorism, perhaps I can allow myself a few more words to try to make the point clearer. Dogmatism, fanaticism, and assertiveness may as easily be evidence of doubt as may tentativeness, confusion, and diffidence. So that if we were to engage in the misguided project of trying to draw up a list of "doubt behavior," we would have to include them in it. And if we were to put on such a list, as I suppose we must, all those forms of behavior that might in some particular circumstance or other be indications of doubt (or any other "inner process" or state), almost nothing would be left off.

Worse: lists compiled in this way for different "inner processes" would turn out to be pretty well identical. For we know that one person's way of expressing affection may be another's way of expressing disdain or exasperation, or whatever. And we know also about Freudian inversions, displacements, unconscious symbolism, and so forth. This may suggest anarchy, but, on the contrary, these notions involve pattern, and pattern must always be there or we shall have no lead into the feelings we are claiming are misexpressed.

But a connected point must now be made. It is that even in the case of the particular individual, the split between feeling and action, belief and practice can only be a *prima facie* one which further examination (perhaps deep and extensive) will close by revealing an underlying connection beneath the apparent separation and disparity.

Look at it like this: species or social norms provide a pattern of expectation ("by-and-large people show anger thus . . .") and the individual frustrates those expectations. They may either pretend or conceal anger, or, because of their peculiar history or special features of the situation, they may show anger in idiosyncratic or aberrant ways. They may be neurotic, drunk, schizophrenic, immature, menopausal, bereaved, father-fixated or what-have-you with the result that their ways of showing some feeling are not the paradigmatic ones. But when we put these reasons for aberrant expression together with the other evidence we may have for his/her emotional state, we see (it is hoped) that the apparently aberrant ways are in fact intelligible as to how a person of this sort placed in these circumstances might be expected to act. So there turns out not to be a real gap after all.

Despite the repeated attempts to wring a license to talk of "inner" and "outer" from "our own case," it seems that it is to the concrete individual in their very concreteness and specificity that we must trace both the ultimate authorization and the ultimate sense of that rather misleading pair of expressions. One might put it that the paradigmatic forms of behavior, how people generally act, the standard syndromes, are just what license us to talk about what is called "our own case" at all. (Without them we wouldn't know what "our own case" was a case of.) But if we examine carefully the license that we get from recognizing those individual deviations from the (by-and-large) standard forms, we shall see that it is a limited license and limited in two ways.

Because it depends precisely on the contrast between paradigmatic and the aberrant, it is incapable of giving us a license to talk of a generic or intrinsic separation between "inner" and "outer." Making the dissociation itself generic would destroy the very contrast between the individual and the standard or generic on which it is based. That is, one of the two categories that we are trying to separate depends already on the very connection we are trying to destroy. The whole notion of the *inner* gets its content from paradigmatic and standard connections between behavior and affect. The notion of *anger* could have no content and use if there were not classic ways of displaying anger, ways which allow us to make judgments, and attributions of the term. What we can't do is follow the behaviorist in attempting to forge a definition from those classic forms of display.

The fact of individual deviations and that possible gap in particular cases cannot therefore create the problem the behaviorist is trying to solve, namely, the supposed gap between "inner" and "outer" the behaviorist is trying to close (and sees as a generic one). Nor will the fact of those individual deviations allow the materials (the "inner"-purged notion of *behavior*) from which to forge definitional links to (or else substitutes for) what are wrongly regarded as an otherwise inaccessible "inner."

The aberrant gives us the idea that the connection between "inner" and "outer" is not a necessary one, but in an era that would allow us a choice only between necessary and no connection, the behaviorist aims to reestablish a necessary connection by elevating certain behaviors to definitional status. It is this aim that causes the trouble. The job can't be done, nor does it need to be done. So long as we hold to the notion of classic or paradigmatic expressions of certain emotions, desires, or whatever else of the "inner," we can talk about "deviations" and seek understanding and access to the emotions that are being expressed in a non-standard way by a particular individual in particular circumstances. That is, we can look for distorting factors that have twisted the normal expression into distorted forms. And we have to keep in mind that there are cultural differences in the ways in which certain emotions are expressed.

The behaviorist has no place for that notion of deviation and the non-standard. By insisting on a definitional connection, a necessary connection between behavior and affect, a behaviorist can say only that the definition has been satisfied or that it has not.

But even in the case of the particular individual, the apparent misalignment from which we start must turn out to be only a *prima facie* split which further facts and analysis will ultimately overcome and explain. For if we were to give to even that individual misalignment an absolute status, that is, if we were to regard the disparity between an individual's thought or feeling and their actions as an ultimate surd and in principle incomprehensible, we would be saying that there is *no* syndrome or pattern to which it can be reduced or under which it can be comprehended, and that there *will* be none and *can* be none – no matter how and in which direction our understanding advances and develops. And this is an impossible claim to substantiate. (I have argued this point, or a cognate one, in chapter 4, "Miracles.")

And just here I would like to make an analogous point for use later when we come to take up the question whether a mad doubt is still a doubt. It is that what we are pleased to call "madness" also involves form and pattern. It is not simply absurd or incomprehensible behavior. The term "madness" is not just a dust-bin category into which we can tip anything and dispose of it, which we can't make out (as the terms "ritual" or "religious behavior" seem often to have been used by the poorer sort of ethnographer or social anthropologist). If it were such a term for residues and leftovers, we would constantly be having to grub back into the dust-bin to fish out those pieces of behavior which later and more powerful and insightful theories allow us to understand. But we don't often have to do this. Certain forms of behavior are still counted as schizophrenic, for example, despite the fact that someone like Gregory Bateson may show us how to see them as poetic perceptions or metaphorical expressions of the actual situation of the schizophrenic.[2]

What is worse, to use the term "mad" in that dust-bin way would not be to characterize the behavior referred to. It would only be calling attention to our own shortcomings of understanding in relation to that behavior. But in fact we recognize that sort of behavior as a *sort*, initially, perhaps, in terms of simple syndrome and pattern, but later, with more insight, as systematically distorted, displaced, and counterproductive, or sometimes as grandly metaphorical and even expressive of things that most of us don't dare notice or face in our own situation or in ourselves. Ultimately, that is, we see that behavior as explicable, whether the forms of explanation we seek are functional, historic/episodic or a combination of the two.

The point of all this is that when we come to consider so-called "mad" doubts, it is by no means obvious that they are to be treated as doubts at all. On the contrary, whatever it was that inclined us to call the doubts "mad" would precisely incline us to see the behavior in which they were supposed to be embodied as really a displaced expression of something quite different. And one must resist the temptation to think that we call beliefs or doubts "mad" simply because they are ill founded or even radically ill founded.

In the sense intended, religious beliefs are radically ill founded (this is a remark about evidence and proof, and the nature of religious understanding, not a profession of atheism), but they are not thereby mad. On the other hand, the paranoids' suspicions are (as the commonplace has it) self-founding (and therefore founded). Their suspicious behavior *does* cause people to peer at them and avoid them, even lock them up. So they were right. But even that doesn't stop us calling them "mad."

But here we are talking at a level of generality that makes the points almost ungraspable. Also their connection with our central problem is a bit unclear. Let's go back a bit.

Now, it is of course quite right that the problem of the reality of the "doubting" that Descartes enjoins has drawn us into a discussion of behaviorism. There is a sense in which we have to settle accounts with that program and its assumptions in the course of getting to grips with skepticism and the Cartesian hyperbolical doubt. But to do this adequately we need also to start with some rough distinctions among skepticisms, because the skepticism of Pyrrho, Cusanus, Bayle, and maybe even Hume is opposite in nature and aim from that of Descartes. For them, skepticism is the outcome of philosophical inquiry and reflection, which serves to show the frailty of human faculties. Bayle and Cusanus want in this way to demonstrate the need for faith as well as humility, whereas the others want merely to curb dogmatism and arrogant pretensions to knowledge and certainty. With Hume there may be the additional point of furthering tolerance as part of a movement toward liberalism – (though he could hardly have put it that way himself.)

None of this will do for Descartes. For him, skepticism is a starting point and a method, and its aim is opposite. His doubt is recommended as a cathartic that will clear the system of dross and help us to reach that clarity and just that certainty which the others despair of, and to reach that certainty without reliance on faith or dogma or on the views and discoveries of others. His program may be individualistic, but it is more like the old American ideal of the rugged individualism of the self-made man than the urbane, tolerant individualism of Hume. (The picture of Descartes as the intellect's John Wayne may be a pretty amusing one, but it can provide its insights too.)

However all that may be, the point we have to take here is that the problems involved in skepticism as the starting point and method of inquiry are radically different from those associated with the skepticism which is being recommended as an intellectual or a life posture as the result of investigation and argument. I hope that some of the more important differences will come out as we go along. At the moment perhaps it is enough to notice that those whose aim is to argue to, rather than from, a skeptical perspective would hardly describe as "hyperbolical" the doubt they recommend.

Descartes, of course, does so describe his recommended doubt, and this is because the aim of his doubt is precisely to undermine or transcend itself. But it is essential to his whole program that the doubt he proposes should not turn out to be hollow and incoherent *ab initio* (as I would like to make out). His doubt must be merely wrong, and shown to be wrong by facts that it itself reveals. (This distinction is parallel to the one that lawyers make between a contract that is void and one that is merely voidable. The one never was a contract; the other was, but can be set aside through facts that perhaps existed but were unknown at the time.) Whatever "hyperbolical" may mean (and that is one of our problems), it has got not to mean "incoherent and self-inconsistent." This raises problems about whether the *Cogito* shows a self-inconsistency in the doubting. I don't want to go into these in a discussion whose subject is Cartesian skepticism and not Descartes generally.

One could make the sort of point I want by saying that at least it is Descartes's view that we have to thank Providence for the fact that we can get beyond the *Cogito*: we might not have been able to. God, or at least the idea of God and reflecting on it, can help us set aside the doubt. Therefore it is Descartes's view that the doubt was real and merely voidable, not self-inconsistent and void *ab initio.*

What I want to do is to contribute to the project of showing that there is no such stance as the one that Descartes proposes that we take up, and for that reason that there can be no Cartesian method of doubt. (This project is obviously not the work of a day.) What I want to bring out is that there is and can be no sense given to the word "doubt" in the context of Descartes's notion of "hyperbolical doubt" – that is, in the notion and use of doubt as a philosophical tool, a tool of conceptual analysis. The suspicion is that the notion of doubt and of doubting has been emptied of content in being transferred from its ordinary homely circumstances in everyday life and projected into the context of *hyperbolical doubt* and given the grand role that it has there. And in this I would see a precise parallel with the fate of the notion of *simultaneity* in the attempt to take it from its home surroundings in the description of commonplace local events and to give it a cosmic and absolute significance. As Einstein showed, it lost all content in the process.

Now, there are two lines open to someone who wants to make good a suspicion like that, both of which I want to explore. One of them is to question the realizability of any such doubt, its enactment or embodiment in actual behavior. The mildest test of coherence and possibility here (one far short of the stringency of the principle of plenitude – which equates "can be" with "will be in the fullness of time") is the Aristotelian test: that "the positing or assumption of the thing's realization involves no contradiction or other impossibility."

That is essentially Cherry's question, though I think it has to be posed in a way that seems at first sight to differ only slightly from his request for "minimum conditions of ascription." As I have indicated in my criticism of behaviorism, I regard that as too severe a request and one that could not be met for the case of ordinary doubting, much less "hyperbolical" doubts. I ask only that a concrete case be describable, one that we can agree should count as a real case of hyperbolical doubt, and that we could defend, in some looser way, the classification of it as a case of doubting. To put it that way may seem to have sold the pass and to have placed our dismantling project in an impossible position. But we shall just have to do our best. One is not going to catch the Cartesian program with an argument that snaps shut like a trap.

The other line of approach is one that is only temporarily and slightly artificially held apart from the first one. It involves a scrutiny of the process of attenuating the notion of *doubt* while generalizing it and abstracting it for use in Descartes's program of methodological doubt. What I would like to make out here is that there is, and is necessarily, in that process of attenuation a point at which the notion of *doubt* loses all content.

As I argued in chapter 3, Cantor had to attenuate the notion of *number* in important ways in creating the notion of a *transfinite number*, and a great deal of mystification and confusion was created in many people's minds by their failing to notice that it was an *attenuated* notion he was operating with. Nevertheless it remained a notion with content, and the content was in that case given by the calculus in which it was embedded – the transfinite arithmetic. And there are enough analogies between that calculus and the ordinary arithmetic of finite numbers to justify the retention of the terms "number" and "arithmetic" in this new setting.

We must look at the notion of *hyperbolical* or *methodical doubt* in an analogous way. Is it a concept with content? If so, what is it that gives it its content? In taking on the problem of artificial intelligence in chapter 5 and the behaviorist assumptions of Turing's "imitation game" I suggested that this sort of doubting was a game merely, and that we didn't know the rules. The question now is: are there rules which we have failed to figure out? Is there a game at all?

Geach has preserved for us a deep quip of Quine's that "It doesn't matter what you believe, so long as you're not serious." And that is precisely the point. If it doesn't matter it doesn't matter, and you can believe what you like – or doubt it.

But has a belief that is not serious any right to be called a "belief" at all? Or a doubt? It is one thing to give mouth to certain words; to give sense to them is quite another thing, and to give assent to them is something yet again. Though there is a connection. It is the nature of this connection that is a large part of our problem. One can go on to ask: is the lack of seriousness of the Cartesian doubt a conceptual necessity? Or only a human constitutional necessity as Hume has suggested?[3] Or perhaps only a practical prudential necessity as Descartes himself seems to have believed? Asking why no one has even been a successful skeptic of that kind may help us with the question of whether the skeptic is even a successful figment of the philosophical imagination.

These remarks suggest a further line of questioning in relation to the method of methodological doubt. If it turns out, as it may, that the only limits that are set on what may or may not be subjected to methodological doubt are logical or conceptual limits, then that method would seem straight away to be disqualified for its intended use in revealing to us just those conceptual or logical limits. The sense of those logical limits will determine for us the range of the possible doubting and not *vice versa*.

But before pursuing these lines, I would like to turn aside in a moment to make a comparison between the Cartesian method of doubting and the Platonic dialectic, which is in a sense its mirror opposite. For (paradoxically), though I am skeptical whether the skeptic is even a successful figment of the philosophical imagination and doubt that the method of doubt is a genuinely possible method in philosophy, I think that both the skeptic and the method have done a great deal of mischief (for all their unreality), and have been responsible for much that is sterile and trivial in philosophy.

In chapter 8's return to the artificial intelligence problem I quote a remark of Ryle's that "good sense flies out of the window when the problem of minds and machines is brought on," suggesting that a similar effect could generally be observed in the presence of the skeptic and the mechanistic determinist. And I have tried before now to trace its pathogenesis. Why the sudden loss of bearings and common sense, the access of artificiality, and lack of judgment? Why do we suddenly find people putting aside their normal good sense and in Lucretius' words "putting their head where their feet should be" and seeming to view the world upside-down?

My own view is that a kind of falsity and dishonesty entered philosophy when Descartes made hyperbolical doubt a canonical method of philosophizing and asked us to reason from doubts that no one does, or could, hold too seriously. Compare the Platonic dialectic, which, though it allowed discussion to start from "mere opinion," demanded that opinion be sincerely put forward and held by one or other of those taking part.

That is, the dialectic involved an interaction between actual views of actual human beings. And in this way supposed to lead, in the fullness of time, from mere opinion to knowledge. Aristotle adapted the dialectic for use in the study as well as the market place or the symposium, but nevertheless allowed discussion to start from what merely appeared to be the case: "to the many, or to the wise." For him, as for Plato, these views were only provisional starting points for critical examination, not absolute starting points, not principles or assumptions of the discussion. They were, precisely, views put up for critical examination and generally ended by being rejected, in the Socratic dialogues anyway. Aristotle, on the other hand, almost never simply rejects those opinions of "the many" and "the wise." They may be modified and qualified in the course of his examination, but they are almost always incorporated in some form.

But just as Aristotle would not concern himself with examining opinions which were merely fanciful or extravagant, so Socrates would not occupy himself with a contentious and insincere respondent. Nothing is to be gained, no progress made in talking to such people, the philosophical fencers, interested in cleverness and show rather than in understanding. The only thing to be done with them is to tie them in knots and leave them, making one's escape.

For Descartes escape is not so easy. In forgoing an actual opponent (who, incidentally, would not allow his "other minds" problem to arise) he and his method have to make do with an internalized opponent, a kind of *daimon*, the "mauvais et malicieux génie" with whom he wrestles like St Teresa with her doubt.

At the same time Descartes is inviting us to a kind of falsity and double-mindedness in recommending and even admonishing us not to take seriously the doubts with which he wants us to work. And in this connection he says some curious things. Particularly I have in mind *Principles* I, III, which tells us "not to make use of these doubts for the conduct of life, but only [*only*!] for the contemplation of truth."

One layer of oddity lies in talking of *using* doubts "in this way or that," as though one could first have a doubt and then decide what to do with it – decide whether or not to accede to it today, or whether to apply it in this area or that. The other layer of oddity lies in the contrast Descartes draws between the "contemplation of truth" and the "conduct of life" as though these two had nothing to do with one another and could be separated just like that.

One sees here, already in his methodology, the source of the Cartesian split between thought and action, between body and mind. That split is not so much a consequence of his method as a presupposition of it. But more importantly for our present purpose, it should be noticed that by these particular oddities of talk, Descartes is cutting away the anchorage of his notion of "hyperbolical doubt" in our ordinary notions of doubting.

To see this more forcefully, start with a remark of Peirce's, "Doubting is more difficult than lying." "Indeed yes!" one wants to say, with a sense of logical incongruity that brings to mind the exchange between Alice and the White Queen – the one in which Alice is told firmly that believing even in impossible things is just a matter of trying. "I daresay you haven't had much practice. When I was your age, I always did it for half-an-hour a day. Why, sometimes I've believed as many as six impossible things before breakfast."

The whole problem of belief (or doubt) and will rises before us here, and the question of whether belief and assent or doubt and dissent are properly *acts* at all and subject to will and choice. Not everything we do is an act of ours and subject to choice. After all, we grow and die and occupy space without being offered any options, and without these things being visited on us either – except maybe the dying.

So perhaps belief and doubt are like that – things which are neither acts and subject to choice nor things undergone and subject in no way to choice and will. We can't choose whether to grow or not. But we can do things that will affect growth – eat well or badly, exercise, and so forth. Of such a nature, presumably, are spiritual exercises as well as the mantras and mandalas of the meditators – aids and indirect means that we hope (but only hope) will help us attain what cannot be attempted directly, simply willed, or done. A certain diet, equally, is no guarantee of, or even a necessary requirement for, proper growth.

Though clearly there is a connection such that it makes sense to follow the diet with that aim.

Descartes seems to make the connection between will, belief or doubt simple and direct. I say "seems" because of some uncertainty about the relations between his notions of *belief* and *doubt* on the one hand and his notion of *judgment* on the other. And there are difficulties over his concept of *will*, about which he says some puzzling things. He says, for example, that he cannot prevent himself from believing what he clearly conceives as true, and yet that his judgment is both willed and free. But in the *Principles* "affirming, denying and judging" are simple matters of willing. (The word he uses is "modes.")

He would therefore presumably have a short way with St Teresa and her doubts about the God to whom she was desperately praying for faith. If judgment is a simple act Descartes would, or ought to, feel justified in telling her to stop being so neurotic and just *believe*. And if that did not work the first time, he could then direct her attention to his ontological proof of God's existence, after which she could have no excuse.

In the event, he would probably have done none of those crass things that his views would seem both to license and to require. But if not, that would be a tribute to his human sensitivity, not his views.

My interest in this imaginary encounter is the gulf it reveals between Descartes's notions of *doubting, believing,* or *suspending judgment* as acts that we can perform to order (for example, in pursuing some philosophical goal) and our ordinary notions of *doubting* and *believing* or *suspending judgment,* none of which can be turned on or off at will. This already should make us suspicious whether the "hyperbolical doubt" of the skeptic should be treated as a species of doubt at all or even treated as some other attitude or state of mind.

But before vexing ourselves with this question we ought to ask whether there is or could be any attitude or state of mind at all that the phrase "hyperbolical doubt" refers to, or whether in the use intended by Descartes, it is just an empty set of words, and represents no attitude or state of mind that we could possibly take up even for the purposes of advancing an argument or exploring a conceptual boundary.

We can, of course, make up phrases *ad lib* by sticking words together in grammatically acceptable ways and even go on to make a show of giving those phrases a use by laying down some syntactic rules that set out what will be counted as well-formed or ill-formed sentences involving them. But that is not enough to give such phrases a sense and a genuine place in a language. They would so far be only decorations. For, the syntactic rules defining "well formed" and "ill formed" will not at the same time define *sense* and *nonsense*, which are notions of a different kind.

Now, at this point I want to look again at the question of anchorage, and in particular to focus again on the possibility of separation that Descartes wants to insist on between his operation of doubting and the conduct of life. For our ordinary concept of *doubting* does involve a connection with action and abstention such that it would be nonsense to tell someone that she ought to doubt the safety of her car's brakes but that she should in no way let that doubt influence her actions. But the program of the First Meditation is precisely to try to root the notion of hyperbolical doubt in ordinary life and connect it to our ordinary notion of doubt. And, interestingly, Descartes is careful to try to turn aside the charge of madness that he recognizes might be brought against the program of doubting that he is suggesting we undertake. He is not going to be counted among those "whose cerebella are troubled and clouded by black bile." On the contrary, his object is to present those doubts as reasonable and well founded in ordinary experience.

But it is here that his program runs into a wall, because in so far as a doubt is reasonable and well founded, precisely to that extent it is unreasonable not to act on it or take it as the basis of action or abstention. We would even call it madness in severe enough circumstances not to act on a well-founded belief or doubt. The connection with action is intrinsic and central to the notions of *belief* and *doubt*, which are not just idle and empty incantations we say over certain propositions.

But it is crucial to notice that the connection between belief and action is not a deductively strict one in either direction. That is, we cannot insist, as Cherry wants to in taking on board the behaviorist program, or insist either on necessary or sufficient conditions of ascription of doubt.

In this connection, it is perhaps worth remarking that neither is the connection between a theory and any particular observed occurrence a deductively strict one in either direction (*pace* Hempel). The background and surroundings of any particular event will be inexhaustibly complex (hence the tell-tale three dots in the formal statement of the deductive-nomological model in representing the antecedents that have to be satisfied before we can deduce any particular outcome and make any prediction on the basis of our deduction). We have a strict deduction only when all the antecedents have been shown to be fulfilled. This, of course, is not possible when they are an indefinite, infinite or unspecified collection. Nevertheless, a theory may tell us what to expect on the whole or in outline, so a person's beliefs will give us some general expectations about their behavior in certain circumstances. Though only general ones – and for the same reasons, namely, that the individual and the circumstances of any particular piece of behavior are inexhaustibly rich.

However, we do say also that people's beliefs are shown by their behavior, though again we cannot make the connection into a deductive one and say (as Hare would have it in *The Language of Morals*) that someone's beliefs or principles are to be *deduced* from their actions. Even several bits of behavior taken together won't provide the basis of any strict deduction, and for the same reason – the inexhaustible complexity of the individual and their circumstances. Although, on the whole, the more pieces of behavior we look at the better the chance we have of getting it right, there is no end to the process or any guarantee that we have got it right. (The analogy with theory and experiment is useful here too.)

The upshot of all this is that Descartes cannot be inviting us to engage in *real* doubt of any kind, for doubting is embedded in the whole context of reasons and actions, and reasons for actions or abstentions, so that it would make no sense to suppose a form of doubting that was constitutionally and *per se* cut off from that context. But if not *real* we might be tempted to think that it was "pretend," "feigned" or "play" doubt that Descartes really had in mind.

We might be tempted briefly, but not for long, because *pretense, play* and any of that associated family of notions all involve the exact opposite of what Descartes wants and needs. That is, they all involve acting as though one had a doubt, without actually having one, whereas what he wants is the opposite: namely, that we could have an actual doubt without acting on it.

What about *imaginary* doubt? Mightn't Descartes be asking us just to imagine that we are doubting this or that, or perhaps simply to imagine and suppose that this or that is the case? (He does, after all, ask us to suppose that we are asleep.) Well, he might be asking us to imagine or suppose something. But then the question is whether that operation will do the kind of work he wants, namely, that of revealing logical structures and conceptual boundaries. What we can imagine is no sort of guide to these. I can imagine, for instance, that I have proved Euclid's fifth postulate or that I have trisected the angle, as well as that I have no body or that the frog has turned into a prince. (As Hobbes, for example, imagined, and even believed, that he had squared the circle, which of course he had not, and as we now know could not have done.)

What Descartes is trying to do is to provide an alternative or an equivalent to the Aristotelian test of possibility mentioned earlier (does the assumption of the thing's realization or actual existence involve an impossibility?), but he has chosen an unfortunate and useless substitute which gratuitously inserts an extra layer of possibility into the test and involves possibility claims that are particularly difficult (maybe even impossible) to test adequately. They are the claims that it is or is not possible to doubt something.

If someone wanted to take as a premise to an argument the claim that he can doubt that he has a head or that the room is real, or something of that kind, and we tried to take that claim seriously (while doubting it), how could we assess it as a claim? Would it be fair, or helpful, to challenge him to make good his claim by actually going ahead and doing what he says he can do? And how would we then tell if he had actually succeeded?

Consider the following little drama: "I don't think you can doubt any such thing – let's see you do it." He shuts his eyes, concentrates, looks worried, says, "Hold on, I almost got it." Then, brightening, "Ah, there, made it! – I doubt I have a head." The absurdity of this little dialogue is an indication that something quite different is going on here, something that is completely misdescribed in bringing in the notion of doubting at all, or the more difficult notion of the *ability* to doubt something. These notions are not doing any real philosophical work here at all, despite the initial appearance.

When we do find ourselves able to assess claims of the possibility or impossibility of certain suppositions successfully, it is generally by other means, particularly the Aristotelian test. A specially interesting example, interesting in two ways, is provided by Descartes's innocent request in the First Meditation that we "suppose we are asleep," a key move in the argument of that Meditation. Of course we can do no such thing.

The notion of *supposition* cannot be combined with *sleeping* or *dreaming*, except that in the opposite sense I might perhaps dream that I was supposing something in a dream argument. But the supposition Descartes is asking us to perform is not a dream supposition but a genuine one, and this requested supposition is in conflict with what it is that we are supposed to be supposing – namely, that we are not in a position to make real suppositions at all, only dream ones. This piece of thumb-catching induces a certain sympathy with Hobbes' remark that Descartes may have been a good enough mathematician, but "his head did not lie for philosophy."

Now, it is obviously interesting and important to note a flaw in a central argument of the *Meditations*, particularly an argument by which

Descartes is trying to absolve his program of doubting from a charge of madness. Nevertheless, what I really want to focus on here is the form of the argument drawing out the impossibility of Descartes's requirement. I think that careful attention here can teach us some important things about that ghost-figure *the skeptic*, and the whole style of philosophizing that has given it birth (and to which it has given birth).

As a preliminary point, notice that, abstractly considered, the supposition that we are asleep is not in itself a contradictory one. It involves no conceptual incoherences and may not be demolished by methods of pure conceptual analysis. In fact someone might make that supposition quite happily. A porter outside the lecture theater, hearing it go quiet, might ask a colleague to suppose that, tired out by a weekend of conference excesses and filled with Sunday dinner, we had all dropped off. Only when the requested supposition is self-referential in a concrete sense, that is, when we are being asked to make a supposition about ourselves, only then does the act of supposing that we are asleep come into conflict with the content of the supposition.

This point can perhaps be generalized by looking at a particular form of argument that Aristotle uses against those skeptics of a deep order who wished to deny, or doubt, the law of contradiction – Protagoras, the Heracleiteans and especially Cratylus. (Cratylus, we are told, carried things even further than Carneades and ended by only sitting and wagging his finger.) Aristotle called that form of argument *apodeixis elenktikos*, which is usually translated "proof by refutation," though "proof by cross-examination" would not only be closer to the Greek but would bring out better the nature of the argument.

For this form, like the dialectic, requires an actual opponent and requires of the actual would-be skeptic that "he say something that is significant both to himself and to another (this is essential if any discussion is to follow, for otherwise such a person cannot reason either with himself or with anyone else)" (*Metaphysics* 1006a23). Aristotle then argues to show that the act and fact of significant speech involves the real acceptance of the (verbally denied) law despite the words of the man's mouth. (He introduces here his useful distinction between *eso* and *exo logos* – the words of the man's mouth as against what he is inwardly committed to, what is implicit in his words and particularly his actions.) If someone tried to be really consistent in his denial and, like Cratylus, refused even to say anything, Aristotle would describe them as "no better than a vegetable." And these days, if we met somebody like that we would probably describe them as a "catatonic" – unless, of course, we came to the conclusion that it was a philosopher trying to make a point. Time would presumably tell.

But in practice if we met someone who seemed to be having actual doubts about whether the ground would hold them or whether the room was real, we would hardly react by putting a copy of the *Meditations* into their hand. We would probably start with the assumption that they had taken or had been given LSD or some other psychotropic and would probably try to calm them, would give them some Valium, and wait it out. And if that didn't work, we would probably treat such a person as a schizophrenic. Nor would that reaction be in the slightest unreasonable because we know that argumentation would be of no avail with someone who was really in doubt about all the things which were the basis of the life we knew, and showed the reality of that doubt by not entering, or not being able to enter, into that life at any point. There would be no beginning of argument or reasoning, no common language in which to converse.

8 Fool's intelligence

Gilbert Ryle once remarked that "Good sense flies out of the window when the problem of minds and machines is brought on." And when one surveys the Armies of the Night charging and counter-marching in the intellectual fog and dust in that neighborhood, each with its crippling weapon that never quite reaches the heart of the enemy, one can only agree and wonder why this should be.

The suspicion is not long dawning that it is because the problems of machine intelligence and artificial intelligence have not only conceptual roots, but ideological ones as well. That is, they are grounded in and express not a scientific view or theory, but a view that stands outside and looks over the sciences as a whole, taking them to be the only comprehensive and legitimate form of understanding and explanation. The connection will not be obvious between that world-view and the belief that we might one day be able to build a machine that was intelligent or create intelligence by artificial, technical means. I shall shortly say a bit more about that world-view based on the sciences, and how it is connected with the classic problem of "mechanical" or "artificial" intelligence. Firstly, we need to get clearer about the nature of the problem itself.

Though cognate, the problem of *machine* intelligence and that of *artificial* intelligence are different problems. The one calls for clarification of the concept of *machine* and its relation to the notions of *use* or *purpose*; the other for a clarification of the notions of *making* and *artifice* in contrast to *natural* or *chance* production. Chapter 5 deals with the problem of "machine intelligence." Here we shall be concerned with "artificial" intelligence, the attempt to produce or imitate intelligence.

Many workers in the field of artificial intelligence and some commentators from outside the field seem to think that the problem is a purely scientific one that hard work and technical advance will solve.

One day we will be able to produce (and maybe mass-produce) machines or other artifacts that everyone but the hardest-bitten dogmatist will recognize as being intelligent. Some, taking a cue from A. M. Turing, add to this a sort of linguistic relativism, claiming that AI work itself will force linguistic changes in the way we use the word "intelligent," changes that will overwhelm even the doubters, leaving them with no way of expressing their dissent in a world in which the word "intelligent" has come to be applied regularly to machines without those tell-tale quotation marks that signal the metaphorical.

First, however, I hope to make out that we have not got here a definite scientific project with a clear outcome and a project aimed at a calculable chance of success. For one thing, projects of that kind do not get funded by the creation of university departments. If a group of scientists, however distinguished, were to approach a university council, senate, and the other appropriate bodies with a proposal to found a department for the purpose of pursuing a finite scientific problem with a definitive outcome, they would have a poor chance of success. They would surely be asked what was meant to be done with the department when the problem had been solved and the technique developed. A research team or other *ad hoc* body would be the appropriate format for that sort of finite problem. The founders of departments of artificial intelligence seem to have known, either instinctively or explicitly, that this was an area of research not bounded by the single goal of producing intelligence by art, despite the suggestion in the department name.

For another thing, if the aim of AI departments' work were really to devise a technology for making intelligences, then they would have about as much prospect of success as Departments of Circle-Squaring. For there is a conceptual antithesis lying at the center of the notion of *mechanical intelligence* and its associate, the notion of *artificial intelligence,* which I am going to try to bring out later by looking carefully at the notion of *making* and the notion of *artifice* to try to bring out in turn a relation that these two concepts already bear to the notion of *intelligence,* a relation which stands in the way of the suggested combination.

Secondly, we need to say something about the seductive suggestions of the "linguistic relativists," whose program, as Bertrand Russell might have said, "exhibits all the advantages of theft over honest toil." But theft is a piece of individual initiative which, if turned into a general program, destroys its own basis, namely, private property. Just so, linguistic relativism ends by destroying language itself, because we can say whatever we like if we are allowed to appeal to the possibility of linguistic changes that will in future license what we say. Such a program could license, for example, our Department of Circle-Squaring through an appeal to the possibility of changes in the meaning of "circle" or further developments in the techniques of squaring.

Just now, with the shadow, or even the reality, of George Orwell's "Newspeak" thickening amongst us, we need to defend the language, its clarity, and its precision, against those whose interests are served by confusion and dust.

Still, the genuine productive work within AI departments must be distinguished from the things that are said about it from outside by way of assessing its social or philosophical significance. The commentators may be actual outsiders or AI workers themselves in their off-duty hours. The assessments may run from the ideological to the poetical. They may come out of a poetical vision, out of muddle or out of a desire to impress the impressionable or gull the gullible, whose name is legion.

This difference between the secular, daily work of AI and what Ryle would have called the "Sunday pronouncements" of its practitioners and others is crucial. To make it clearer, we need to identify and characterize a visionary use of the sciences that has been with us almost as long as the sciences themselves. "Scientism" is a convenient label for this programmatic and visionary science-based religion. It is a complex syndrome of ideas and attitudes whose chief marks are reductionism, determinism, a kind of "theologizing" of science and a tendency, even a necessity, to talk about "science" rather than "the sciences," by the introduction of absolute notions, and the deification of Nature (capital "N," please, to signal its transcendent nature), as well as a general "mechanization of the world-picture."

Scientism lives more in the future than in the present and takes little note of the past except as the basis of gigantic extrapolations that generally look to the end of processes that are actually endless, generating thereby questions that are not susceptible to scientific answers at all but are questions of quite a different order and demand a different sort of answer. An example here is the "origin of the Universe" conceived as a question about absolute origins. At the moment the candidate explanation is the "Big Bang," which is meant to have started it all off. But this can hardly be a final explanation that will satisfy astrophysicists and theoretical mathematicians for all time. As soon as enough work has been done to understand and describe the Big Bang sufficiently, the question will pose itself: "What went *bang!*?" And so on . . . Astrophysicists don't yet ask that question for the good and substantial reason that they haven't yet got the materials to make it into a substantial question, one that would define a research program. I don't know how long that will take, but it will surely happen.

And a similar line of argument will run for any "ultimates" and "fundamentals" that are offered up as the final resting places for scientific investigation, analysis or theorizing.

In the pre-quark early 1960s I gave a series of lectures on Scientism, to which at that time I gave the title "scientific fundamentalism." It was the period when what were then being called "fundamental particles" – the mesons in their infinite variety, pions, muons, etc. – were beginning to organize themselves into hierarchies and relationships reminiscent of the periodic table. In view of that, I felt, and said with some confidence, that it was now only a matter of time before some "more fundamental" particles would be proposed in order to explain the periodicity and order that had emerged. This was for me the inevitable result of the logic of explanation and theorizing here. For the title "fundamental" that those particles had carried for a while told us about the state of our knowledge of them rather than about their actual position in the order of things. I did not have to wait very long for that prediction to be realized. Within a year or two quarks had been proposed and articulated to explain that order and those relationships in just the way I had imagined.

"Scientism" as I have been using the word could almost be defined as the rejection of that point. It insists that there *must* be an end to those processes of analysis, explanation, and theorizing and then insists on the right to talk about conditions at the limit. This is not itself a scientific point of view. It could not even be described as a theory or a view about the sciences. And it is one that could not itself be called "scientific," for it goes against the evidence obtained from the actual history and practice of the sciences. It really has to be described as a religious and theological movement of thought with exactly the form of St Thomas Aquinas' famous *quinque viae*, arguments for the existence of God. It is an attempt to create a comprehensive world-view out of the scientific enterprise and feeds on the secular, practising sciences to stoke its visionary fires. Those practising sciences generally get damaged in the process since the real nature of their projects, achievements, and problems gets obscured, and the sciences often get lumbered with "absolute" notions (such as absolute space and absolute time) that cause much mischief before they are finally exorcised.

Scientism stands to the concrete practising sciences and their achievements "as onanism to sexual love" (to reuse Marx's brutally vivid words). One had thought it somewhat in retreat, damaged, and dented by developments within the sciences themselves. Relativity,

Uncertainty, Gödel's theorem,[1] the destruction of hopes of reaching particles that were absolutely fundamental have all in their several ways trammeled that fantasy of a comprehensive and complete account of everything in natural scientific terms, a fantasy which sails majestically under a flag with "Materialism" written on it.

Yet Scientism lives on, its dreams revived by the computer age and its hopes fixed on departments of artificial intelligence, which, if they could make a machine intelligent, would in effect be showing that intelligence could be explained mechanically. "Artificial intelligence" is only De la Mettrie's "L'Homme Machine" in modern dress. It seems that in each period the dominant scientific advance kindles yet again hopes of complete explanations and total understanding within a single unified mode (for Scientism is nothing if not monotheistic).

However, this time and in this form Scientism has gone straight for the heart – humanity itself and its intelligence, something that earlier generations had generally tried to exempt, even employing heroic measures to do so. Descartes's "two-substance" separation of mind and body was one such heroic attempt to save humanity from being run over by the steamroller of scientific explanation, its freedom flattened and stuck onto a deterministic map. And like most such heroic measures, it caused more trouble than it avoided.

But not all AI workers are worshippers in this particular church, nor need they be, nor need they accept its proffered false perspective from which the would-be problem of the "ultimate origin of intelligence" not only looks like a sensible, soluble one (which it is not) but a scientific one into the bargain (which it certainly is not).

Many may see their project as that of showing the ultimate origin of intelligence through a reductive analysis that will show how to get intelligence out of what is not intelligent. Others have put aside that grandiose and empty goal and are getting on with some honest and interesting work. Marvin Minsky has shown them the way by a clear and sensible statement of the aims of AI as "getting a machine to do what in a man would require, or be evidence of, intelligence." That is a very different project from trying to *make* intelligence.

Making and mimicking are two different and in fact incompatible enterprises, just as pretending anger and stirring oneself up to anger are, or feigning sleep and being asleep are incompatible. In the same way, Christopher Pinchbeck never thought he was actually making gold. Even if he had gone to great lengths to produce an alloy that passed all the known tests of his day and gained an Assay Office hallmark, he would have produced only fool's gold and have been guilty of the crime of "passing off." In the same way, Frederick Winslow

Taylor's "scientific management" teams do not turn unskilled workers into skilled by defining their work in terms of mechanical routines and bodily movements that produce the result that skilled workers would using judgment, skill and initiative. Quite the contrary. The work has been "de-skilled" and the worker degraded.

Nowadays we can make gold, really make gold, out of what is not gold. We have the technology. But you don't (and can't) get there by mimicking or simulating – that would be just *faking* gold, not making it. Just so, computer simulation of intelligence will no doubt produce many interesting and important results, and, used properly, could help us to solve many of the problems that machines and mechanization are setting for us in our lives, and might even lead to some real social gains in the fullness of time. (At least we can hope.) What it is *not* going to do, however is to produce genuine intelligence. That line of march, simulation, can produce only *simulated* intelligence, "fool's intelligence." The fantasy is not only a myth and a distraction but a symptom of a malaise and a danger too.

I have tried to isolate and identify a certain cast of mind that sets scientists chasing after theological questions that don't admit of any scientific answer or any answer in terms of a theory at all. That turn of mind seems to have posed the question that some people in the AI field see themselves as addressing: the problem of understanding and explaining the ultimate origin and absolute beginnings of intelligence itself, how it may arise out of what is not intelligent. They think (wrongly) that they could go some way to solving this problem if they were (*per impossibile*) to make non-intelligent things intelligent by deliberate and repeatable contrivance.

They are wrong in this because intelligences created by human artifice would still be intelligences created by intelligence – that is precisely what it would mean to call them "artificial." If we were to accept (as I think we should not) that there is a genuine problem here in trying to account for "the origin of intelligence," it would have to be the problem of seeing how intelligences might contrive to create themselves out of some preexisting state of non-intelligence. That is the only proper sort of answer that that question of origins could get.

But I want to make a suggestion here that, if accepted, would vitiate all the discussions and arguments about artificial or mechanical intelligence as contributors to a would-be problem about the ultimate origins of intelligence. I want to suggest that the problem itself is not a theoretical one at all, or open to understanding in terms of a theory, but a practical one that has already been solved by humanity in practice and in practical life.

As this is a point of view that is not going to recommend itself to academics whose stock-in-trade is theoretical understanding, I don't expect an easy passage for it even though I think the point is a correct one and one that can illuminate these dark areas.

It has a parallel in a central point in Aristotle's *Ethics*, a point whose centrality has not often been seen because of our era and profession's insistence on intellect and theory. Aristotle says that the good man becomes good by doing good. But he is not good in that, and because he has done good (it could be accidental), or even because he did the good out of a desire to do good (it could be a one-off impulse and not a settled disposition). Nor is his goodness a matter of adhering to some good principle (which would be the general ethical point of view of our time with its insistence on theory), for this leaves us with the *akratos*, the undisciplined man, who is not good despite all his perception or theoretical grasp of the good and even desire to do good. Even though he both sees the good and wants the good and does the good sometimes, we would have to say that his doing good has an accidental character; it isn't a settled part of his nature. He is, as one might say, a moral spastic; he is unable to move in the way he wants; he lacks a knack, an ability to act well in a consistent and repeatable fashion.

Now, just as a good person has to make themselves good (no other can do it for them), so, I want to suggest, humanity has had to make itself intelligent. Homo Erectus didn't become "Sapiens" by external imposition, nor (despite the words of the US Constitution) can humanity have been "created" free. Freedom has to be achieved just as intelligence has; unless you want to stick with the "negative" notion of freedom (absence of constraint) and are therefore willing, if consistent, to call a slug or a worm "free"; in which case your notion of freedom doesn't amount to very much. And neither of those things happens by accident, either; they have to be won.

But isn't the notion of humanity making itself intelligent too paradoxical to be understood? How can the non-intelligent make itself intelligent? Doesn't the act of making already imply intelligence? *Imply*, yes; *require*, no. And in saying that, I am inviting you to look at the problem in the light of the Aristotelian example above. There are two aspects of that example I want to bring out. One is that the act of making itself has a double aspect – the maker and the thing made. And the maker in the act of making not only makes the thing but makes himself into a maker. This is a point of Marx's, too – when he says that humanity produces itself.

In creating anything, humanity creates itself, makes itself into maker, produces itself as producer. And here I have deliberately followed Marx and used the species term "humanity." For this "production" is not going to be the matter of a grand epochal moment, not the work of some individual of genius who sees the light and seizes the bone, stick or stone and makes it into a tool. Generations, millennia would probably be taken up in a slow painful progress from happy accidents to the acquisition of a knack, a skill that enables the thing to be done deliberately and at will. Only then can we describe it as a "making" and not just a happy accident. Think of the child learning to speak, or to whistle, and the progress from an accidental production of the sound to slowly increasing success in the struggle to do it again. Finally the thing can be done confidently and at will.

But the child's struggle takes place in a context of already existing skills and practices, with the example and encouragement of others, their corrections, and rewards. Humanity, of course, had no such pre-existing context, or even the knowledge that there was such-and-such a skill to be acquired.

And this leads to the second aspect of the Aristotelian example I want to insist on. For we don't properly say of someone that they have produced something unless they can do it deliberately and at will. Short of that, they can't be counted as an artificer or the thing as an artifact. The accidental result of something I do is not counted as an act, product or artifact of mine. Also, humanity as a species can't be counted as producers or as intelligent until those skills can be taught, passed on by example or by deliberate instruction.

Consider those things we call "tools." From one point of view they are just physical objects or even collections of unrelated physical objects. They get to be tools only in the context of existing practices which give them a use and a unity related to that use. The welding set dropped (however gently) into the jungles of New Guinea loses that status and that unity because the practice of welding does not exist there. (Of course, the situation is ambiguous because the practice does exist elsewhere. Perhaps we need to make use of that impossibility the "time machine" and have it drop our welding set into ninth-century Anatolia.) The electrodes might be used for one thing, the leads for another, and the mask for ritual purposes and perhaps the transformer might become an object of veneration, like the packing-cases of the "cargo cults" of post-war Micronesia.

The first thing to notice is that the object that we with our practices and skills would describe as "the welding set" has here ceased to be a tool or even a unity. It has been absorbed into another set of practices, in this case, religious ones. The second thing to notice is that it is the existence of those practices and skills among us that gives the thing that status as "tool," as a welding set.

I should really say a lot more here to defend these points in the face of the tendency of our individualistic era to posit a single "born genius" who suddenly sees, solves the problem, and shows the way. And much more discussion is needed to expand and elaborate the role of teaching and passing on of skills in mankind's self-creation as creators, and in the existence of practices which are capable of defining and underpinning the role and nature of those physical objects that are designated "tools." But that will have to wait. In any case it would be out of place here, where the only object at this stage has been to show that AI work has nothing to contribute to the problem of understanding the self-creation of intelligence.

That problem of the "self-creation" of intelligence, I have been claiming, has got to be a practical problem, solved already by mankind in practice and by doing, and not a theoretical problem. And by this dark saying I mean no more than that there could be no theory about how such a thing was done or was to be done, nothing which could stand in advance of practice, and guide it in the way theories are supposed to. For that suggestion would run right up against a brick wall of paradox, requiring, as it would, a prior existing intelligence to apply the theory. Practice has here got to precede theory and theorizing.

You can, of course, say that theory is implicit in any practice since practice has got to be guided and regular action and thereby committed to a recognition of regularities in the things it is working with. Only the presence of that regularity and that (at least implicit) recognition of regularity will mark out a practice from random and accidental movement. I think I can accept that point well enough and could perhaps take on board and even extend it by saying that it shows that the two notions *theory* and *practice* are correlative and dialectically linked notions. The two things come into being together and you can't have a practice without an implicit theory, or a theory without implications for practice.

But there is another paradox here that has to be brought out. It lies in the very notion that there could be a technique, a technology, for producing intelligence, a formula for forcing intelligence on recalcitrant, or at least uncooperative, material. (Though if we are going to be really careful of our language here, as we must, we should say "noncooperative," for the notions of *cooperative* and *uncooperative* involve intelligence already.)

For, to be intelligent is precisely to be able to embody one's own projects, plans, purposes, and intentions in actions and products – able at least generally and for the most part. We hardly call "intelligent" the person who can never bring off any projects or make anything right, just as we don't call the *akratos*, the morally undisciplined person, a good person whatever their hopes or intentions. As for the genuine spastic, the more we understand the physiological basis of the spasms that distort practice, the more easily we can see the intelligence embodied in what earlier generations saw as irrational jerks and inarticulate sounds.

When I insist, as I want to here, on the primacy of practice and making in the assessment of and in the conception of intelligence, I may seem to be in agreement with the behavioristic assumptions of the seekers after artificial intelligence. But there is a sting in the tail of that insistence, one that ultimately paralyses the "false" AI project in paradox. It lies in a further insistence: on the dazzlingly obvious fact that it is the intelligence of the maker or doer that is embodied and shown forth in the thing made or done.[2]

And here we can see that "false" AI project broken on a crux. For the notions *artifact* and *intelligence* are also correlative notions and dialectically linked. Artifacts are just those things that have been shaped by, and therefore embody and exhibit, the intelligence of the artificer. But the artifact will also have many *accidental* features and properties. Any feature of the artifact that was not intended, foreseen, and deliberately brought about through the application of a skill or technique will be an accidental feature.

The accidental features may be welcome and useful, they may be unwelcome or even disastrous, or else they may be matters of indifference. What they are not is a part of the artifact as such. They are not part of my intentional contriving of the thing made. What I have made, the artifact itself, consists of just those features and properties that have been put there by contrivance and design. I can take credit for them, but not for what I neither intended nor expected. *Chance* and *artificial* are opposed notions, just as *intelligence* and *artificial* are connected ones. What is *chance* is not *artificial*, and what is *artificial* is not *chance*.

The intelligence of whatever is said to have its own intelligence has got to be self-made and cannot be put there by another. The point could be summed up in philosophical terminology by saying that there is already an internal relation between the notions of *artifact* and *intelligence*, one that excludes the possibility of any further or different relation. In particular there is no room for the possibility of an artifact embodying its *own* intelligence just in so far as, and precisely because, it is an artifact. It is in the nature of intelligence to be embodied in products and actions, and in the nature of products, artifacts, and actions to embody the intelligence of the producer or actor. If it is intelligent, I can't have made it so, because the intelligence it showed would in that case be mine and not its own.

Perhaps we need here to challenge head-on the whole traditional conception of intelligence that has come down to us from Descartes. This conception has dominated the way we have looked at the mind and at human intelligence – as something separated, existing in abstraction from practice, standing over and above and outside it. Maybe we need to insist not only that the two notions *intelligence* and *artifact* are correlative and dialectically linked, but that, looking from the other side, there can be no application for the notion of *intelligence* where there are not artifacts, practices, products, and production. And correspondingly, there can be no application for the notions of *artifact, practice, act* or *product* without the implication of, or presumption of, a producing intelligence. Intelligence is what appears in products, actions and artifacts. And on the other side, actions, artifacts, and products are just those things that exhibit and carry the implication of a producing intelligence.

There are, of course, resonances here with that famous passage of Marx and Engels in the *German Ideology,*

> Men can be distinguished from animals by consciousness, by religion or anything else you like. They themselves begin to distinguish themselves from animals as soon as they begin to *produce* their means of subsistence, a step that is conditioned by their physical organisation. By producing their means of subsistence men are indirectly producing their actual material life.[3]

My own view, set out earlier, puts perhaps this same point by saying that in producing *anything*, humanity produces itself as *producer*, creates itself *creator*, makes itself *maker*, though clearly "means of subsistence" would be historically the most likely first candidate for production.

A quick survey of the ways in which things can come into being may help nail down and secure these points. Roughly, we can distinguish three ways: naturally, artificially, and by accident. And, very roughly indeed, those things are called "natural" which regularly come to be of themselves and without any outside help and contrivance. The artificial is what does involve outside help and contrivance. It results from the application of skill, technique, and intelligence. No doubt natural forces and materials will have been used, but they will have been brought together in ways that would not occur in the ordinary way of things in the absence of intentional action. The *accidental* is what is neither contrived nor regular and predictable of itself. It will be the result of the happy or unhappy coincidence of forces that don't ordinarily come together on their own.

Human intelligence is unique in not coming to be under any of these three heads. I am not saying other species may not come to take charge of their own development in the way humanity did. All one can say is that despite help and encouragement, so far none has. The chimpanzees that have been raised with human families have shown some interesting development as individuals, but this has not been transmitted, so far as I know, to other members of the species. It may yet happen or even be happening by degrees too small for us to make out. In any case I see nothing to rule it out. And in this connection it is interesting to put the question whether those chimpanzees raised with humans should be considered as potential candidates for the title "artificial intelligences." Taking that question seriously and not giving a pat answer can reveal much to us about the problems involved in coming to the conclusion that the intelligence exhibited by something is to be counted as its *own* intelligence rather than that it is really the intelligence of another working through, and exhibited in, that individual or thing. Myth and literature, and sometimes life itself, provide many examples of individuals who are so manipulated by another (Svengali and Trilby) that their actions do not exhibit their own will and intelligence, but those of another.

But here we have to confront another confusion infecting the whole discussion of the notion of *artificial intelligence*. For there are two distinguishable notions of *intelligence* and two quite different applications of the word "intelligent." One is a "species" concept that applies to whole species, as when we might say, for example, that the chimpanzees are showing some signs of developing intelligence, while flatworms or may-flies are not. The contrast term for this use is "non-intelligent" rather than "stupid."

The other notion of *intelligent*, for which "stupid" is the contrasting term, is one that applies to individuals within a species (so far only humanity) that has already earned the species-designation "intelligent." The may-flies as a species have not got that species-designation "intelligent" and therefore individual may-flies cannot be called either "stupid" or "intelligent." The application of the epithet to individuals within a species allows for a whole range of gradations between "intelligent" and "stupid," while the species-notion makes only the simple division between intelligent and non-intelligent without any such gradations of more or less. (This does *not* imply that there was a grand epochal moment when humanity passed, as a species, from the one state to the other.)

One of the residues left by the retreating Enlightenment is a belief in the possibility of human progress in intelligence, which may tempt us to think that there may be gradations in the species-notion of intelligence. I shall say no more about this than to recall the nice irony of Will Cuppy in his chapter on Charlemagne (from that great work *The Decline and Fall of Practically Everybody*): "Way back in the Dark Ages, people were not very bright. They have been getting brighter and brighter ever since, till they are like they are now."

The notion of *intelligence* with its contrast *stupid*, which applies to individuals, does not apply to species. While the may-flies may not be intelligent, they are not stupid either. They are just not intelligent (or, if you like, are non-intelligent beings).

Of course, we often do use such words as "stupid" anthropomorphically, for example, to describe a species that has adopted what we regard as a poor evolutionary strategy. But there are many layers of anthropomorphism in that sort of talk.

That sort of anthropomorphic viewpoint and style of talk can provide insight and even inspiration, as when Robert the Bruce saw perseverance and determination in the spider's efforts and drew new strength from that. There is certainly no ground or justification for forbidding its use in AI or anywhere else. But we must be clear what sort of talk it is. What we must *not* do is take that metaphorical talk literally and lose a sense of the style of talk we are engaging in and the proper purposes of its use.

Superstition arises when the figurative is taken for the literal. Almost worse than that, we lose the value of both sorts of talk when we rub out the line between the poetical and the literal or prosaic. We end up with bad poetry and sloppy, inaccurate prose that is incapable of making clear distinctions or saying anything definite. One could charge some AI ideologists with producing nothing but bad poetry.

Let us now turn back to the would-be notion of an "intelligence constructed by contrivance and technique." In the light of some of the above discussion we can perhaps now see an interesting moral paradox there too. For the would-be producer of artificial intelligence would at the same time be trying to *claim*, and trying *divest themselves of*, responsibility for their product and its behavior. My artifact is my product. I made it for a purpose, and if I made it well it will serve that purpose, which is *my* purpose, and so its performance in serving my purpose is my responsibility. The intelligent being, on the other hand, is precisely one that can have its own purposes and projects separate from mine and is presumed to be responsible for its own actions. It is sometimes thought that being unpredictable in its behavior would be evidence of a separate will or point of view on the part of a machine. It is not.

I can, of course, easily design a machine that is in principle unpredictable in its action: the insertion of a simple randomizing element will do that. But in being unpredictable it would be behaving precisely as I intended; it would be embodying my exact intention. And I would hardly escape responsibility if the machine were to wreak havoc (say it was part of an automatic landing program for an aeroplane).

I might also mischievously deliberately design a malfunctioning machine, one that might have the aim of inducing a paranoid sense of being "got at" in anyone who innocently tried to use it. (Only if it worked perfectly for them might I for a moment feel *I* was being got at.)

A brilliant example of such a contrivance was the unassembleable deck-chair that the *Candid Camera* team devised some years ago and then, quite mischievously, put into the hands of a pretty woman in Hyde Park. Then they cheerfully filmed the slow erosion of the confidence of officiously helpful males who rushed to her aid thinking they would quickly put the thing to rights for this "pretty young thing" and then struggled without success with the fiendish device. Then, following an erosion of confidence, came the awful realization that they now had the problem of how to extricate themselves from the situation without loss of face.

In all those cases the maker's aim, intelligence, and skill are embodied and exhibited in the thing made. But what about the machine that seems to go beyond the skill of the designer? The standard example here is the chess-playing program that outplays its deviser.

Despite all the fuss made about such examples I see no reason to pay any particular attention to them. After all, it is the whole point and nature of machines and tools generally to extend, magnify, and go beyond unaided human power. The simple jack lifts more than I can, but I see no reason to get worked up over that, any more than to fall down and worship the aeroplane because it can outfly me. They are all human contrivances and cause for pride and not abasement. And when we get, as we shall, machines that design machines, that design machines, etc., we mustn't lose track of the fact that *we* stand at the head of it all, and that those machines are all doing what *we* intend – unless they are malfunctioning or badly designed.

Let's now go back to Ryle's remark and try to understand the sterility and the rather false passion of the debate over AI and machine intelligence. One reason for all the passion is that the debate is completely idle and the volume has been turned up on passion to conceal that fact. It is not a practical issue for anybody. None of the participants is trying to decide how to behave in the presence of some machine or other artifact (though I have heard of people who turn off the television set in the bedroom before undressing. Perhaps our discussion and its results might help them overcome that modesty). The workers in AI, however, are not waiting on the outcome of the debate to decide how to conduct themselves in relation to the machines that are the subject of their research. No one is really in a quandary as to whether to treat certain machines as moral agents, whether to allow them to form unions, and to press for their rights or better working conditions.

Another reason for both the passion and the sterility and lack of resolution is that AI has been coopted to do quasi-religious duty in the service of the mechanical world-view that is a central feature of the Scientism that was born with our era. The passion is exactly what might be expected in religious debate, even though the subject and the question is one that pretends to be scientific.

I have wanted to shift the whole perspective and alter the terms of discussion to ones which can expose the root incoherence of the myth embodied in the "false" AI project and yet bring out what is right about that picture too. For it is at the same time deeply right and infuriatingly wrong. For amid all this self-congratulation of humans as the intelligent devisers whose intelligence shines out in their products, there are darker themes as well.

Machines may embody only our own intelligence, not their own, but that does not prevent that embodied intelligence from being turned back against humanity in ways that are already of the utmost seriousness for our whole human existence. Never have we been in greater danger from our own products.

The destructive possibilities of the weapons systems we have made are just too numbing to take in. And the military and governmental apparatus we have devised piecemeal have grown so complex that they seem beyond comprehension and control. We have built up a world economic system that has brought with it poverty, idleness, and starvation on a completely new scale. That system's underlying profit-based conception of "rationality" and choice is on the way to destroying the environment and the very conditions of our continued health or even our existence. That same system of "rationality" and choice is implicated in the evolution of conditions of production that make work generally quite unpalatable, demeaning, and destructive of intelligence itself, as skilled work is replaced by routines devised by "industrial psychologists" applying Frederick Winslow Taylor's "principles of scientific management."

It may look quite out of proportion and inappropriate to set down in this landscape the analysis we have been making of the shamanistic mystifications and conceptual dust-raising of some of AI's camp-followers and off-duty workers. They often see themselves as just having a bit of fun playfully dazzling laymen with alarming pictures propped up by *façons de parler* which are issued as promissory notes and are never exactly redeemed and made good. But don't be fooled by that air of playing the fool. The apparently playful myth of the machine with its own separate intelligence expresses with deadly accuracy the alienation and false-consciousness of our era, an era marked by the extent to which we present our own products and institutions to ourselves as if they came to be spontaneously with their own direction. They twist our lives in ways not intended by anybody and we end up confronting them as the embodiments of some alien force of nature.

But AI mythology not only expresses that false-consciousness perfectly, but helps solidify it and make it impenetrable, turning our eyes firmly in the wrong direction, muddying the waters, confusing the issues and subverting clarity of language and thought just when we need a monumental effort to understand and regain control over those forces we have created and can no longer comprehend. If intelligence is shown and measured by mastery and control over the environment and conditions of life, over our own political and moral development, then the human race is not so much creating rival intelligences as losing its own as each of these things seem to slip from our grasp and we come to see ourselves as victims and not as initiators.

9 Language and the society of others

The solitary language user is again stalking the critical fields of Europe (and America, one should add). This pre-social individual, abstracted from all social and historical context, has been seemingly revived after what many of us saw as a death-blow dealt by Wittgenstein in his analysis of the notion of *following a rule*, and his related discussions bringing out the impossibilities of a "private" language – what has come to be known as Wittgenstein's "private language argument." Just what a "private language" is has become the issue: did Wittgenstein show that language use and rule-following essentially and necessarily involved others, and were therefore necessarily social in character (thus showing that to be human and to be rational was necessarily to be social – as Aristotle had it)? Or did his arguments bear only against the notion of a language which was essentially and necessarily private, one which could not *in principle* be taught to another?

Now, it might seem that the idea of a language that *could* not be taught to another is a nonsense which does not need arguing against, but the proponents of the latter reading (Baker and Hacker,[1] Colin McGinn,[2] for example) see Wittgenstein's argument as really being about "private objects" (as sensations have often been considered) and the possibility of referring to such things. The "private" unteachable language would be one purporting to refer to such objects, which one could not teach another about because they were not part of common experience. This reading of Wittgenstein detaches his discussion of private language from his discussion of rules and rule-following and locates it in the discussion of private objects and problems of reference.

And so this latter (one is tempted to say "revisionist") reading of Wittgenstein seems to rescue the notion of the abstract pre-social language user from the conceptual dust-bin to which many of us thought it had been consigned. This abstract being will be allowed to use language in their pre-social isolation just so long as that language, though untaught to the user, could be taught to another. (Notice that the original user will not have *learned* the language – which would imply its preexistence – they will have *created* it.) The structural analogy between the untaught teacher and Aristotle's unmoved mover is not a coincidence but comes from the foundational role of each in an account of things.

Colin McGinn has in his argument called in the support of God's powers – in particular McGinn claims that God has the power to create a language user isolated from any social contact and therefore not dependent on such contact for their ability to use language. God is a dangerous ally in philosophical argument, especially when one is trying to delineate conceptual possibilities. He can give one too much of a free ride. Still, if we take McGinn's suggestion really seriously and examine it very carefully, we may be able to get some useful mileage from it nevertheless.

In examining this "revisionist" reading we are going to have to look carefully at the distinction insisted on between a language which is *necessarily* spoken by one person alone (not allowed) and one which is only *contingently* restricted to one speaker (supposed to be a genuine possibility). We are also going to have to look at the relation between rules and actions which are in accord with them, at the same time insisting on the connection between the ability of our creature to use language and their ability to engage in behavior which could be described as "following a rule."

But first let's try to see what is at stake here and what are the sources of the temptation to believe in this mythical creature whose like, we are certain, has never existed in the history of the human race. (Of course, we have the myth of Romulus and Remus suckled by the she-wolf, a myth which was, significantly, a foundation-myth of the beginnings of Rome.) And there are the accounts of "wolf-children" in eighteenth-century France, but these don't help us much. They certainly don't provide us with an argument from *existence* to *possibility* for the pre-social language user. No, that possibility has to be assessed in the absence of empirical evidence, independently of it.

Why should we care so much about the possibility of this abstract, pre-social, yet rational creature, this creature without historical context – even though we are sure that they never really existed? The short answer is that this creature is part of the foundation-myth defining the view of society and of humanity that has been dominant in our era, dominant because it expresses, in its way, some salient facts about that era.

But that answer needs expanding. Firstly, "our era" here means: the era that had its first beginnings in the process of dissolution of the feudal era and the dissolution of the particular ways in which, under feudalism, people were bound into relations of subservience and obligation by custom and law. That new era took a significant leap in self-definition in the seventeenth century, and it is here that we first meet the pre-social individual – with Hobbes and his "Contract" theory of society. Hobbes regards society as an artifact, that is, something created by intelligent creatures, and so begins the view that has continued down the centuries (and was most recently expressed emphatically by Margaret Thatcher) that society is a construct out of individuals, that the individual is prior to society. This view appears also in the doctrine of "methodological individualism" as a tool of social and economic analysis.

Hobbes' "Contract" theory of society was a generalization from, and actually reflected, new social realities. The free laborer's contract for hire had replaced villein's obligations of service, the *corvée,* and the other feudal customary, or legally determined, methods of extracting a surplus from the labor of the serf or villein. Common land was fast disappearing, and with it communal structures. These were being replaced by the individual proprietor whose relations with others were governed by contracts of hire, or rent – that is, by market relations as buyer or seller of labor, land or goods. His counterpart was the "free" laborer whose living, that is, his *existence,* depended on contractual relations with the hirer of his labor.

From the vantage point of these changes it was natural to see the emerging society as constituted by contractual relations between "free" individuals and to express that vision in the myth of the *Social Contract.* That vision posited a mythical pre-social humankind: "man in the state of nature" or Rousseau's "man who is born free," a pre-social assemblage of separate individuals who set about constituting society because they individually see the advantage. But for this, speech is necessary. "Without speech," Hobbes says in the *Leviathan,* "there had been amongst men, neither Commonwealth, nor Society, nor Contract, nor Peace, no more than amongst Lyons, Bears, and Wolves."

In Hobbes' founding myth and vision, speech is seen as a precondition of society, a condition of agreement, not a consequence of it. And the individual too is seen as a creator of, not a creation of, the society of which they are a constituent part.

And this individualist myth of the primacy and priority of the individual *vis-à-vis* society has also set the agenda for most of the philosophy of our era and culture. Philosophers have been called upon to give an account of how knowledge of the world and of other minds is possible to this individual, born isolated with nothing but native endowments and experience to call on in this momentous task. Ethical and political theory also have been called on to take this individual as the starting point, and their job-description has been to kit them out with rights, or claims, or soundly based judgments of good and bad, right and wrong, of worth or worthlessness – and all this on the basis of the individual's original endowment of needs and capacities, or the attitudes and desires that they have developed in isolation.

Given all that it has riding on it, all the philosophical weight it has had to bear, one is not surprised to find the philosophers circling wagons when the notion of the *pre-social individual language user* comes under attack.

What may seem surprising, but really isn't, is that this notion has not come in for more attack, or at least serious examination. It is precisely *because of* its foundational role in our society's self-image, defining and perpetuating it and helping to shape its institutions, that the notion has not been carefully discussed and analyzed. A serious examination would require, or lead to, a point of view standing outside the prevailing world-view, not an Archimedian point such as Descartes sought, but at least a dissenting one.

That Wittgenstein had come to such a point is, I think, indicated by that remark in the *Remarks on the Foundations of Mathematics* in which he allows himself to talk of "the sickness of a time."[3] This sickness is one infecting our vision itself and so is visible only to someone already on the way to recovery.

Because this post-feudal world-view (sometimes titled "liberal individualism") is generally shared, it and its founding conceptions do not strike people as problematic. And most English-speaking philosophers have been trained up in a tradition and a conception of tasks that begins with Descartes's individualistic exercise of withdrawing into himself to slough off the socially received and to build up his picture of the world for himself out of his own internal resources.

Locke and Hume continued working within this established conception of the task of philosophy as that of accounting for our knowledge of the world as something possible to each of us individually, in isolation, having only our own individual resources to work with. Hume, for example, in the *Enquiry* discussion of the "acquisition of the idea of *cause and effect*," asks us to "Suppose a person, though endowed with the strongest faculties of reason and reflection, to be brought on a sudden into this world." This person is precisely our pre-social individual endowed with thought and reason (and,

Wittgenstein would insist, with language). Hume's definition of our philosophical task is to show how such a creature of the imagination could come to the idea of *cause and effect* on the basis of those endowments plus sense experience. Most conspicuously, the very existence of the problem of "other minds" for modern philosophy implies a conception of philosophy's task as that of deriving the social from the pre-social and the positing of the pre-social individual thinker and language user as starting point.

Aristotle, who antedated and stood outside this world-view and self-image of humanity, regarded humans and their knowledge as irreducibly social. For him, knowledge proceeds from teaching and learning and reflecting on preexisting knowledge, both of these things implying a social context. But he could hardly provide a critique of the notion of a pre-social linguistic individual since that notion had not been put forward by anyone. Though there is the basis of a critique in his argument in the *Metaphysics* IV (1006a23 *et seq.*) against those, like Cratylus, who would deny the law of contradiction. The suggestion there is that such people will not be able to say anything significant to another and *therefore not to themselves either.*

Marx was someone who managed to find himself a foothold outside the prevailing world-view, a point from which he could mount a critique. But he was not concerned, except tangentially, to criticize the notion of the abstract pre-social individual. He regarded it as an ideological fiction, part of a time-bound and historically conditioned world-view which was trying to present itself as an eternal truth. For him, this pre-social rational creature "belongs among the unimaginative conceits of the eighteenth-century Robinsonades."[4] ("Robinsonades" are those whose flights of imagination begin with Defoe's Robinson Crusoe, the isolated individual creating his world for himself.) These conceits have reappeared in twentieth-century arguments about the possibility of a *private language.*

For Marx, the myth of society being formed by and out of individuals presents the reverse of the actual and historical truth, namely, that it is only gradually and through a process of history that individuals have achieved some kind of self-recognition and self-distinction, have been distilled out of the social matrix which has brought them to this point. "Human beings become individuals only through a process of history. . . . Exchange is a chief means of this individuation. It makes the herd-like existence superfluous and dissolves it."[5] And he also makes suggestive but not developed remarks about the impossibility of the isolated pre-social language user that have some resonances with both Aristotle and Wittgenstein: "An isolated individual could no more have property than he could speak."[6] And in the *German Ideology*: "Language is practical consciousness that exists also for other men and *for that reason alone* it really exists for me personally as well" (my italics.)[7]

Marx did not feel the need to dissect this fantasy of the pre-social individual with speech and reason. For him, it, and the myth of the formation of society that it served, were ideological conceits that reflected in a distorted form (and helped to preserve) certain central aspects of our actual social life – in particular, that our life is dominated by market relations of exchange and by the commodification of labor, art, religion, caring, and whatever else you care to name. Ultimately the only effective argument against those fantasies was criticism in the streets which would bring changes in those fundamental social relations of which they were a distorted reflection. Then the fantasy would disappear of itself.

So it was left to Wittgenstein to struggle *philosophically* with this notion, to pull out its presuppositions and to try to break the charm of the many mutually supporting conceptions forming a web that ensnared us. But he had no illusions about the efficacy of his work in bringing about a cure. In the same place in the *Remarks on the Foundations of Mathematics* in which he speaks of "the sickness of a time" he speaks also of "the sickness of philosophical problems," which get "cured only through a changed mode of thought and of life, not through the medicine invented by an individual." And the history of the treatment of his work and the failure to see and come to terms with its radical critique bear out his insight. The mode of life and therefore the mode of thought have not changed, and the sickness remains.

So much for the historical background and the ideological significance of the notion of the pre-social language user. We must now engage philosophically with the notion itself, using the materials with which Wittgenstein has provided us. But this background has, I hope, helped to make clear the deep historical significance of Wittgenstein's enterprise, as well as showing the source of the attraction of the notion and the tendency to return to it again and again as a seemingly "natural" notion. It may also help us to see the special force and significance of an important remark near the end of the *Philosophical Investigations*: "What has to be accepted, the given, is – so one could say – *forms of life*."[8] That is to say: *forms of life* are what you start with, the social.

But now we must wrestle with this wraith ourselves, this posited pre-social language user, and somehow test its possible reality without being able to give it a concrete history and characteristics. The trouble is, you don't know where you are with wraiths and they can draw you into a fairyland where stones speak and frogs turn into princes and your tests of real possibility go soft.

Let's start by marching boldly into the lion's cage and peering resolutely into his mouth. That is, let's take up Colin McGinn's suggestion that God could create an isolated language user and set them in some remote part of the Earth (if even He could still find one) or on some other planet. If we are not struck dumb by God's awesome power, we can ask some detailed questions about this "gift" of language.

But first we are going to need a rough catalogue of types of regularity so that we can see where we want to place rule-following and language use and go on to ask whether the place we would want to assign the proposed "gift" of God could be made to match that of language use.

Firstly, there are what we can call "natural" regularities, for example, the properties of materials – the boiling point of water, or the magnetic properties of iron, the course of the planets, and of the seasons. The generation of living species can probably be placed here amongst the natural regularities without making the category too heterogeneous for our use. Here, too, can probably go those regularities of behavior of animals and insects, some of them quite complex, which we call instinctive. They can go in here too because those regularities called instinctive seem also to be given with the species, even though they are perhaps not bound up with the species with the same intimacy as the properties of materials are with the materials. The latter enter into our very identifications. What doesn't boil at 100°C we are hesitant to classify as pure water. The courtship behavior of cranes or the extraordinary instinctive migrations of the Monarch butterfly from the eastern United States to one small valley in Mexico, on the other hand, do not enter in the same way into our identifications of those species. Nevertheless, instincts are species-wide and are *given with* the identification of an individual as a member even though they do not form *part of* the identifying process. (Instinctive behaviors are in fact a nice example of the Aristotelian notion of *property*: something that belongs to all without being part of the definition or essence.)

In general contrast to this are those regularities of behavior which are acquired or imposed during the lifetime of an individual member of a species. And the manner of that acquisition gives rise to some distinctions which are crucial for us here. We can leave to one side the magnetization of iron or the tempering of steel and concentrate on the living.

One sort of acquired regularity of performance we describe as *skill* – the potter's ability to turn out a uniform set of cups, or a singer's ability to hit a note precisely. Another sort of regularity is *habit*, such as always taking a certain route or buying a certain brand. A third sort is the *conditioned behavior* of the laboratory rat, pigeon or human. We are going to have to distinguish carefully between these types of acquired regularity of behavior – resisting the coaxing of those professional muddiers of waters who, out of a misguided zeal for simplicity, would have us roll them all up together.

In *conditioning*, the new regularities of behavior are imposed, perhaps irresistibly, by what seem to be natural processes. If an experimenter arranges it that a small jet of air hits the corner of my eye whenever I hear or see or feel something, then, in spite of myself, in a short time that signal itself will cause me to blink and I shall have no choice in the matter – either as to the blinking itself, or as to the acquisition of that new pattern of behavior.

By contrast, a *skill* is something not imposed. It is acquired and generally involves application and practice by someone who wishes to have that skill. The acquisition is at some level voluntary. This may sound a hollow claim to the small boy pushed unwillingly to the piano teacher and called in from play to do his practice, but he must *at some level* be willing to acquire the skill, or it would just not happen. (Perhaps he just wants to keep a badgering parent quiet.) This distinguishes it from conditioning.

No doubt, teachers faced with recalcitrant classes may sometimes wish for some natural process by which algebra or Latin grammar could be irresistibly imposed on their unwilling charges, just as Geach's imagined schoolboy wished for a brain operation that would give him those skills by a mechanical process in which he took no part. That dreamed-of process would be one which he could neither resist nor advance. He would be the completely passive object on which the process worked. (We are going to have to look further at that fantasy. It turns out to be identical with McGinn's fantasy of God's "gift" of language.)

And skills are distinguished not only by being voluntary in their acquisition but also by being voluntary in their exercise on any given occasion. The singer does not *have* to hit the note precisely even though she could. Nor must the grammatical person always write grammatically.

No doubt, some skills, the results of much drill and practice, become in time, as we say, "instinctive" or "second nature" so that it becomes hard for the singer to sing flat, or the boxer not to raise his guard when someone playfully feints. But here we are passing over into the realm of *habit*.

Habits can be both good and bad. Whereas skills are approved and sought (by the practitioner anyway) and subject to will, habits are acquired mostly by inadvertence (not by *imposition*, which would imply that they could not be resisted.) But unlike conditioned reflexes, habits are not so impervious to will that they cannot be resisted or broken. However, some habits, like smoking or drinking, can pass over into chemical dependencies which take more than just willpower to break or resist. There are possibly metabolic changes here which are analogous to the magnetization and tempering of steel which we put to one side earlier.

After this rough sketch, let's get back to God and the pre-social language user to ask about the nature of God's "gift" of language to that isolated individual. Hobbes is interesting on this topic, because he does not make even Adam into such an isolated individual. In Hobbes' account God is the "first author" of speech and he *instructs* Adam "how to name such creatures as he presented to his sight." We are not told by Hobbes how this instruction proceeded, but can take note that *instruction* is a social notion involving a social relation between teacher and pupil. So on Hobbes' account, Adam was neither isolated nor a pre-social language user, and Hobbes derives all the rest of human speech from this one source.

It is perhaps not helpful to ask how God in His pre-Adamic isolation could create speech for Himself which He then teaches to Adam. God's powers are not something we can rightly take the measure of. But we can ask what McGinn might mean by saying that God has, without teaching (a social relation), endowed some isolated creature with speech. Since this imagined creature is, it seems, taken to be human, the regularities it exhibits in sound patterns and behavior are not to be assimilated to *instinct* – that is, to regularities given with the species itself. In that case no language learning would be necessary amongst the rest of us, since *instinctive* behavior is precisely contrasted with *acquired*.

Also it is important to note that the notion of a *mistake* of the sort corresponding to the notions of *rule-following* and *language* does not attach to instincts. It may appear to because evolution has tailored instincts to serve species' survival needs and so a deviation from the instinctive pattern leads to reduced prospects of survival. But a mistake defined as such by a failure to serve natural, or self-set, needs or goals is quite different from a mistake in following a rule which is essentially arbitrary – as the rules and usages of language are. Wittgenstein reminds us of this difference in *Zettel* §320, where he points out that cookery rules are not arbitrary in the way that the rules of language and of games are. This is because the rules of cookery are set by the end or goal of cookery, which is to produce tasty and/or nutritious meals. I don't have to engage in cookery, and it is not an activity imposed upon me, but if I do engage in it, then the rules I follow are no longer arbitrary. They are in part given by the natural properties of the foodstuffs and the facts of human biology. The latter are a matter of discovery, not fiat.

And so it is with all skills involving the manipulation of materials to some end, everything from pottery to producing electricity by nuclear fusion. But the rules of games and of language are not like that. If an individual or group decides to concoct names for things they have come to distinguish, they do not then have to go on to experiment to see if certain names "fit" or not, whether the word "rain" really works all right. There are no mistakes lying in wait for the coiners of names, mistakes of the sort the cook or the potter may run into. (This or that sort of clay warps or cracks in firing, etc.) In linguistic matters the rule is arbitrary and the mistake is defined by the arbitrary rule and not by some naturally imposed sanction that could call the rule itself into question. The potter's pot collapses and/or explodes in firing as a result of natural processes, and it is those which define the other sense of "mistake," which is that of "ineffectiveness" in relation to the potter's goal of producing a serviceable pot, or else the move is a mistake because it is something damaging or disastrous.

[Here, properly, we should set about settling accounts with Chomsky and his contrary claim that there is a natural and even biological basis for at least the grammatical rules of language. But the problem with Chomsky's innatist view is whether it has any content at all, and taking up that question would take us well out of the line of our current one.]

It may be tempting to try to find a parallel sanction for linguistic lapses and so eliminate that distinctive sense of "mistake," folding solecisms in with mistakes in cookery, pottery or nuclear power. A natural candidate would be "failure of communication." But notice that this is a *social* matter, not a natural one, and is therefore not a sanction that will be visited on our supposed pre-social language user. [We are going to have to come back to this question of sanctions and the definition of *mistakes* in talking about the supposed *untaught teacher* of language and in taking up the topic of the relation of *rule* to *action*.] The sanction appropriate to this distinctive sort of mistake, the solecism or "incorrect speaking," is ridicule and correction.

The twentieth-century Robinsonades generally trade unconsciously on the confusion between mistakes defined in terms of needs or goals on the one hand and those mistakes that are solecisms defined in terms of arbitrary rules on the other. When they try to kit out their isolated Crusoe with some rules, these rules usually involve using a sign which is going to help Crusoe distinguish or recall which berries are edible and which poisonous, and so Crusoe will certainly know when he has made a mistake. However, this is not a mistake in the relevant sense.

Now let's return to our God-created pre-social individual whose language could neither be *taught* to them by God (or it would be social) nor, it seems, be *instinctive*. The teaching would violate the supposition of the creature's pre-social isolation. On the other hand, to qualify for the description "instinctive," regularities of sound-making or mark-making would have to be species-wide. More important, the notion of *instinct* does not involve or allow for the notion of a *mistake* in the sense appropriate to language, namely, that of *solecism*. Lapses in instinctive patterns are mistakes only where and in the sense that there are damaging natural consequences which will be visited on the lapse, and even there it is a stretched and dubious use.

It would not do, either, to say that God has imposed regularities of sound-making or mark-making, by, for example, conditioning. Conditioned responses or reflexes have no more room for the notion of a *mistake* than does instinct. It is not at all appropriate to say that the pigeon has made a mistake, only that it has been inadequately conditioned.

What about the fantasy of Peter Geach's school-boy who wishes for the brain operation that will give him the ability to do algebra or write Latin? Would it make sense to pray to God to give us these skills? Could He alter my brain in some appropriate way so that I found myself able to write Latin verse?

The mechanist in all of us pulls us toward saying "yes." Yet we might diminish that pull somewhat by asking for a little more detail: just how good might those verses be that I found myself able to write, and in what style might they be? Or might they be quite original and unlike those of any particular author or period? Would I be able to progress in, and develop, that ability which we are supposing has its source in the brain alteration?

More important than all this, we have to ask whether the notion of a *mistake* can get a foothold in this fantasy picture. If God by means of the brain alteration *causes* me to have the ability to write Latin verse, then He will in effect have imposed on me, somehow, the rules of

Latin grammar and versification. But can we make sense of the idea of a rule being imposed on me in this way?

A rule is something I can be in a position to follow or not. I may come to an awareness of a rule implicit in my actions and come, through the awareness, to have that choice. I may deliberately violate some rule which I am well capable of adhering to. I may speak ungrammatically or cheat in a game. Or else, when intending to follow a rule I am not so well in possession of, I may make a mistake. That is, a misalignment between rule and action may be deliberate or not.

In this picture of God imposing a rule-following ability on me, there may seem to be room for a deliberate violation but not for a mistake. My making a grammatical "mistake" in my writing would mean simply that God had not done the job well. He will not have really imposed that rule properly.

But is there even room for the notion of a *deliberate violation* of a "rule" that we are imagining has been imposed upon me without my cooperation, acquiescence or knowledge? (I cannot be allowed awareness of the process of imposition without spoiling my supposed pre-social isolation.)

To violate a rule deliberately, I have to be in possession of that rule and not in *its* possession (as I would be if it were imposed on me externally and non-socially, causally, and where the word "regularity" would be more in order.) The imposition of a "rule" (whether this is done by conditioning or biologically) involves the imposing of conformity with the rule. It leaves no room for either voluntary or involuntary lapse, either mistake or deliberate violation. The white blackbird or the fruit-fly that develops a second pair of wings, the hydrocephalic or the bearded lady of the side-show have none of them made "mistakes" in those aberrational developments. There is a causal story behind each of them and no room for the notion of the *voluntary* or the *involuntary*. One of that pair of notions can apply only where the other is in order too. And where neither is in place, the word "rule" is only a misleading substitute for "regularity."

If we don't opt for the Hobbes' story which derives Adam's speech from the social relation of *instruction* by God, God is not left with many options: only conditioning, physiological mechanisms or something akin to instinct, none of which allow for the possibility of mistakes, and even less for the possibility of deliberate violations. If I fail to blink at the conditioned stimulus, I have not made a mistake. It is the conditioning process that has failed. (Maybe I have resisted the conditioning, which implies that I *have* been aware of the process and the regularity it was intended to impose.) So none of these residue options will do the job required.

Nor will physiological mechanisms allow room for the notion of a *mistake*. If my pupil fails to contract in bright light, neither it nor I have made a mistake. One might look for some factor disturbing the normal physiology, belladonna, for example, but hardly invoke the inadequate grasp of a rule as explanation. That suggestion would be laughed out of court.

And if I learned to control that physiological process or any other, such as my breathing or heartbeat, normally regulated without my being aware, that would not be the deliberate violation of a rule, but simply the voluntary control of a normally involuntary physiological process. Were I to damage myself by an ill-considered exercise of an unusual ability to control, say, pupil dilation, that would be a "mistake" only in the sense of a mistaken thing to do from the point of view of my own good, not a "mistake" in the sense of a "violation of a rule." The physiological mechanism and the regularity it exhibits or brings about have no point of contact with the rules exhibited in speech or even the regularities in skilled performance, or the regularities exhibited in activities that are sometimes described as "rule governed."

These considerations really show the door to Colin McGinn's pre-social language user created as such by God, for we should notice that our argument makes against any form of *imposition* of grammatical ability, whether by brain alteration or any other means that fails to engage with me as a human being, that is, *socially*. Not even God can *cause* (in the sense of *force*) me to be linguistic, using means, that is, which treat me as just a physical or biological system. If God is to get me to be grammatical or linguistic or to understand chess, He is going to have to engage with me as a person, as Hobbes suggested, instructing me by showing me my mistakes, *defining for me* what a mistake is in each of these practices.

McGinn called in God's powers by way of trying (unsuccessfully) to establish the "conceptual" possibility of an individual who has language without being taught it. This would be a language which is teachable but untaught, neither taught *to* the user nor taught *by* the user (since either would involve a social relation to another person.)

Still, this untaught person must be *capable* of teaching the language which they have without having been taught it. Something like this is common ground between McGinn and Baker and Hacker, though Baker and Hacker use a more guardedly abstract phrase, saying that the individual must be capable of "coming to agreement" with another or a group in the individual's use of rules (whether linguistic or other). But what can this be but my teaching them my language or my rule?

We have to ask one final question: whether there are other ways in which I might come by language by myself, or institute rules for myself without any social connection with others. Can I establish rules that stand over and above and outside my practice, against which an isolated *I* can measure that practice? The rule has to stand as "other" to my practice. How can I do that for myself, be *other* to myself, stand as guide and teacher, correcting my own practice? Clearly, I cannot. I must have a genuine *other*, or others with whom I am in communion, others who can correct me and tell me when I have committed a solecism, made a mistake.

Wittgenstein's view was that without an independent being to gainsay me, whatever I said would go. If I said I had followed the rule, that would be OK. And if, on the other hand, I said I hadn't followed the rule, that would be OK too. There would be no external check and therefore no rule. And no other self-applied *meta*-rule or ritual can play that role of *other* to my performance, for it will be in exactly the same fix as the original rule, and no more external than it.

If whatever I say goes, then I've said nothing. It is mere random babble, of no use to myself or anyone else. Though I hope to have brought out the social nature of language and of the associated notion of *solecism*, I must leave this discussion with a warning that it needs to be supplemented by a discussion of the notions of *skill* and of *practice*. For it is only through these notions that we can get to the idea of behavior and performance for which the rule is implicit rather than external (even though that implicit rule is open to being formulated and externalized.) Without practices whose rule is implicit and unconscious, rather than external and explicit, we shall get into the difficulties discussed in chapter 2, caused by the fact that every external rule and formula is open to interpretation. The series this generates must come to earth in a performance, reaction or judgment that is made without reference to any external rule or formula.

10 *Deus sive natura:*
science, nature, and ideology

As feudalism made God the source and the justification of its particular social arrangements and the guarantor of their eternity, so the bourgeois/capitalist order that dissolved and supplanted feudalism has used *nature*, drawing science into its ideological orbit, using science to found the new era's dominant world-view. My complaint against the concept of *nature* that has thus been given God's work to do is that it does not present itself honestly as a religious notion. It covers its transcendental tracks and dresses in secular clothes. The notion of *nature* that has thus been imposed on us and the notion of its *laws* pretend both to stand over and yet to lie within, and even to constitute, the physical, secular world. That pretense to both a transcendental and a secular status can't be maintained for long under examination, and what is surprising is how little critical examination it has been given.

The seventeenth century is usually and usefully described as the time of a great secularization of thought and life in Europe. The rise of the secular states, the scientific revolution pushing theology to the margins, and the logic of the market displacing the sanction of the Church in determining the ways in which social life would be ordered are all processes usefully summed up in the term "secularization." Descartes was a major contributor to this process of secularization and to the formation of that conception of *science* which stands opposite that theologized conception of *nature*. But the tasks that were given to science and the role it was drafted in to play in this revolutionary new world ensured that it took on some of the character of the religious and theological notions it was being called on to supplant. This is hardly surprising.

I would like to take a close look at the process by which *nature* was elevated to quasi-divine status and given a role that placed it both within and without the world. And I would like to look also at some representatives of a class of concepts in this area that I would call "absolute," concepts that have been given roles that try to combine the transcendent with the secular but produce only confusion. This is by way of trying to draw out the incompatibility of those two roles.

In his British Academy Lecture "Ceasing to Exist,"[1] Peter Winch has focussed our attention on an extraordinary passage in Descartes's Meditation III and has done us a great service thereby. It is really quite an extraordinary passage, and a great deal is to be learned by looking at it carefully and also by asking how it was that the passage was allowed to pass at the time and subsequently. For there are things in it that are quite outrageous, and Descartes goes to what can only be described as "heroic" lengths to dislodge the ordinary conceptions of *existence* and *change* with which we operate in our everyday lives. First, the passage:

> For all the course of my life may be divided into an infinite number of parts, none of which is in any way dependent on the other; and thus from the fact that I was in existence a short time ago it does not follow that I must be in existence now, unless some cause at this instant, so to speak, produces me anew, that is to say, conserves me. It is as a matter of fact perfectly clear and evident to all those who consider with attention the nature of time, that, in order to be conserved in each moment in which it endures, a substance has need of the same power and action as would be necessary to produce and create it anew, supposing it did not yet exist, so that the light of nature shows us clearly that the distinction between creation and conservation is solely a distinction of reason.[2]

As a piece of argumentation it hardly does Descartes credit. To adapt the saying of the late Dr Goebbels: I want to reach for my Browning when "the light of nature" is wheeled on (presumably to foreclose argument.) Naturally, "the light of nature" shows us something clearly. That is no doubt the precise function of such a faculty in life and in argument.[3] But just what it is that we are supposed to have been shown so clearly by it here is not so clear. That is, just what is it that we are shown by the light of nature when we are shown that some distinction "is solely a distinction of reason," and just how damning an indictment is that supposed to be? Is it supposed to have shown us that the words "conservation" and "creation" do not mark a real distinction at all but are only two different words for the same thing?

We could hardly accept that for our ordinary uses of the words. A conservator of paintings is hardly thereby a painter. And some painters have deliberately created works that would self-destruct after a time –

by way of defying the conservators and the whole process of the commodification of their art.

So, in their ordinary senses, the words "creation" and "conservation" mark a distinction that is real enough. And Descartes has not introduced us to any other senses that could be at issue. Though it is a fair guess that it is some notion of "absolute" creation that is intended, a creation *ex nihilo* of a sort that could be attributed only to God.[4] This would be not an everyday, but a theological, sense of "creation" and of "conservation," the counterpart of the absolute "ceasing to exist," the destruction *in nihilum*, that is the subject of Peter Winch's lecture. The question is whether either of these absolute notions has a legitimate secular use, or whether they have a place and sense only within a religious and theological context.

That is essentially Winch's problem in relation to the notion of *absolute destruction* or what he calls "*bare*" *ceasing to exist*, and he attempts to show that it cannot be given a secular use and sense. Unfortunately his strategy for doing this is to make a heroic effort to root the notion of *absolute destruction* in ordinary life (*via* a story of Isaac Bashevis Singer) and find that he is unable to do so. This failure may induce sympathy for his view that there is no such secular function for the notion, but it hardly shows that there cannot be. We shall have to go into all that later. For the moment there is much more to be extracted from the passage above from the *Meditations* that we need to stop over.

In addition to Descartes's attempt to bamboozle us with "the light of nature," there are two other things in the passage that deserve a close eye. The first can really only be described as an attempt to brow-beat us. Descartes tells us that

> It is, as a matter of fact, perfectly clear and evident to all those who consider with attention the nature of time, that a substance has need of the same power and action as would be necessary to produce and create it anew, supposing it not to exist.

If it isn't "clear and evident" to us (which it isn't), then Descartes wants us to conclude that we haven't considered with sufficient attention "the nature of time."

He himself does not offer us that account of the "nature of time" which would make his conclusion "clear and evident." This is in a way surprising and in a way not. It is a surprising omission given the purported role of the account in establishing what is for him an important and, for those on whom the "light of nature" does not shine so brightly, a controversial thesis. It is, on the other hand, not surprising because it is pretty clear that no account of "the nature of time" could do the shoring-up job required. Descartes is bluffing as well as brow-beating. And it is not a very good bluff, either. Who could imagine that any account of "the nature of time" could be so clear, firm, and uncontroversial as to be a foundation of anything at all and much less anything so unintuitive as the claim (whatever it may mean) that the "distinction between creation and conservation is solely a distinction of reason?" The unintuitiveness of that claim is something I want to come to now.

Take the first sentence of the passage: "For all the course of my life may be divided into an infinite number of parts, none of which is in any way dependent on the other." How can we understand this? Taken one way, it describes a mental illness more radical and destructive than any described in the clinical literature. Oliver Sacks' patient had a memory-span that was at least measured in minutes and could give some kind of limited continuity to his life.[5] For this infinitely fragmented Descartes there could be none – no continuity, no "course" to his life, no life, no Descartes. For, what reason would we have to give a common name to the myriad instantaneous independent beings who are somehow supposed to constitute this metaphysically decomposed Descartes?

And are we being asked to take in any way seriously the claimed independence of the fragments into which Descartes has decomposed himself (and the rest of the world, presumably)? Of course we can't. We can't make any serious use of this picture, can't put it to work in any way in our life. It is an idle fantasy. Anyone who did really see the world in this way would be unable to operate at all, would suffer from the most appalling form of mental illness.

No doubt Descartes would admonish us, as he does in *Principles* I, III in relation to the "hyperbolical" doubt, "not to make use of" this picture "for the conduct of life, but only for the pursuit of truth."[6] One wonders how it is possible to pursue truth by starting with a proposition that is manifestly false and believed by no one.

In the Socratic dialectic it was possible to pursue truth starting from a proposition that was false – so long as that proposition was sincerely believed and put forward by someone who was willing to allow it to be analyzed, criticized, modified or rejected. None of that is true of Descartes's claim of fragmentation. No one sincerely believes it, and Descartes is not putting it forward for analysis and possible rejection. On the contrary, he has erected barriers against its analysis and bulwarks against its rejection. It is meant to be a foundation of his analysis and he is determined that it should not be rejected. Hence the browbeating and trickery, the pretense that some absent account of the nature of time could make it all clear, evident, and solid enough to act as a foundation for a whole edifice.

I am certainly being hard on Descartes in all this, and that is because I am doing him the honor of treating him as a contemporary with contemporary relevance rather than as some quaint historical curiosity who is to be described and elucidated for our diversion but not confronted, that is, not taken seriously.

But it is not just by way of honoring Descartes that I am taking him seriously. I think that something deep and important is going on in the passage that is occupying us, something that has had a profound effect on our way of looking at things, and, I think, has led us into a number of traps and blind alleys from which we are going to escape only by retracing our steps. Put briefly, what I would like to make out is going on here could be described as the first steps in a process which may be called the "theologizing" of science.

The notion of *science* itself, as something over and above the individual sciences, is a product of this process and the theological tasks it is meant for. The notion of *science* takes on a transcendent character because it is given transcendent work to do. What do I mean by this?

Perhaps the best way to begin is with a point of Tony Palmer's. If we ask of each of the sciences what it studies, cryogenics, say, we get the answer: "the properties of matter at low temperatures." Thermodynamics? "the transfer and conversion of heat energy." Ethology? "The behavior patterns of animal species;" and so forth. But if we now put the Socratic-style question, and ask: "But what does *science* itself study?," we shall get the answer: "reality," or perhaps more modestly, "nature." But the notion of *nature* that stands opposite science here is a transcendent one, one that determines the transcendence of this notion of *science* and the way in which it stands "over and above" the particular sciences like a Platonic Form.

I think we can see the process of forging such a transcendent conception of *nature* at work in our passage from the *Meditations*, and this will go far in helping us to understand the passage, its pivotal role, and the reasons for the heroic energy that Descartes applies to the task of undermining our ordinary notions of the continuity and self-sufficiency of the everyday things of this world. The concept of *nature* that Descartes is helping to found is one that is familiar to us, the conception of *nature* as standing over and above and outside the happenings of this world, a nature which is thought of as having "laws." These "laws" also are thought of as having an existence independent of those happenings and are conceived as "regulating" or "determining" them. (And thus "determinism" had an easy birth.) It is precisely because *nature* is being groomed to take over from God and science from theology in *explaining* the order and regularities we find, rather than merely describing them, that it has to be given this external, transcendent status.

To unravel the metaphor and reveal the transcendental, essentially religious character of the talk of "nature's laws," one has only to try to take this talk seriously as a *physical* account of anything. That would mean holding their operation, the "causal link" between the "laws" and any happening, open to physical investigation, asking questions about the forces involved, etc. Of course, the thing's impossible and one would hardly get a grant to undertake it. In fact no one would last long in the scientific community who even thought of such a project. That is, at some level everyone knows that such talk is talk of a different order, not talk within the sciences, rather talk about them, taking a view of them from outside, offering us a picture and a metaphor. But that knowledge has not been faced and formulated, nor have its consequences been drawn out.

This conception of *nature*, because it tries to keep one foot in the secular while elevating the other to the level of the divine, is in the end an incoherent one, one composed of incompatible parts. It has no practical role within the sciences, and can be given none. It is a picture merely, a fanciful way of looking at the world, a poetical way of looking that, when mistaken for the literal, generates pseudo-problems such as determinism and that other pseudo-problem "the uniformity of nature" that hangs round determinism's neck like an albatross.

It also generates such spurious concepts as *the preternatural* and *lusus naturae.* These all are spurious, one should add, only in so far as they are defined in contrast to and, therefore, depend on the transcendent status of this concept of *nature,* while pretending, like it, to have a secular application in the ordinary, daily world. They are trying to run with the hare and hunt with the hounds, and are as incoherent as the concept of *nature* and the "naturalism" or the "mechanical world-view" (which is its theology) against which they are set. Therefore they cannot carry out the task they are given, by Roy Holland,[7] for example, of setting a limit on and curbing the pretensions of this naturalism to explain everything in the natural world from a position outside.

Naturalism's pretensions have to be unmasked, not countered with would-be examples of the "inexplicable" (whose inexplicability would have to be absolute and shown to be such if they were to carry out their designed task of puncturing naturalism's claim to transcendence and pretensions to completeness.) We shall have to return to the problem of bringing out the incoherence of the notion of *absolute inexplicability.* This is by way of supplementing the discussion in chapter 4.

To move along the process of giving the notion of *nature* this transcendent status, Descartes had to try to break the grip of the ordinary conceptions of *change* and *identity through change* and particularly the notions of *substance* and *nature* with which Aristotle had attempted to put our ordinary ways of talking into some perspicuous order. Putting our ordinary talk into a clear order is not all easy going, but the lower slopes of the notion of *substance* and the Aristotelian notion of *nature* are gentle enough. Substances are the ordinary things of our lives with which we work, which we recognize, identify, and follow through changes – growth, decay, alteration, even metamorphosis of the sort that insects and other creatures go through. With this ability to recognize and to follow something through changes goes the notion of *nature* as a repeatable and expected pattern of development and change, a pattern which is also part of the means of identifying the thing as of a certain sort or species. (If it doesn't boil at 100°C our identification of the stuff as water is thrown into doubt, and if what we took to be an acorn grows up into a pear tree, we think again.) These Aristotelian notions of *nature* and of *essence* are also implicated in our distinction between *change* and *destruction.* If we can no longer identify what is in front of us as the same sort as it was and find that it no longer behaves, reacts or develops in the same way, when we no longer have a person, but a corpse; no longer have wood, but ash; no longer a house, but rubble, then we have destruction, not change. (Notice that Descartes's proffered way of looking at things requires relinquishing this contrast between *change* and *destruction.* Every change becomes a destruction and replacement.)

Now we come to a point which is crucial. It is Aristotle's description of nature as "an internal principle of movement and change." This is crucial in two ways for the project of understanding the transformations that were being wrought by Descartes and others, and for getting a clear view of the transcendent conception of *nature*, which through their efforts has come to dominate the modern era. The first point is that in the Aristotelian conception, *nature* is in no way a transcendent notion. For Aristotle, *nature* is located in, rooted in, the concrete things of this world, not in Heaven. It does not stand "over and above" the world and the things in it.

The second point is perhaps even more important, and, for us, perhaps harder to grasp. It is that, in describing nature as an "internal principle" Aristotle is not, emphatically *not*, putting it forward as some kind of internal, distinguishable entity which "causes" or "explains" the thing's behavior (the kind of view that Popper, for example, has attributed to him.)[8] Aristotle's "internal principle" neither *causes* nor *explains* the thing's behavior. On the contrary, calling it an "internal principle" simply says "don't look outside the thing for an explanation when it is behaving naturally." And to this we can add "and don't look *inside* either." In fact, don't look for an *explanation* at all. The natural is for him simply what is there, what actually happens "by and large and for the most part."

To ask for an explanation of the natural, an explanation of what is there, is to ask a question of a different order, a question that takes us outside the natural world as it stands. The question could be taken to be either a historical developmental one that looks for an evolutionary answer from biology or cosmology, or one that looks beyond the secular world of change for an answer that was religious and transcendental. In the latter case the terminology of "question and answer" is perhaps inappropriate and misleading. It might be better to talk of "expressing an attitude to the world" because the "question" itself is trying to go outside the world as a whole for its answer.

There are strengths and limitations in this Aristotelian conception of *nature* and *the natural* which we shall have to come back to. I have given my brief sketch of Aristotle's attempt to give perspicuous order to ordinary ways of talking about change, or destruction and creation, in order to give some background and indication of what it was that Descartes was trying to overthrow by such heroic efforts, fragmenting himself and the world in the process, and requiring an outside agency to reconstruct them both at every instant. For Aristotle the source of movement and change lies within the thing (unless the change is a violent incursion or has its source in human manipulation) and no outside agent is involved.

That is *what* Descartes is trying to overthrow. The next question is why? Why did he feel that he had to obliterate the distinction between change, on the one hand, and creation and destruction on the other? Why did he want to locate the source of change outside the thing and outside the world itself and to regard that type of change as normal rather than as a violent incursion by an external force?

Well, it may be surprising to hear that I have some sympathy with Descartes's efforts even though I think his methods were wrongheaded and subversive of good sense and have landed us in muddles and sent us up blind alleys. What is most serious is that we can't take his talk or his picture seriously and use it in our life. As I have said, no one could even approach grasping the world according to that picture of fragmentation. Even a distant approach would constitute a crippling mental illness. In this way Descartes has initiated a style of philosophizing that cuts philosophy off from life and from the language and ways of talking that arise out of that ordinary life. He can hardly be forgiven for that.

On the other hand, despite my sympathy for Aristotle's style of philosophizing as trying to articulate and make perspicuous our ordinary ways of talking, and despite my view that his particular analysis here is on the right lines and that his non-transcendent concept of *nature* as an "internal principle" is a valuable one and a good starting point, I have to go on to say that the concept needed further articulation and development before it was adequate to the scientific enterprise that was struggling to be born. It is unfortunate that Descartes did not attempt that development. But in a revolutionary period the valuable is often thrown out along with the corrupt.

And, toward the end of the reign of scholasticism, the concept of *nature* had itself become corrupt. Paradoxically, this corruption can be seen as a result of the struggle of the new scientific enterprise to be born. In those revolutionary times explanations were being sought where simple description and acceptance had previously stood. The concept of *nature* (whether Aristotelian or transcendent) encompasses what is simply *there*, what has to be accepted. So, if you asked why iron or steel hardened on being quenched and were softened by being cooled slowly whereas copper or bronze were softened by being quenched and were tempered by beating, you might be told: that's just the nature of ferrous metals; the nature of copper and bronze is different.

But in this new age, manipulation was becoming the goal and so causal connections were being sought and the notion of *cause* was correspondingly being changed from its Aristotelian sense, from a formal, logical/conceptual, ordering notion to an instrumental/manipulative one. As part of this search, Aristotelian notions such as *nature* and *essence* were being "entified" – turned into separate "things" which could stand in causal and explanatory relations to whatever "had" the essence or nature (their "host," as it were.) The purely formal, organizing notion of *essence* was given a causal/manipulative role and was now looked on as something that could be seized on and used for manipulatory purposes. The alchemists sought "quintessences" as separate somethings, substances that could be extracted and compounded so that they would have the power to transform some other stuff into some other sort of stuff (gold was the usual aim). This was a sort of profane, secular imitation of the doctrine of Transubstantiation.

Thus, terms that for Aristotle had the purely conceptual, logical function of putting order into our ways of talking were now recast into an explanatory, manipulative role. In one way, the results were, of course, a ridiculous parody of explanation, a renaming parading as explanation. Thus the efforts of Molière's student in *Le Médecin malgré lui* to "explain" opium's known properties in terms of "dormative virtue" amounted to the same empty gesture. In another way, however, these empty gestures at explanation at least pointed the inquirer in the right direction. What was mistaken for a goal arrived at was in fact a directing signpost. In a primitive way these "entified" versions of the Aristotelian concepts defined a research program.

But even that primitive research program did not suit all the emerging sciences equally. The entified notion of *essence* certainly defined the alchemist's research program. The conception of an *essence* as a separable, extractable something, something that "made" (i.e. forced) its host to be whatever it was (gold, for example), sent the alchemists off on a trail that we now regard as false and even ridiculous, though it did result in the development of useful techniques of refinement, distillation, and extraction, and some concepts (*calyx* was one) that proved valuable in the subsequent development of chemistry.

But that research model was of no use at all to the physicists studying the motion of projectiles, pendulums, falling bodies or the inclined plane. These were the real growth-points of seventeenth-century science, and they could not be bound by this constricting model of explanation and of research based on these pseudo-Aristotelian concepts.

Descartes and the other "reforming" philosophers were setting about liberating the new sciences (whose new aim was manipulation and control) from the constricting alchemical format that this parody of the Aristotelian system had become – the search for "essences" and "quintessences" that could transmute "gross matter." (Oddly, even Spinoza, who had an important part to play in this liberation, "has heard of someone" who was able to effect such transmutations.)

The Aristotelian conception of *physis* as a principle of motion and change internal to the things of the world arranged by species not only became a fatuous parody when recruited to the project of explanation and manipulation, but seemed totally unfitted for and even to stand in the way of the other great project of the seventeenth century – the mathematization of Nature. Aristotle's own notion as it fitted into his own project was therefore simply ignored or misunderstood and reinterpreted to suit the new one.

Unfortunately Descartes did not follow out the logic of the drastic means he used to break the grip of this pseudo-Aristotelian model of explanation and research and to transform the notion of *nature* into something unitary and transcendent. If he had, he might have come to see how his rejection of the notions of *continuity* and *change* in favor of those of *destruction* (or *disappearance*) *in nihilum* and *creation ex nihilo* conflicts with deep-running principles of the new sciences. One of them had already been explicitly formulated by Descartes's time, the principle of the conservation of matter: "Matter can neither be created nor destroyed." This had already been formulated by Hobbes (and perhaps by Galileo), but it really goes back to Democritus.

Now, one of the first questions we have to ask here is about the nature and status of this "principle" (which we would nowadays have to reformulate as "the principle of the conservation of mass/energy") together with those others of a similar standing: the principle of no action at a distance, and the principle of the uniformity of nature. Our question has to be: do these "principles" make large substantive claims about the world, or express assumptions or hopes that might be dashed? Or are they, rather, formal, regulatory principles that tell the scientists how to go on, how to go about painting their picture of the world (with the result that the picture they paint comes to have a certain character – not by being dictated by the character of what is being depicted, but by limitations imposed by the way they are going about depicting it and the means they have at hand)?

From what I have already said above, it is probably no secret that I take the latter view (which was also Wittgenstein's). That comes out in my rejection of determinism and the problem of the uniformity of nature which is its obverse twin, as both of them pseudo-problems generated by the same wrong picture. And it shows also my rejection, as spurious, of the notions of *the preternatural* or *lusus naturae* in so far as they also are derived from the same picture (this despite the fact that they are trying to counter false claims made for a mechanical world-view that depends on that picture.) To bring all that out we are now going to look carefully at the credentials of some notions that pretend to an "absolute" status: *absolute creation*[9] and *absolute, or "bare" ceasing to exist* are the ones we will start with because of the pivotal role they have in Descartes's contribution to the project of prising nature loose from the world and projecting it into the heavens (or at least out of the world.)

We shall take these notions by themselves to begin with, but they really belong with a whole class of "absolute" concepts that were brought on the scene in the process of giving nature a transcendent status, and science a quasi-theological role as its exponent: absolute time, absolute space, the (absolute) origin of the Universe and (absolutely) fundamental particles. To this list must be added *absolute inexplicability*, a notion that will occupy us later as being implicated in the notion of *"bare" ceasing to exist.* (Where you have *creation* and *destruction*, you have an agent and therefore some kind of an explanation. A "bare" ceasing to exist would lack both a residue and an explanation.) These "absolute" concepts have much the same history. That is, they start off as humble notions in humble surroundings with ordinary uses which give them their sense and show their usefulness. They are then taken from these ordinary surroundings and projected into new ones, where it is assumed that they will carry with them all their old sense and their old uses. This is generally not the case. Though sometimes scraps of the old sense remain. For example, some, but not much, of the ordinary sense of the notion of *number* got carried forward into Cantor's conception of *transfinite number.* The sense that remained was given by the calculus that he devised for those numbers, the transfinite arithmetic. This had (just) enough analogy with ordinary arithmetic to justify retaining the name.

On the other hand, when the notion of *simultaneity* was taken from its ordinary surroundings in ordinary life or in the laboratory and its function there of dating events, measuring time, arranging meetings, etc. and given Universe-wide work to do, it was not able to carry its old sense with it (or any sense.) But it took Einstein's analysis to show that.

Similarly, I argued in chapter 7 that the notion of *doubting* lost all content when Descartes removed it from daily life and from its role there as reason for action or abstention and tried, with his notion of *hyperbolical doubt*, to give it a grand metaphysical role that deliberately cut it off from "the conduct of life."

The notions of *the (absolute) origin of the Universe* and of *(absolutely) fundamental particles* (or whatever else it is proposed to start with absolutely) are up for a similar job of dismantling. But each of these absolute notions raises its own particular problems and there is no general principle we could appeal to in order to deal with them all at once. We have to go case-by-case. I have given the earlier examples only to show that there is a job to be done and to give some idea what kind of a job it is that we have to do on the notion of *a bare cessation of existence.*

Perhaps we had better start by noticing that we *do* in fact have ordinary uses for the notions of *bare cessation* and *bare coming to be.* A flame goes out, a love dies, a sunset darkens, the seasons pass, a skill is lost, a memory fades. When the flame goes out it leaves nothing of itself behind. There is nothing it has "turned into." Though its effects may persist for a time. And so with the others. On the other side it is easy to see falling in love as a "coming to be" *ex nihilo*, something gratuitous, undeserved, in no way "on the cards." As with artistic production, there will be a background, a history, but that background neither causes nor explains the leap into the new. That leap is gratuitous, in that sense absolute.

But it is not that sort of ceasing and coming to be that Descartes is proposing and Winch opposing. It is the appearance and disappearance of material things, their *absolute* disappearance, not by their being destroyed in the ordinary way of being transformed into something radically different: house into rubble, wood into ash + carbon dioxide + heat, etc., but by the total disappearance of the material of the thing. And not its transformation into energy either.

It is certainly a deep regulatory principle of the practice of physicists (most conspicuously fundamental particle physicists) that all matter has to be accounted for. No theory would be accepted that didn't balance the books. Any theory that posited or required that particles (or energy) came into being out of nowhere or disappeared into nothing would not be considered. Are the physicists being narrow-minded in this? Or rash? Mightn't they be *forced* to accept that some particle (maybe only a tiny one) or the increase of energy (just a little) came into existence out of nothing? Or went out of it without trace?

Firstly, progress in fundamental particle physics would be brought to a halt in its investigation of the structure of matter by means of destructive collisions in accelerators without this requirement to balance the mass/energy books. There would be no restrictions on the theories one might propose, and no way to choose between them.

To understand the nature of the commitment of physicists to this principle, consider the history of the neutrino. This particle was first proposed by Pauli in 1930 to fill a gap in the mass/energy accounts for beta-decay. At that time and for some considerable time afterward, there seemed to be no hope of detecting neutrinos, and they were often described as "theoretical constructs" or even as "mere" theoretical constructs by some physicists and philosophers of science. Still, neutrinos remained on the books for a generation while theoretical work was done on their relation to other particles and on the possibility of their confirmation. The War, of course, switched attention to neutrons and their role in fission, but finally in 1956 a great detection effort was mounted, involving the assembly of a large tank of carbon tetrachloride and the detection equipment in an abandoned gold mine two miles below the surface of the earth. Finally, neutrinos were found a home in a different story – the understanding of the collisions detected in that gold mine – and so were taken as "confirmed."

I give that bit of history to show the strength of the physicists' commitment to the principle of the conservation of mass/energy. Actually, I would rather reformulate that and say that it shows the strength of their determination to defend that principle. Why are they so determined that they are willing to continue the search for a generation and commit such effort and resources to an entity whose only claim to existence is that it is required by that principle?

In the end, what is at stake here is not just fundamental particle physics, but the whole scientific enterprise. The conservation principle is implicated in every part. Without it, the laws of motion would go. We could not count on Newton's third law, for example: "Each and every action is accompanied by an equal and opposite reaction." The reaction might be suddenly and arbitrarily augmented or diminished through a sudden addition of mass or energy out of nowhere or its disappearance into nothing. With the loss of those laws of motion would go astronomy, and dynamics of every kind, aerodynamics, electrodynamics, and so on. And, of course, there would be a cascade effect bringing down every other branch of the scientific enterprise because of the implication of those laws in every part.

And it wouldn't be just the scientific activity and understanding that would collapse. The assumptions of our practical world would be scuttled too. The Weights and Measures Department, for example, could hardly prosecute for short weight if a trader could enter a defense that "some just disappeared into nothing." And how could they be sure of their test weights? Could we avoid "bare cessation" as an explanation of shortages in the till or in inventory? The thief or receiver could presumably deny a charge of "handling stolen goods" by claiming that the thing "just appeared" on his premises.

And one could go on and on. For no part of our life would be untouched by the belief that it was possible for things to appear out of nowhere and to disappear into nothing. And so we have to go well beyond what Peter Winch says of the notion: "My objection to the idea of a bare cessation of existence is that it has no basis in *any* general understanding of things, naturalistic or otherwise."[10] It is not just that the *origins* of the notion are suspect and defective (which it is, as I have tried to indicate in analyzing the motivations of Descartes's infamous argument above); it is rather that the consequences of admitting the notion into our stock of explanations would be utterly destructive of understanding and of the assumptions on which our practical life is based.

It is for this reason that we can say that no serious use can be made of the notion. It cannot be incorporated into our ways of understanding the world and operating in it. And for this reason we can go on to claim (what Winch disclaims having done) that we have shown the impossibility of a "bare cessation of existence." We have shown that the thing is impossible through showing that the term can have no serious use or sense. There can be no "bare cessation of existence" such as Descartes requires for his argument and such as Isaac Bashevis Singer's character Zalman conjures up in the story.

And in saying that, I am not making a sweeping and extraordinary claim about "the way things are." I am making what might, I suppose, be called a "formal" or, as Wittgenstein would call it, a "grammatical" point. The *thing* cannot exist because the phrase cannot be given a serious application. It is a beguiling creation of the imagination that cannot be lifted out of the context of fictions, fantasies, fairy stories, and dreams and given real work to do in our life. It cannot be admitted into our stock of explanations because it would undermine and destroy the whole context of understanding and practices into which it was being injected. It would leave only arbitrariness and confusion. And for that reason we have to say that the notion is without sense and can't have had sense from the beginning.

Perhaps it would be helpful to make this same point from another direction by going back to the neutrino and to the conservation law that called it into being and kept it alive for a generation, eliciting such theoretical and practical efforts together with money and manpower in the drive for its confirmation. The role and the status of that law and several others are easily misunderstood in a way that is cognate with the belief that the pseudo-concepts *bare cessation* and *coming to be* might have a genuine application, a role outside the bracketed context of stories, dreams, and fantasies.

If the conservation law were making a grand, Universe-wide factual claim (as its logical form might suggest), then it would be open to factual exception, and our two concepts would stand as descriptions of just those possible exceptions that would require the rejection of the law. But if it really did function in that way – as a vast claim about how things were – then it would be a most extraordinarily shaky claim whose truth would always be provisional, even tentative. For how are we to know how things are ordered in distant galaxies and at remote periods? How would we dare erect so much on such an ill-tested base? How could we dare commit astronauts to orbits calculated by methods and laws that rested on such an unproven conjecture? Of course we are not doing any such thing, and that picture has got things upside-down.

At one level, every scientist knows that the conservation laws or the laws of motion don't have that character of large-scale conjectural claims. They are not up for testing. They define, they relate concepts, and they regulate theory building and the interpretation of results. They make no claim that might be falsified.

In his essay "The Classical Mechanics"[11] Henri Poincaré has a beautiful little analysis of the impossibility of putting Newton's second law, "force = mass x acceleration," to any empirical test. The concepts are so inter-defined that it is impossible to get an independent determination of each of them in any particular case. Yet that law lies at the base of dynamics and through dynamics much of the rest of physics and a great part of the other sciences.

In the same way, no one would think of proposing a test for the conservation law for mass/energy. The laughter would be deafening. The reason is that if the conservation law were really up for testing, then nothing at all could be relied on for use in the testing. The conservation law does not, and could not, have that sort of status. It does not tell us "how the world is," but rather determines our use of the notions *matter, mass,* and *energy.* It helps settle for us what is to be counted as a material, physical thing (being subject to the law) and what has some other status, like the flame, the likeness, the love, the frontier, the skill, the opportune moment, and the myriad other things that can come to be and disappear without there being a question of balancing the mass/energy books.

I suppose that if you really wanted to, you could say that in an indirect way and in a manner of speaking, the conservation law shows us "how the world is" – in the same sense, that is, that I have claimed above to have shown that a "bare cessation" could not exist. But the real content of that claim was that it had been shown that the would-be concept *bare cessation of existence* could not be given a serious use and accepted into our stock of explanations and means of operating in the world. For it would be destructive of them and would have left us in chaos and arbitrariness. It would be better, however, to say that it could not be introduced into our stock of explanations because *there is nothing to introduce.* There is no concrete sense to the phrase.

But we are putting a tentative and exploratory foot on the road to misunderstanding and confusion in wanting to use an expression of the form: "showing how the world is" in relation to the conservation laws, a law like the principle of "no action at a distance" or the "principle of the uniformity of nature." None of these should be looked on as having any empirical content. In that direction lies confusion. They are, rather, defining and regulatory in their role and function. And it is for this reason that the would-be notions of *the preternatural* or *lusus naturae* (in their transcendental senses) fall to the ground, having no application as working descriptions of anything or even a "possible" anything. The pretense to application that these pseudo-concepts have is parasitic on a misunderstanding of the nature of the "uniformity of nature principle" as making a vast empirical claim. If the "uniformity" principle is not making an empirical claim, it can have no empirical exceptions, and those concepts can have no application or sense.

The same goes for the notion of the *absolutely inexplicable*. That notion is parasitic on the mistaken belief that nature (maybe "Nature" with an important capital letter) can be completely bagged and sorted, that there is an end-point to the scientific enterprise when all the explanations will be in, when there are no more problem areas, and no more lines of research open, when there are no more new theories to be formulated or new concepts to be put forward. Only then could we talk about something that is permanently and necessarily left out. The empirical evidence goes completely against such a conception. It shows an exponential growth of unsolved problems and of new research areas and the notion of a *closure* to be something in the mind of the myth-makers. But has it even a legitimate place there?

If we keep firmly to the view from where we are as ordinary struggling humans, trying as scientists or whatever else to make sense of the world and to live in it, I think we can see that the notion of an end-point in that struggle has no sense, that we could not come to a point in the scientific enterprise which declared itself as an end to that enterprise. What would that point be like? Would it mean that everything was understood? What could we possibly mean by "everything" here? Would it mean that we had a "complete" set of the concepts in terms of which problems could be formulated – and knew it to be complete? How could we know such a thing?

Scientists, particularly fundamental particle physicists and cosmologists, often find themselves up against something that looks like an end, a barrier, an absolute starting point. That is almost inevitably the case when something has just been proposed to explain a range of phenomena, as the "Big Bang" was proposed to explain the distribution and properties of energy and matter in the Universe, and as atoms were proposed in modern times by Dalton in trying to elaborate a distinction between a physical mixture and a chemical reaction and to explain the simple proportionality in reactions he regarded as chemical.[12] At the time they are proposed, and because of the role they have then as explanations, not as something to be explained, such things are starting points, and they may well look like absolute starting points.

There was no possibility for Dalton to raise any serious questions about the structure of the atoms he was working with. He was struggling to make some theoretical sense of their behavior in reactions and in mixtures of gases, to formulate his law of partial pressures and to understand its working (which he understood as being the result of "repulsions" between atoms of the same sort, mediated by phlogiston.) In that climate, atoms could seem be to nothing but absolute starting points, the unexaminable beginnings of theorizing and explanation. That is the understandable, and laudable, reaction of a working scientist who is not going to be diverted into what, at that stage, could be only pure speculation, speculation, that is, that could not be articulated further or incorporated into testable theories, speculation that could have no practical place in their work.

But again we come up against a phenomenon we have been meeting all along. What really belongs to the enterprise and its state of development and the role a concept has there (*pro tem*) gets projected outward and made into an objective property of the thing. The atoms get described as "unsplittable" and as "fundamental building blocks" of the Universe. Those descriptions have no genuine descriptive role for the working scientist, only for the ideologist of science. The ideologist of science may need those notions for the project of building a world-view that will rival and displace the religious world-views (particularly Christianity's). For the working scientist, on the other hand, the real content of the application of such phrases comes to no more than "I can't deal with that now. Leave me alone."

But of course, as we all know, the scientists *were* able to deal with it later. First, the chemists working with the notion of *atoms* in their accounts of chemical reactions (largely through Avogadro's work with gases and his hypothesis that the same volumes of whatever gases at the same temperature and pressure contained the same number of molecules) were able to develop the notions of *atomic weight* and that of *valency* and finally, and above all, Mendeleyev was able to employ these brilliantly in setting out his periodic table. It was at this point, when enough had become known about them, that atoms changed their role and status from *explanans* to *explanandum*, and the physicists moved in to look for models of their structure that could account for what the chemists had found.

The lesson I want to get out of all this is that character of "absoluteness" that is projected onto the thing (the atoms) really belongs to their place and role in a body of explanation. That role is a historically limited one, so that the assigned character has to be withdrawn in the end. And the same fate lies waiting for whatever is drafted to fill that sort of role for a time. So long as not enough is known about it, it will be safe in its role as *explanans*. But its very employment in that role will lead to a slow buildup of information about it. It will inevitably acquire various properties that will eject it from the role of *means of explanation* into that of *the thing to be explained*. At that moment, it loses its "absolute" status.

And this story also may help us to see how ill-founded is the notion of *closure* for the scientific enterprise. I should add here that I keep using the expression "the scientific enterprise" and not "science" by way of trying to keep at bay the transcendental viewpoint from which the notion of *closure* may look not only sensible but tempting.

It is no doubt easiest to think of progress as the nearer approach to some end or goal, and it is not at all easy to grasp a notion of *progress* that defines itself in relation to what has gone before rather than in relation to what is yet to come. The notion of *nature* as something transcendent and therefore final and complete in its splendid separation from the secular world which it rules and governs through its "laws" is not only a notion with which we have been imbued, but a notion tempting in itself. It also reflects a conception of progress that has been with us since the time of Plato and the theory of Forms, which put the perfect and the transcendent ahead of the things of this world as in some sense their "cause." Descartes also declares himself of this view when (also in Meditation III) he puts the notion of the *infinite* prior to the notion of the *finite*.

Tempting though this viewpoint may be, it has nothing to do with the sciences – except by way of trying to use them for quasi-religious purposes. That is, it has no role within the sciences, no use there. When some theory is judged better than another, it is hardly because it is seen to approach some ideal. How could the scientists have such an idea to use in that way? As Humphrey Lyttelton once said in reply to a dumb question about where jazz was going: "If I knew where jazz was going, I'd *be* there!" The notion of *better* has got to be defined retrospectively for scientific theorizing (as well as for many other human enterprises.) One theory is better than another if it allows us to do more, to understand more, than the previous ones. And it could be no other way. There is no "best" it can be approaching.

No doubt we shall keep coming back and back to that transcendent view of nature as something complete and finished off, as separated from and "above" the mass of particular things and happenings that make up the world, as the "cause" of how things are. We shall return to it almost, but not quite, as "the Dog returns to his Vomit and the Sow returns to her mire." Not, that is, as a part of our nature, but rather as part of a climate of thought and a web of ideas that has us ensnared. I have tried to bring out Descartes's part in the weaving of that web. But I have given no more than an oblique hint as to why our era wrapped itself so willingly and so warmly in it that the web became imperceptible, like a mediating skin whose role in perception is not itself perceived. Understanding the eagerness with which that viewpoint was accepted is a job that remains to be tackled. It will be attempted in chapter 11, where there is an examination of the individualistic assumptions and program for philosophy and the historical reasons for them. That vision of humanity as separated, isolated individuals put a special pressure on philosophers to propose a transcendentally determined reality that would stand outside each and all, the same for all, a common focus that would unite them.

11 On misunderstanding science

You've seen to an almost unprecedented extent what I've been up to. I couldn't have identified my position so clearly at the time I wrote *Structure*.

Letter from Thomas Kuhn

I am going to lay my cards on the table and say that I don't think there is any room in philosophy for theories and theses. So I get nervous and suspicious when the "isms" come marching by. One that makes me particularly nervous is "Scientific Realism." The reason for that is that I think that historical facts extraneous to both philosophy and to the sciences have been a major subterranean motivation for the belief in what might be called an "ultimate reality" as a goal of, or limit on, scientific work. If we describe that "ultimate reality" as a goal in the sense of something worked toward, and as a limit in the sense of what it is that gives us something to measure our theories against and test their adequacy, then we can see that it is a very appealing notion, one that seems to solve a lot of problems at once.

Unfortunately, I don't think it is as simple as that, and we can see why if we consider why we should be suspicious of the notion of theories and theses in philosophy. Theories, theses, beliefs, and opinions are all propositional in character. That is, they say how things are and how they might not be. That is what gives them their true/false status. In relation to that we need to ask whether the world could change in any way so that Scientific Realism would become true (having been false) or so that it became false (having been true). Since pretty obviously it could not, we have to say that Scientific Realism is not a theory or thesis and that something else is going on here, something that is being obscured and misrepresented.[1]

To get at what is going on and the nature and source of the obscurities I think we are going to have to go a long way round, to look at an alternative way of analyzing scientific development and progress and to consider what kind of work the notion of *reality* does both in the sciences and outside them.

I want to start by looking at the radical shift in viewpoint, method, style, and conception of what it is to understand the sciences and scientific development proposed by T. S. Kuhn in the 1960s. I want to try to bring out just how radical a challenge he was issuing to a conception of the sciences themselves, what it was to account for their development and what progress in them consisted in. The conception which he was challenging can really be said to have dominated our era from the time of Descartes.

Thirty years ago in his *Structure of Scientific Revolutions,* Kuhn made a plea for a new conception of what it was to understand science and scientific development and progress, one to replace the conception of the task as that of supplying a logical model of that development and progress. That "logical model" conception had dominated the field and defined its aim from the beginning – and still largely does. And we have to ask why. And we have to ask why the *historical* conception that Kuhn proposed was largely misunderstood and then buried and tiled over with "isms," so that Kuhn is now often seen through the wrong end of a telescope, a reversed telescope, moreover, that is focussed on a distorting mirror. That is, his careful argument and analysis, his setting out of the concrete detail of the circumstances and the arguments surrounding several crucial moments of scientific development and his demonstration of the inadequacy of the usual "logical models" to make sense of them have all been boiled down and evaporated and reduced to some kind of "ism" – in this case "irrationalism" or something of that kind.

All reductions of that sort, the reduction of a complex argument to an "ism," involve turning the telescope around and looking through the wrong end. One can see the advantage of this kind of procedure in that it allows you to avoid dealing with the detailed arguments of the position that has been so reduced and abstracted, but that single advantage doesn't seem to be enough to account for the current dominance of a style of philosophical argumentation that can be described as "ism shuffling." Perhaps a historical account is needed here too.

But of course, the notion of a *historical understanding* is one that is profoundly alien to our era. For that era, scientific understanding has been the dominant mode, to the point that other forms of understanding are thought to need legitimating by a reduction to the scientific. We at least *think* we know what scientific understanding is – even as we struggle to give an account of it with no evident success. But the notion of *historical understanding* is quite beyond us and our impulse is to try to reduce it (in the manner, perhaps, of Carl Hempel) to a poor sort of scientific understanding that appeals implicitly, and perhaps illicitly, to hidden laws and generalizations that would "explain" things if only they could be identified and formulated. Hempel simply assumed that there was only the one kind of explanation (derivation or deduction from a generalization or law) and took his task to be that of showing how history and historical explanation could be reduced to that model. If you have ever seen history written in that style you will know what dreadful stuff it is, cluttered up with gaseous generalizations that are utterly unconvincing and easy enough to shoot down.

If we could get over the initial block, perhaps we could have a historical explanation of why it is that the notion of *a historical explanation* is so difficult for us. I think one is available, and I have hinted at one in outline before now, but that is rather a long story that involves some alien notions and I wouldn't expect it to be taken in in one go.

The reaction to Kuhn's work and the particular kind of misunderstanding of it that was exhibited are a very nice illustration of a process that Kuhn was himself describing and documenting in the sciences. It was the dominance of the very model of understanding that Kuhn wanted to challenge and replace that made it impossible for people to take in his message and to understand his proposal.

The assumption has been that there is only one kind of understanding, one that finds the reason for the thing in some larger or more general principle. Understanding something is to have a *theory* of it that derives or deduces it, sees it as an example of, the more abstract and universal truth. Simply because Kuhn purported to be offering us a way of understanding the sciences and their development, it was assumed that he was offering a *theory* of scientific development, and for that reason some "ism" had to be found that would characterize his message. "Subjectivism," "irrationalism," a "sociology of science" and even a "psychological theory" of scientific development were among those attributed to him – apart from that old favorite "relativism."

All these bogeymen have been conjured up to threaten scientific rationality itself and placed between us and Kuhn. Or rather, Kuhn has been dressed up in these bogeyman clothes, given these masks to wear, and made to threaten that scientific rationality with its promise of objectivity and truth. And if the sciences can't give us the truth, what can? It is all too terrible to contemplate. We have a lot invested here. It is the secular equivalent of the denial of God.

To understand the forces making for misunderstanding and rejection one has to get a measure of the full depth and nature of Kuhn's challenge to the reigning paradigm and conception of what it was to understand the sciences, the conception that gave rise to the project of logical modelling. For Kuhn's challenge was completely subversive of that paradigm, and the changes of aim, outlook, and practice that he was calling for were total, a reversal of the previous account.

Since Descartes, a project has been laid before us that has almost defined that branch of philosophy, epistemology, that came into being then, and since then has shaped and directed our search for an account and understanding of the sciences, a theory of their development and progress. The sciences have been the focus because they have been for us a paradigm and the chief hope for obtaining that certain and objective knowledge sought in the post-feudal era, a vision of knowledge which was central to the Enlightenment dream of universal human emancipation.

That project was exemplified in Descartes's *Meditations*, and it laid two demands on any account of knowledge and the means to knowledge, demands that set the standard and defined the adequacy of any account. There had been urgent reasons for making those demands, but the reasons were historical rather than philosophical and came from the individualistic model of humanity that played such a pivotal role in the era's project of eliminating feudalism's remnants in thought and social institutions, and the project of justifying the conceptions and arrangements that were replacing them. That story needs to be elaborated, and will get some elaboration in the next chapter. What is important here is that those demands have been accepted since without serious critique or examination of alternatives.

The first of the demands, describable as a "democratic" or "individualistic" one, was that a method be found that was available to each separated individual to apply privately and severally in the search for knowledge. The second, relating to the knowledge thus found, was that the method would lead all who conscientiously applied it to the same, objective and timeless true view of things.

The historical task here taken on was that of finding a secular alternative to Christendom as a means for bringing unity and a common focus to an increasingly fragmented world of separated individuals. This task was an urgent one in the post-Reformation world, which faced the individuating and secularizing force of the market without a single, unifying Christendom and Church to counterpose it. But that story, as I have said, needs elaboration.

For the moment I would simply like to note how these two demands, the "democratic" or "individualistic" and the "unifying," are implicit in the aims declared by the many books in this century with the titles *The Foundations* or *The Principles* of this or of that: *The Foundations of Logic and Mathematics* (Carnap), *The Foundations of Science* (Campbell), *The*

Foundations of Empirical Knowledge (Ayer), etc., etc. The point of foundations is precisely to be fixed, immovable, and as far as possible, eternal and the same for all. The image of "Principles" is procedural rather than architectural, but the thrust is the same. The object of setting them out in a book is to enable the individual reader who grasps them to proceed by their means to a timeless and objective true view of the world, a view that, because "objective," will be the same for all.

Now we have to look at the way in which Kuhn's analysis and account of the development of the sciences demands a complete rejection of both these demands – not only setting them at nought, but turning them on their heads. Kuhn asks us to see the sciences not as abstract structures of principles and deductions, of observations and postulates that each individual could in principle discover individually, but rather as a human activity and moreover as a communal one. He goes on to spell this out by adding that this human activity is not, as the reigning paradigm demands, the slow and painful uncovering of the divine order (as it were), the objective, eternal laws, order, and truth, that transcends the secular world of growth, decay, and change that we inhabit.

This human activity is, on the contrary, a historically conditioned one, one that is carried out against a particular concrete background of existing theories and models, vocabulary and equipment, hopes and expectations that may come from adjacent fields, prospects, and projects of consolidation as well as being shaped by the standards of accuracy and comprehensiveness reigning in the field at the time.

All these are the historical legacy of the immediate past, its successes and its failures, its projects and its hopes. They form the shaping environment in which any particular scientific activity is carried out. The experimenting and the theorizing do not stand in any strict logical relation to that environment, but they are shaped by it nevertheless in ways that are hardly irrational (so that the charge of "irrationalism" against Kuhn can itself only be described as "obfuscating and unhelpful").

Perhaps the best model of what is going on is the way in which the hand is guided by the model or the scene in making a drawing. There is no mechanical or strict determination going on. (Though one can describe some draughtsman's work as "mechanical," this is an "as it were" meant to indicate that habit and technique have come to displace sensitivity and freshness of vision.) But the hand that is being guided is the hand of an artist with perhaps years of looking and drawing entering into the way in which the eye sees and the hand moves in tune with it. (Setting this down now, I am reminded that many years ago, Kuhn told me that he wanted to turn his attention to art as a way of illuminating the sciences. Perhaps he had just that point in mind. At the time I didn't see what he was after.[2]) The image seems to me to be a useful and illuminating one even though it will not give us the basis of a theory or theoretical account and so will not satisfy those whose vision is limited by the dominant paradigm of understanding as theorizing.

Apart from anything else, Kuhn's radical and subversive suggestion and way of looking has the effect of dethroning the scientists as priests and theologians of this transcendental order (whether ordained of God, or just there) whose job is the uncovering and interpreting of that order to us. That itself would account for some unpopularity and resistance.

To be fair, those pretensions to priesthood are not found much among the general population of practising scientists, though there is sometimes a natural increased concentration among cosmologists and fundamental particle physicists. The very conception of their task as searching for ultimates and origins makes them prone to those pretensions. And there are, of course, the "Sunday scientists" whose stock-in-trade and delight is making just the sort of grand metaphysical interpretations that will impress a gullible lay audience.

But what if Kuhn has not been trying to give us a *theory* of anything? And of course he is not. His message is that *theorizing* is the wrong way to go about trying to understand the sciences and scientific development. The various *theories* of scientific development, attempts to discover universal rules, principles or tests that are supposed to define scientific rationality and account for the development of the sciences, haven't worked and can't work as a description of the historical developments we have before our eyes. His message is the Wittgensteinian one: "Look and see."

But in an era dominated by the scientific model of understanding, "looking and seeing" is regarded as only a preliminary to theoretical analysis, its role limited to providing the data that a theory will have to account for. Without that theory, the dominant view is that there is no understanding.

Kuhn makes an *analysis* of various crucial historical developments in the sciences all right, but it is not an analysis that issues in a theory that gives us what has been so long sought – a logical model of scientific development and progress, an account of scientific rationality that fits our dominant model of rationality as logical and deductive. On the contrary, the analysis that he makes shows that such a logical model of scientific development and scientific rationality is not to be had. Of course scientists use logical and deductive methods – who doesn't? But Kuhn's analysis shows that there is a characteristic pattern of development in the sciences which at certain historical moments involves critical readjustments of viewpoint and the introduction of new procedures and styles of analysis, readjustments, and innovations for which these logical methods and arguments are not determining.

Kuhn's suggested way of looking at the moments of radical change in the sciences brought to the center of the stage the notion of a *paradigm*, the notion of a *crisis* for a given paradigm and, most importantly, the notion of a *paradigm shift*. There has been much huffing and puffing about the notion of a *paradigm*, and at one time acres of journal-space were devoted to it. For some it was the key to the Universe, for others a major piece of obfuscation – mainly because of Kuhn's use of it to show that the really crucial developments in the sciences are not available to logical modelling.

Where the Cartesian project sought a method that would lead separated individuals to a common view and to community, Kuhn says that a community of view and of practice is a condition and a requirement of progress in the sciences. The notion of *paradigm* is involved here because the acceptance of a common paradigm and way of seeing is what makes communication possible amongst a group of scientists. That acceptance is the source[3] of common practices and vocabulary which make them into a community and therefore make progress possible through mutual criticism and discussion, through the repetition of results and experiments, through the adoption of procedures and practices that prove successful – or, just as revealingly, run up against limits and encounter failures.

The notion of a *paradigm* is simple enough, however, and, so long as your project is one of clarification and not theory building, it will not run you into complexities and difficulties of definition, and so forth. It won't bear the whole weight of a theory, and Kuhn doesn't mean it to. (Before long we are going to have to face and examine that conception of understanding as limited to giving a theoretical account.) The reasons for the unavailability of logical determinations in "paradigm shifts" are themselves logical. A key is perhaps given in Wittgenstein's discussion in *Philosophical Investigations* II, IV of the possibility of regarding someone as an automaton: "My attitude to him is an attitude to a soul. I am not of the *opinion* that he has a soul." My attitude is a matter of my whole demeanor toward him involving the rights and duties and customs of my culture. Not something that is simply true or false like an opinion, a matter for argument and proof. Paradigms, attitudes, and ways of looking are not matters of proof and disproof.

To get at the notion of *paradigm*, take the example that Newton gives to illustrate his third law of motion: that every action is accompanied by an equal and opposite reaction, or, as he himself puts it: "To every action there is always opposed an equal reaction: or, the mutual actions of two bodies upon each other are always equal, and directed to contrary parts."

As the sense of this is not obvious to someone coming fresh to it, as were Newton's contemporaries, he offers an illustration. That illustration is in effect a paradigmatic example meant to give the sense of the law, to show how it is to be applied:

> If a horse draws a stone tied to a rope, the horse (*if I may so say*) will be equally drawn back to the stone; for the distended rope by the same endeavour to relax or unbend itself, will draw the horse as much toward the stone as it does the stone toward the horse.

I have italicized the phrase "if I may so say" because this signals the status of what, because of its misleading propositional appearance, might easily be mistaken for a proposition or claim with a truth value. But Newton is not offering us a claim or a theory that is testable and has a truth value. The phrase "if I may so say" indicates that he is clear that he is offering us a *way of looking* at the situation, a *method* of analyzing it, rather than a testable, falsifiable claim about it.

And here we have to say that Newton was a lot clearer about the status of what he called "axioms" and "laws" of motion than were later generations who looked on them as universal, and perhaps providential, truths about the cosmos. It took Henri Poincaré hard work and careful analysis to bring out the fact that what was perhaps the most promising candidate of the three laws for empirical status and testable content, the second law – nowadays rendered as "Force equals mass times acceleration" – was not in fact a testable, falsifiable claim about the cosmos or the things in it. Poincaré showed that there was no way of measuring each of the three components, the force, the mass and the acceleration, independently in any concrete situation and that therefore no experiment could bring the law to the test. And so too for the other two of Newton's three "laws" of dynamics.

Poincaré concluded that what looked like a law or theory, and had the outward form of a testable proposition, was in fact a disguised definition. Naturally he got boxed into an "ism" for his pains – I have forgotten which – and is these days only referred to as the representative of some "ism" or other. I recommend forgetting the "ism" and going back to the actual argument beautifully set out in the chapter called "The Classical Mechanics" in *Science and Hypothesis*.[4]

As will be suspected from what I have been saying, I don't myself think that "definition" is the most perspicuous way of describing the Newtonian "laws" of motion, but would suggest "way of looking" and "method of analysis" would give us a clearer picture of what is going on. What is common to both descriptions, however, is that they bring out the fact that those "laws" of motion are not propositional or theoretical in character. They are not true or false, are not candidates for testing on that true/false axis. They are guides for practice that stand to it much as the model or the scene stand to the drawing. (And my remarks themselves are not theoretical or propositional in character. They are not up for testing and refutation. Though you may persuade yourself and come to the conclusion that they are, or else are not, a valuable way of looking at things.)

Methods and ways of looking are not propositional in character. They are not true or false, and we create great confusion for ourselves if we try to assess them in that way or mistake a *method of analysis* for a theory, a proposition or anything else two-valued and testable. We do assess methods and ways of looking, but in ways that are generally scalar rather than bivalent. The pragmatists merely confused matters by trying to bundle everything up into one package and making no distinction between propositions, methods, and ways of looking. Apart from anything else, the pragmatists' "usefulness," being scalar, is for that reason not appropriate for giving an account of propositions, which are manifestly bipolar. "Usefulness" may be an appropriate way of assessing methods, since generally a single goal or thrust is defined for them. For *ways of looking*, by contrast, there are many other scales on which they may be assessed. Ways of looking may be deeper, more sensitive, funnier, enlightening, unifying, more human, more rigid, more puritanical, more self-serving, sexist, etc., etc., etc.

Now, let's get back to Kuhn's "paradigms" and what is meant by calling them "incommensurable" by way of signalling that logical canons are not available which will force a decision in favor of one of two or more competing paradigms. Of course, one can *use* logical canons to make a decision between two paradigms as one might use anything else, tossing a coin, for example. But that way of making the decision is not the way the scientists work, and it would not advance the sciences any.

The notion of *incommensurability* seems now to be even less well understood than it was in the 1960s and 1970s when Kuhn's work provoked a great deal of journal activity. Hilary Putnam, for example, reduces it (or, if you like, expands it gaseously) to a claim about the untranslatability of the theoretical vocabulary of different scientific "cultures."[5] He then produces a "knock-down" argument that reminds one somewhat of Anselm's way of dealing with "the Fool who in his heart hath said 'there is no God.'" That is, Putnam fastens on what it is that is supposed to be getting denied to show that the very notion of it subverts the denial. The argument is that we can't assert that there is a gap or disparity between the two vocabularies if we can't say something about the gap, and that is to say something simultaneously about both sides of it, and to do that requires a vocabulary which bridges it – QED.

A snazzy little argument. Unfortunately, like most snazzy little arguments it doesn't reveal much to us. Snazzy arguments have too short a way with things to be much use in philosophical clarification. More important here is that it doesn't really touch Kuhn's notion of *incommensurability* because that incommensurability lies in the first instance between paradigms. Since these are ways of looking at things and related practices and methods of working, two different paradigms don't lie in the same logical space. They are not true or false any more than building in steel is as against building in wood, stone, concrete or reed. One or other may be a more appropriate building technique given the available skills or materials, the use of the building or appropriateness to its surroundings, or the exigencies of wind and weather, and so forth. And here again we have a range of scales for assessing the activity, project or technique.

Any incommensurability of vocabulary between different scientific practices derives from the incommensurability of the paradigms that guide those practices in which the vocabulary is embedded and from which it draws its sense. The disparities in vocabulary are not the cause of, basis of or reason for that paradigmatic incommensurability. Things run the other way round and the incommensurabilities of vocabulary derive from that incommensurability in paradigms and ways of looking.

The piece of incommensurable vocabulary that Putnam takes as an example and then proceeds to hammer is that of "temperature" as used by the seventeenth-century scientists with only proto-thermometers to measure it by and the word's use and meaning in our own time, in which there is a range of methods to measure it. This turns out to be rather a soft target that Kuhn offers up by certain things that he incautiously says about changes in the notion of *mass* from Newton (for whom it was conserved) and Einstein (for whom it was not). What Kuhn says can be said to be "incautious" only in that it offers up this soft target to an unsympathetic interpreter, as Putnam is here. Putnam would not have had such an easy time bridging the incommensurabilities if he had been considering differences in vocabulary, viewpoint, and practice embedded in, say, the homeopathic model of disease and treatment and those of what is called "the medical model" by the people who view it from amongst the alternative strategies.

It might have been better still to have considered the vocabulary gaps revealed in the story of the Indian of northern Canada who had no difficulty believing his informant who told him that as a result of the Apollo Mission men had been to the Moon. He was in no way surprised or particularly impressed. "My uncle, the shaman," he said, "has been to the Moon many times."

Finding a bridge between the vocabularies and the life and whole world-view connected with those two ways of talking would not have appeared such a simple business. One can, of course, take the easy way of the hard-nosed and say that the Indian and his people inhabited a delusional fantasy world in accepting the notions of shamanistic travel to the underworld or to the heavens.

That is, of course, an option. What it does not do, however, is to find a bridge between two incommensurable outlooks and ways of talking. It simply denies sense to one of them. And, given that that way of talking of the ascents of the shaman or his descents into the underworld is rooted in a whole way of life and set of practices, that denial of sense to it is not very persuasive or convincing.

The task of bridge building between incommensurable outlooks and associated vocabularies is in no way made easier by the disparities of viewpoint and ways of looking being contained within a single individual. A nice case here is that of the young Trobrian Islander who went to Port Moresby to the university there. When he was in Port Moresby engaged in his studies and the university world, he said, he *knew* that ghosts didn't exist. When he was back home in the Trobrian Islands, he *knew* that they did. They were part of the world-view and the practices of the society that he had reentered. To ask which of these seeming incompatibles he *really* believed is perhaps not helpful here. Though it certainly is possible to recognize when someone has rejected a point of view and practices from which a certain vocabulary draws its sense and its strength, leaving that person mouthing formulaic words that no longer have life or force.

With our Trobrian Islander it could go either way. He might become so identified with the Port Moresby world that he found himself unable to reenter his native world to take a genuine part in its rituals and practices and ended up merely going through the motions, like an unbeliever in church for whom the invocations, the prayers, and the practices have no meaning and are only a dumb-show. On the other hand, he might be so pulled by the tribal identity and solidarity that the urban, essentially secular viewpoint of Port Moresby lost its hold. I have no information about the subsequent history of the actual individual interviewed. He might even have continued to move between these two irreconcilable points of view.

Each of us employs a variety of vocabularies with disparities of that sort across which bridges cannot be built – political, moral, medical, aesthetic, religious, scientific vocabularies, all associated with and taking their meaning from different areas of our life and practices that have quite different places there. On the whole these different practices and ways of viewing the world are not in competition with one another, except that they may compete for our time and attention. On the whole they have not got vocabularies that have the deceptive appearance of overlapping – though there are certain notorious exceptions – words from different practices that have the same form and enough analogy between their functions in those practices that they get taken to have exactly the same function and meaning. Much confusion results from that identification and literal transfer, confusion which generally needs careful philosophical unpicking.

Transfers from one such sphere to another can be made deliberately for poetical effect, or to make a joke. Transfers that are made without knowing or noticing are a source of confusion rich enough to supply philosophy with its *raison d'être.* An example is the confusion endemic in the sort of AI talk we looked at in chapter 5 and chapter 8, talk which involves the unexamined transfer of the notion of *purpose* from the human to the mechanical world and the description of certain machines as though purposes can be attributed to machines in the same way that purposes can be attributed to people. But the purpose that a machine has is given to it by its human designers or its users, and may be withdrawn or changed if the use of the machine is forgotten or a new use is found and preferred.

The reduced and derivative nature of that transferred attribution of purpose to the machine infects the attribution of all the other "human" attributes up to and including "intelligent" and "creative" and shows them all to be transferred and metaphorical uses, whether poetry, joke or mere confusion. The "creative" machine or program is not creative on its own behalf and according to its own lights, but only according to *our* aims, purposes, and standards. That fact is overlooked in the eagerness to transfer the human epithets to the machine. Only confusion results from this, even though all the participants in the "great debate" about AI know at some level that they are only kidding one another. The underlying form of the debate is: "Prove to me that I'm kidding you." What I mean by that is that no one of the participants is willing to "put their money where his mouth is" and to show that they really believe in the "sensitivity," "intelligence," or whatever of the machine by behaving in a way appropriate to that belief. If they were to, they would be carted away.

It is Descartes who has licensed this kind of stuff with his method of "hyperbolical" doubt that asks us to "employ" (whatever that may mean) doubts that no one feels or could act on without being rounded up and put into an institution. I regard Descartes as having done immense damage to the practice of philosophy thereby, and with his "method" having created problems wholesale that his method was incapable of solving, and, more seriously, having infected philosophy with a kind of insincerity that has turned it all too often into a dumbshow, a stage-battle between puppets, abstractions, and "isms."

But here we are getting away from the main line of our problem, which was to elucidate the notion of *paradigm* as a way of looking and as a guide to practice, pointing out how paradigms are necessarily incommensurable in the way practices are. They may be competing all right, but in that competition they will get assessed on a whole range of scales and not simply as true/false, in the manner of beliefs, opinions, assertions, assumptions or anything propositional in character. Practices and ways of looking can't be measured on that single true/false scale, and as a result logic and observation will not settle the choice and force the agreement amongst scientists. One can *recommend* a way of looking or a practice and point to a whole range of different and completely disparate things which may make it attractive (or not).

Perhaps now, after some of the things that have been said, it is possible to have a clearer grasp of what Kuhn had in mind in saying that community and agreement among scientists, a common vocabulary, practices and standards, are a *condition* of progress and fruitful work and not a consequence of it.

But one has to be careful here, because the relations are not ones of strict logical priority but the characteristically zig-zag dialectical relations of a concrete historical development. That is, at one stage the rough agreements in practice, vocabulary, and standards and conception of the problems that have come from the allegiance to a single paradigm make possible fruitful work and successes (or significant failures) that in their turn lead to finer and closer agreements amongst practitioners, and so forth. If, by contrast, we pursue the "foundational" approach, looking for strict and absolute priorities, we are only heading for confusion. Actual historical development is not like that and cannot be made to fit that requirement.

But now we have to face the problem of scientific progress, a problem which is thought to arise particularly acutely for Kuhn because of his presentation of the sciences as a historical human activity and his emphasis on internally set standards and norms, his emphasis, reminiscent of Wittgenstein, on agreement in paradigms, practices, vocabulary, and even judgments. These may be what it is that welds the scientists into a community, and enables them to communicate with one another, but doesn't that leave their activity without any external check and therefore any external reference? They may be able to compare results because of this ability to communicate, but if this ability requires a common way of looking at things and this common vocabulary requires "agreement in judgments," aren't we left with an internally organized activity which has no more external reference than dancing has? Wittgenstein, for his part, tells us only that this requirement of "agreement in judgments" for the possibility of communicating "seems to abolish logic, but does not really do so" (*PI* §242). He leaves us there.

What is worse, Kuhn even suggests that at certain historical junctures, the development of some particular science might have gone another way. Does that view of the sciences not remove from them any claim to an external, objective reference? I don't think so, even though a first view may give the impression that the sciences are a cozy old-boy network admitting or rejecting whom they want and settling things among themselves. We shall have to come back to that. But first we shall have to say something about the problem of scientific progress itself, because the notion of *progress* itself has its own entanglements that make it pretty well intractable for almost any view of things.

The first cause of trouble we have to look at is a conception of progress that is powerful and has exercised its fascination since Socrates used it as an argument for the existence of the Forms. This conception of progress sees it as necessarily involving a final goal and the nearer approach to that goal. That conception underlies and gives urgency and a particular cast to the whole debate on "Scientific Realism." It requires us to think that there is something that one might call "ultimate reality" which in some way or other the sciences are approaching.

There are two things to be said about that. One is that though progress is sometimes like that, defined and assessed in terms of a goal that is aimed at, it is probably less often like that than it is a matter of an improvement over a previous condition. If I have progressed in drawing or playing the piano or running or doing philosophy, there is no implication of an ultimate skill I am approaching. If I am making a table, that is a different matter. There is a point at which it is done, and my progress in the task of making it is measured by that: "It's only half-done," "Nearly done," "A couple more hours" . . . etc.

The other thing that must be said about that conception of scientific progress as an approach to some ultimate true picture (or whatever "ultimate" you want) is that if it is taken seriously and not just as a metaphorical, allusive, poetical or (dare I say it ?) religious way of speaking, then it seems that coherent sense cannot be made of it. For one thing, we have to notice that the would-be "goal" is a transcendental one and beyond reach. There could be no point at which the sciences or the scientists could come actually to have achieved it, come to have grasped that "ultimate reality" in all its fullness. That notion can't be given sense. But then, if the end or goal is not achievable, what sense can we give to the notion of *approaching* it that was meant to be involved in our idea of scientific progress?

In mathematics we can, of course, talk about an asymptotic approach to something, one that never reaches the thing however long continued. We can talk about it there because the limiting value, the asymptote, is defined and therefore the notion of *approach* is defined; we can talk about getting "as close as we please" and so forth. But in this would-be notion of the progress of the sciences toward an unreachable goal we have not got, as we have in mathematical case, an independent means of defining, describing or characterizing the goal in a way that will allow us to give any sense to the notion of *approach*. With the "approach" notion of progress, scientific progress becomes an intractable problem for everyone.

Popper had a sense of this difficulty, which arose for him because in his attempt at logical modeling he had only the two categories in which to put theories: "falsified" and "not yet falsified." This simple division was incapable of giving him any measure of progress. To get round this he tried to introduce a scalar notion of *verisimilitude* which he wanted to define in logical and mathematical terms. Roughly, verisimilitude was to be measured by taking all the deductions from the theory that turned out to be true and all the deductions that turned out to be false and noting the excess of the one over the other.

As a measure it ended up in that never-never land to which the logical modelers often retire. The notion of *all* the true deductions or of *all* the false deductions are never-never-land notions. The operation could never be carried out because the would-be classes are infinite and, in addition, they are not infinite in a way that would allow comparisons between those classes on the model, say, of Cantor's "Diagonal Argument." That is, the notion of *verisimilitude* that Popper offered turned out to be not only unworkable but meaningless. When I pointed that out in 1971 in *Analysis* I got a chilly reception from the Popperians, who, after much argument among themselves came in the end to the same conclusion.

But in concentrating on the impossibilities and inappropriateness of the mechanical test I see now that I missed something deeper and more important about Popper's notion of *verisimilitude*, something for which he should be given much credit. It lay in the aim of that notion, which was to give us a test of *improvement* so that we didn't have to say that one theory was "better than another" because it was "closer to" some mythical "ultimate or final picture." Though Popper did not provide us with a useful answer, he did something deeper and more important. He provided us with a more useful question or project in directing us away from the "approach" notion of progress toward the "improvement" model.

Because of the impossibilities in the "approach" notion we have to scrap it and to try to get a better grip on the "improvement" conception. This seeks to define progress in relation to what has gone before instead of looking vainly to an ideal something lying in a future that we know will never arrive.

But that change of direction removes one of the supposed functions of the notion of *reality*, and we need to look hard at the work that the notions of the *real* or *reality* are actually given in the daily working of the sciences.

The answer is "not much if any." It is not in itself a substantial term. Its role, as Austin pointed out in *Sense and Sensibilia* is pretty well confined to negating other terms with real content such as: "toy," "stuffed," "simulated," "imitation," "fake," "artificial," "makeshift" or "poor." Even those old favorites of epistemology, "dream," "mirage," "hallucination," "illusion," are all specific in themselves and are not to be bundled up into one bag, as they used to be by the epistemologists, and defined as perceptual lapses from the real. A dream is not an illusion, and a mirage is not a hallucination. They all have their separate senses and work to do, whereas the notion of *real* has only the job of denying them and gets what sense it has from what is denied. The gun that is real as against imitation is one that can be fired. The Scotch that is real wasn't made in Japan. The leather that is real was not produced from petroleum.

In the actual working sciences the job of the notion of the *real* is chiefly to contrast with the suggestion that some result was "an artifact" of the experimental situation. For a time chemists pursued something that came to be called "polywater" – a form of superfluid water that appeared in minute quantities in certain experiments. In the end they decided that it "didn't really exist," that it was an artifact of the experimental situation. Though you *can* say that polywater turned out "not to be real," that is a less helpful and clear way of expressing things than it would be to say that what was thought to be a new form of water turned out to be an artifact of the experimental situation. Much the same goes for the recent furore over "cold fusion," which was itself interesting in that it tended to divide the physicists from the chemists, who were more prepared to consider the possibility. The ungenerous have suggested that this was because the physicists had invested huge amounts of time and oceans of money in the plasma approach to fusion. They too had had that same artifacts problem that had led to premature claims of having achieved the production of energy by controlled fusion. For the moment, the consensus on cold fusion is "artifact." However, my grapevine sources tell me that the Japanese have moved in to bankroll Martin Fleishman's work, so maybe the tallies are not all in yet.

I think I'll stick my neck out here and say that the working scientists could manage to get on with their work quite happily without the word "real." You could put it mischievously and say that there is no real use for it in the sciences. It is only the ideologues of science, the Sunday scientists, who can't seem to get on without it.

My own preferred term for the task of trying to capture and represent the "externality" of the sciences and scientific activity is "objectivity," which for several reasons I think does a much better job of bringing out the nature of the checks and limits that give scientific activity its external reference than does a notion of *the real* or *ultimate reality*, which lies in splendid isolation in the misty distance, never to be really grasped. Part of the problem with the notions of *the real* or *reality* is that they carry with them the inescapable picture of being "pre-formed," so that to grasp the *real* properly is to grasp it only in one way.[6] This leaves us wandering always in darkness in the sciences, because we can never actually reach that "one way" and, as we have made out above, we can't even give sense to talk about "approaching it."

The *objective*, on the other hand, does not lie in the unreachable distance. Quite the opposite: it is what is "thrown down" before us, what we trip over and knock against, on the one hand, or pick up and use, on the other. That is one side of it. The other side is its relation to our projects. What we trip over is a matter of where we are going, and what we pick up a matter of what we are up to.

This introduces something that the notion of *reality* and cognates miss entirely, namely, the *historical* dimension of the objective. What I have in mind here is that the projects that are possible to us develop over time with our past achievements and successes, both as individuals and as cultures. Nuclear fusion was not a possible project for the Greeks, nor was bridging the Rhine for the Neanderthals. Playing Scarlatti or climbing Everest are not projects open to me at my age, even though they are projects that exist and are recognized in my culture. We shall have to come back and make use of that notion of a project *being established* or *existing* in a given culture.

Since the job description for the notion of *reality* was to be eternal and without history as well as single, presenting the same face to everyone, we have really two tasks here: the first is to try to make out whether anything *could* carry out that role for the sciences and the secular world without muddling matters and ending by giving the sciences a quasi-religious role; the second is whether the job needs to be done at all and whether, without it, we can put together a view of the external sources of both limit and possibility. These are not small tasks. For the notion of the *objective* has generally been given that very same old timeless and abstract role as *the real*, and it is hard for us to think of anything as *objective* that isn't the same for everyone and the same at all times. I think there is no hope of detaching the notion of *reality* from that job and those characteristics. It seems to have a natural affinity for the word "ultimate" and a hankering for theology.

On the other hand, I think there is some hope for the notion of *the objective* – so long as we start from the conception of it as "what we encounter" in our projects and activities and work out from there. But we shall have to keep in mind constantly that what we encounter in our activities and our projects is from one side determined by them, by the practices that are embedded in those activities and the way of life and the way of looking in which they in turn are involved. *What we encounter* must not be treated, as *reality* has been, as a notion that pretends to an abstract sense that is independent of and detached from those human contexts of practices and way of life. It is precisely that pretense that removes the notion of *reality* from any role, place or sense within the secular world and projects onto it a quasi-theological role.

These tasks are, however, implicit in Kuhn's project and vision, and we have been circling around them all along. The unwillingness to take them on board has been the reason for the distortions and misunderstandings of his work.

12 History and human nature

The seventeenth century framed an agenda for philosophy on the basis of an inverted picture of humanity, seeing each human not as a social animal (Aristotle's *zoon politikon*) but rather as by nature atomized and separated, an individual first and only later, and as it were accidentally, a social being. That social being of humans was presented as the result of an act of combination of initially, and essentially, isolated individuals, an agreement among those separated individuals that bound them together in a common subservience to a set of laws and rules or to a sovereign body or individual. Anyone who sets out to take that picture seriously will find contradictions and impossibilities leaping out to prevent it. At the merest touch of realism the picture falls apart.

For example, one has only to ask seriously about the language in which the imagined negotiations were supposed to have taken place and the agreement framed, to be sent off on the trail of one set of contradictions. And then, consider the notion of the binding force of the agreement or contract that is supposed to be the origin of all social bonds and obligations. I can hardly bind myself (out of nowhere, so to speak) by a promise to keep promises. If I was not bound already to and by that practice, I am not bound now, by this promise I now make. I cannot in the same act and at the same instant promise and institute the practice of promising and promise-keeping that is its necessary background. My words can constitute a promise only where that practice already exists in a society in which I am a participant.

In the same way the central notions of *contract* or *agreement* cannot be presented as the *origin* of social bonds. Those notions of *agreement* and *contract* and the corresponding acts of contracting and agreeing *require* those bonds as a precondition and cannot produce them out of a social vacuum as the myth requires or suggests. The existence of those bonds and a whole surrounding of practices are required by the notion of *contract* to have any sense and for the action of contracting to be possible.

So the notion of *contract* can hardly be put forward seriously as an explanation of what a moment's not very deep reflection shows to be its own preconditions. Real history can never have gone in that way. Something else is going on here. We are dealing with myth, not history or possible history, or even seriously imagined imaginary history.

But if the Social Contract is a myth only, we are not entitled to ask those embarrassing questions any more than we can ask for a physical account of the luminosity of the Holy Grail in the Arthurian legends, or Loki's ability to change into a salmon in the Norse myths. On the other hand we are entitled, and even required, to ask some different questions, questions of quite another sort, questions about the function of that myth and questions about the reasons for its attraction over the previous centuries and the reasons for its dominance in the seventeenth. We need to ask those questions seriously and to pursue them rigorously because so much of the agenda of philosophy that we are still working to in our time was set then in the light of that myth and its imagined pre-historical, pre-social condition of mankind.

That imaginary pre-social condition would necessarily and by definition, so to speak, be as atomized individuals with no shared practices, institutions or obligations.[1] It is these atomized individuals whom so much of philosophy in the modern era has tried to accommodate and give reality to. A central part of philosophy's job-description has been to show how such atomized individuals could by their own unaided (except perhaps by God) efforts emerge from ignorance and isolation to knowledge of a common world, and through that common knowledge arrive at the possibility of contact and community with others.

Here, I would want to make out, philosophers took on the task of inverting reality in their efforts to give reality to that mythic picture conjured up in the Social Contract. Mistaking the metaphorical for the literal, myth for history, and the picture for the thing generally produces only nonsense and confusion. Here, as I hope I have begun to indicate and hope to bring out further, the project has involved philosophers in thumb-catching on a grand scale, or, if you prefer, in trying to lift themselves off the ground by tugging on the board on which they are standing.

I would also claim that the individualist project involves another attempt at inversion in its treatment of knowledge, language and thought, because, contrary to the requirements of that project, these are social in origin and depend on community with others.

I have argued that previously and shall in what follows. I give notice of that claimed inversion only to show the overall direction of the discussion. But first we have to do something to make good the claim that individualism was in fact the program, then we have to understand the reasons why the myth of a social contract came to have the dominant position it did and thus to motivate that program and the associated view of humanity, and then we have to see whether there were reasons apart from those, which made that atomized view of humanity seem natural.

First it is important to say that nobody set out the program and the job-description so baldly as I have here. It was largely unspoken and unformulated. But the program can be seen as implicit in the answers that were offered, in the methods used, and in what was to be taken as given and could be appealed to in carrying it out.

One can see it, for example, in Descartes's enterprise in the *Meditations* or the *Discourse*. He was there establishing for all of us the possibility of thinking our way out of an initial and original isolation and ignorance by doing it himself for himself under our eyes. First he doubts his way out of a world of hearsay and ignorant tales, and by his method of doubt forces himself into a world that might have as its only other inhabitant the malicious genie. Then he thinks his way back out of that isolation and ignorance (with a bit of help from God). The idea is that if he, Descartes can do it, anyone can. After all, "Good sense is," as he tells us (and a commonplace of the day had it), "of all things in the world the most equally distributed."[2]

To see that Descartes is in fact working to that agenda set by the picture of humanity as aboriginally separated and isolated, notice that in his program of doubting he leads both himself and us to the point where we are supposed to have no reason to believe that there is anything human beneath the cloaks and hats we see through the window scurrying in the rain. He might as well have said "beneath the skin and hair." This completes that isolation which was supposed to have been the pre-social condition of humanity. His aim is then to show in his own person and through his own example how it is possible for such an isolated human being to escape from that isolation by the exercise of reason alone.

The problem that he is thus solving is the problem that set the agenda and directed the efforts of his successors as well. Some of them may have appealed to different resources, to sense experience, and not just reason. But the determining fact about those resources was that they were supposed to be available (along with the universal distribution of good sense) to each isolated individual human atom pursuing the solitary struggle for that knowledge of a common world that would make possible a common language through which to make contact with others.

Both the rationalists, who made *reason* the main resource in that struggle, and the empiricists, who made *experience* the means, agreed in requiring that the knowledge attained be generated out of resources available to each separated individual, resources that were unmediated by social relations such as teaching or training, and undeveloped by social contact.[3] This requirement distorted the understanding both of reason and of experience. Reason became a kind of mechanical calculation, a thing of algorithms, and no judgment. And experience became a matter of sense experience conceived also as a mechanical process. The mechanical character that was given to both reason and experience was not just a product of the dominance of what Dijksterhuis has called the "rise of the mechanical world-view." It was also the necessary result of the requirement that those resources belong to each individual asocially, as original equipment with which each individual has to negotiate a path to knowledge and to social relations. This unreal picture thus had two fathers.

Neither experience nor reason is actually like that, a mechanical process with no social dimension. We are *taught* to discern, distinguish, and identify, to judge distances and quantities, to measure and compare, to hear musical intervals in our culture's scale, to smell when the bread is done or the engine is too hot. Because of her training, the doctor hears the faulty heart valve with her stethoscope where I hear nothing. It's not that I hear it but can't put a name to it. I don't *hear* it, though perhaps I can be taught to.

At one level we know perfectly well that our use of the various senses, seeing, hearing, touch, taste, and smell, involves skill and training, a cultural or occupational background. The common inherited biological structures do not *produce* those abilities and those skills mechanically. The inherited structures are a *condition* only, and they can be a condition for a wide range of abilities that involve the same mechanical structures of the sense organs, just as the same tool, a computer, say, or a saw can be used in a wide variety of ways, and their use may exhibit a vast range of skills. The saw can even be used as a musical instrument.

Our knowledge of the training element in the exercise of the senses is implicit, for example, in the old saw about the Inuit recognizing and naming twenty kinds of snow. And we are aware of the fact that ordinary Japanese are unable to hear the difference between an "r" and an "l." A perception that is obvious to an English speaker takes difficult training for a native speaker of Japanese, whose ears, we can presume, are structurally no different. The bank clerk who can feel the difference between the forged note and the genuine has a sensory skill that I do not have, though again, I may be able to acquire it. T. S. Kuhn, in *The Structure of Scientific Revolutions*, called to our attention the training and the skill that go into the scientist's ability to read a gauge, measure a meniscus, judge a titration. And perhaps we should listen also to some striking remarks by the astronomer Hershel quoted by Charles Babbage in *The Decline of Science in England*: "An object is frequently not seen *from not knowing how to see it*, rather than from any defect in the organ of vision," said Babbage, introducing Herschel's claim that:

> I will prepare the apparatus, and put you in such a position that Fraunhofer's lines shall be visible, and yet you shall look for them and not find them; after which, while you remain in the same position, I will instruct you *how to see them* and you shall see them, and not merely wonder you did not see them before, but you shall find it impossible to look at the spectrum without seeing them.

Many of us will have had that experience of being taught to hear, see or feel something that we could not before. I remember being taught to hear an interval of a third or a fifth, even though that acquired skill had no long term effect on my musical ability, which remains nil. Others may remember being shown the puzzle picture known as "Christ in the Snow" and struggling to see the figure in it with increasing frustration as someone described in words what they were looking for, how it was situated in the frame, and so forth. Then suddenly the figure leaps out either spontaneously or as a result of one's being shown with a finger the eyes, the nose, etc. The seeing of it usually brings a gasp and a wonderment at having missed it and one is no longer able to see the picture in the old way.

As I say, at one level we all know these things, but in philosophical discussions the grip of the individualistic picture is such that they are not allowed in as evidence that our use of the various senses involves skills that are either part of our culture or the result of particular occupational training. One could even offer this phenomenon as a mischievous further example of how certain things are not recognized because of a perspective and a way of seeing that has no place for them.

The requirement that perception be depicted as a passive mechanical process the same for all who have the same equipment requires in its turn that these things be explained away, however convoluted the explanation may turn out to be, or simply not noticed or maybe denied. The determination to put the individual before the social requires that the training and skill element be ignored or otherwise disposed of. (Though I have never seen a serious attempt to mount a biological explanation of the inability of Japanese speakers to hear the difference between an "r" and an "I.") And at the same time that aim of putting the individual before the social imposes just that mechanical view of things, since it is the physiological structures that are given to the individual at birth or through maturation and physiological development. Those structures and that development are presumed to be common between individuals as part of the same biological species.

Those mechanical structures and the mechanistic view are then supposed to represent a working out of the individualistic program's requirement that all sensory abilities be shown to be part of the individual's original, pre-social endowment. At the same time, those biologically common features are supposed to provide us with an explanation of how those individuals working in isolation are supposed to have come to a common view of things which is then supposed to be the source of their ability to communicate and form communities.

I have used the expressions "explanation" and "source" in describing the role proposed for that common physiology in our understanding of the facts of common understanding, meaning by those phrases to mark a clear distinction between that and describing that common physiology as a "condition" of such common understanding. A condition does not bring the thing about, though its absence will prevent it. We may need that common physiology in order to develop those common skills and discriminations in the exercise of our senses, but it is training and acculturation and the learning of a common language that are the developing force. That common physiology does not guarantee, cause or bring about the development of those skills.

Again, this picture which the individualist paradigm and program are trying to work out and impose is an inversion of things, taking cause for effect and effect for cause. The community of practices and skills, of aims and way of life, and the common language and the common view of things are a single package, mutually influencing and developing. We all know that we learned language partly through instruction and correction, but mainly through getting the drift and catching on, by seeing the point, hearing the tone, and getting the reference. Yet, weighed down by the requirements of a picture, some philosophers have allowed themselves the luxury of postulating an internal, pre-social language that is only waiting for the right circumstances to be translated into Gullah or German, Cree or Chinese and become the spoken language of the child brought up in those linguistic communities.

We have to take note of the fact that there can be no evidence for such a universal first language apart from its being required by the picture. Even the common structural features that Chomsky and others have sought to present do not constitute evidence for more than the existence of common features of human life to be counted as human at all, and the common features of anything that is to function as a language and to be counted as one.

Other philosophers, following much the same line, have turned the pre-linguistic infant into a little theoretician, a mini-anthropologist set down in an alien tribe of grownups and trying to figure out the significance or meaning of the sounds that are coming from its mother and other adults in its vicinity. Our little theoretician is meant to be correlating those sounds with features of the immediate environment that are supposed to be, in some way or another, striking, or obvious, or of some interest to the infant.

We are not told in these accounts how our little theoretician comes by the notion of *significant speech* and the idea that the sounds that adults make are meant to be correlated with anything. Without that notion of *significance* this picture can't get us beyond the notion of *conditioning* to that of *speech*. Correlating is an activity that we may engage in or not and may show various degrees of skill at. Conditioning is a passive matter, requiring no skill and giving no opportunity for any. And conditioning does not issue in speech. All this turning and twisting is in the service of the aim of avoiding appeal to social relations and practices in understanding the skills and abilities of human beings.

The fact that this program aims to fill out a picture which inverts reality does not make it any easier to combat. Quite the contrary. Once we have been persuaded to deny some of our very ordinary observations and understandings, the program moves philosophical discussion into a kind of twilight zone where nothing is exactly real and our ordinary sense of things is set at nought. We are, in a sense, lost. This is the effect, if not the function, of Descartes's Method of Hyperbolical Doubt and of the "arguments from illusion" which used to be a popular method in the US and Britain of inducting students into philosophy.

Getting back on our feet and seeing the world the right way up will not be easy. As psychological experiments have shown, we quickly accommodate to inverting spectacles and soon everything seems normal. To find our way out of this twilight zone and reestablish a grip on some realities, we are going to have to go back and identify, and then counteract, some of the strong historical pressures that made the individualistic program seem to be a necessary one to undertake. The form as well as the aim of this examination will offend all of those who wish to see philosophy as a self-contained activity that reaches for timeless truths and is immune from pressures exerted by historical developments in a wider world. Maybe philosophy would like to be like that, but what is certain is that it hasn't been, in spite of all its claims and pretensions to such a status.

Perhaps I need here to give reassurances that the examination of the role of historical developments and historical circumstances will not issue in the kind of unenlightening name-calling dismissals that used to pass for analysis amongst a certain sort of Marxists ("bourgeois individualism" and that sort of thing). The ease and simplicity of that epithetic style has attractions from which even philosophers have not been immune, and we have got unfortunately used to hearing "conventionalist," "subjectivist," "relativist," and the rest, applied in various directions as though they clarified matters. I promise nothing of that kind.

A way of looking at things and a program with associated methods and standards (what Kuhn would call a "paradigm") have been proposed to us and have been accepted and have dominated philosophical practice since the seventeenth century. But *ways of looking* and *programs* are not to be tested on a true/false scale and found acceptable or wanting. A program is not in the running for proof in the way that propositions are; though a program and a way of looking may be exciting, fruitful, and suggestive and it may solve problems and worries that were there before it came on the scene, as well as generating new problems and new goals. On the other hand, it may just run out in sand or people may get bored with it because it has become too complicated, too expensive, or just doesn't seem to be getting anywhere.

But in the seventeenth century there were many reasons why the Social Contract and its implied individualistic picture offered an attractive and exciting program and a new perspective and way of looking at things that would eliminate problems and worries of the time. That picture and program also promised to provide a basis for an understanding of the new social and historical realities that had come about in the great social upheavals of the previous centuries. It offered as well the prospect of integrating the understanding of humanity with the forms of mechanical understanding that were being worked out in the sciences. That mechanical form of explanation and understanding had by then become the dominant one, even to the exclusion of all others.

The aim of that new mechanical understanding was ultimately that of control and manipulation. This brought about deep changes in the notions of *explanation* and of the *causes* that explanations sought. The new notion of *cause* no longer had any connection with what Aristotle had discussed under that heading. The "causes" that were now sought, and that "explanations" were now meant to identify, were something separate and apart from the thing or condition or process, something that could be used to bring it about, to manipulate it or control it. Any purported explanation that could not be used in this way came to be looked on as no explanation at all and as providing no understanding. "Knowledge is power," said Bacon, expressing the new sense that had been given to the notion of knowledge: if it isn't power, it isn't knowledge.

It was natural and even necessary to start with individuals in any account of human abilities, capacities, and achievements that was to fit this new mechanical and manipulatory conception of understanding and explanation. The *social* and the *mechanical* are opposed notions, and any explanation that was going to conform to the new mechanical format would not be able to start with anything but the individual conceived as a mechanism. And this new format brought in its train a new nominalism that denied existence to anything but the individual.

And so we have found a whole constellation of pressures to take the individual as the starting point. There were also strong historical pressures to pose the question of "the origins of society," pressures that at the same time worked against considering whether that question itself had any sense. And that question in its turn brings us back to the individual by requiring us to posit the isolated pre-social individual that the "Contract" turns into a social being.

The prospect and the aim of being integrated into the "mechanical world-view" that had come to dominance with the scientific revolution, by adopting mechanical forms of explanation, was only one of the forces that came newly to bear on philosophers from the surrounding historical context. There were others that came from new social structures that were emerging, and from the need for a political theory that would "delegitimate" feudal institutions.

The seventeenth century was a time when political theorists and philosophers had to come to terms with the immense social changes that had been taking place over the previous centuries. Those changes involved not only introducing new legal and social structures and institutions but new aims, values, virtues, new standards, and ways of assessing actions and proposals. A society that had been organized as a military hierarchy supported by a more or less subsistence agricultural economy was giving way to a commercial order of property owners and laborers who were producing commodities for the market. Wholly new institutions, practices, and laws were needed to accommodate and embody fundamental changes in social relations, relations that were now increasingly mediated by money. Wages and rents were replacing direct obligations to serve that came with birth. Land could now be bought and sold as well as labor. But the buying of labor required that the laborer be free to sell it, free, that is, from the feudal obligations of service, the *corvée*, and so forth. And as a result of these new needs and pressures, the feudally instituted obligations came not only to be restrictive but to seem unnatural and unjust. But a new framework of thought was needed to bring this out and to make it clear.

These changes forced a fundamental reassessment which the philosophers saw as posing the question of how social institutions *as such* are to be justified. But a question about the justification of a social institution that is raised in a completely general and abstract way so that the question encompasses any and every system of social relations and obligations necessarily leaves aside all historical and social context and confronts us with the abstracted and separated individual yet again.

The notion of a *Social Contract* seems to be the only type of answer to the justification question posed in this way. Having put aside all social context in which there might be practices of justification and reason giving, we are necessarily left with individual agreement with others to adopt certain institutions or accept a certain authority. This agreement is presented as creating *ex nihilo* the basis of justification. And this picture in its turn seems to force an appeal to the notion of a universal human nature, and to the "original endowments" of the bare, forked, human animal. This is because the Social Contract theorists, who are standing outside all this process, or, if you like, are making this story up, have laid on themselves the task of presenting the story as a "natural" one grounded in the facts of human nature. How else could it be recommended? It is also a logical requirement of that story because of the relation of the two terms "natural" and "social." When you have stripped away the social, all you have left is the natural.

There are two questions embedded in all this that we are going to have to come back to. One is whether the notion of the "origin of society" is one that can be given sense any more than the project of "justifying" all its institutions can. The latter project is trying to eat its own tail because *justification* is itself a practice and an institution and already a social notion. That is, justification can only take place within a framework of standards and procedures that are already part of the life of a society. Those practices of justification can't reach behind themselves to justify themselves and their own procedures and standards. That kind of thumb-catching is an inescapable result of the task the Social Contract theorists had taken on board. They were trying to lift themselves up by pulling up on the plank on which they were standing.

The new response to this problem was deeply subversive. It was to take the notion of *reason*, which had been seen as something essentially human and the distinguishing feature of humanity, and to present it as something abstract and mechanical, something that could be captured in an axiomatic system of logic. Reason was now seen as something that was paradigmatically exhibited in mathematics, something standing outside of humanity and its practices. Euclid's geometry was for the seventeenth-century philosophers the ideal. Their view of it was of an external, self-sustaining, and self-authenticating system, proceeding from self-evident axioms by incontrovertible logical steps to undeniable conclusions. And the new drive, which was the opposite side of the AI coin, was to mechanize human thought. It led to a view of logic as having its own independent force, the view which was the subject of chapter 2. The next chapter will look at the tangles and intractable problems that this view gets into in trying to give an account of the foundations of geometry, the sense of its terms, and the so-called "self-evidence" of its starting points.

The other problem in this project of giving an account of the origins of society is one raised by the necessary appeal to notions of "human nature." We have to ask about the role and function of a whole class of concepts, "natural endowments," "God-given" or "innate capacities" or whatever, and the notion of "human nature" itself. We must ask whether they can have any genuine explanatory role at all, since they all function logically pretty much like the "occult qualities" of which the seventeenth century was so censorious. We shall have to ask just what sort of thing we are being told when we are told that something is "natural" or to be put down to "human nature." It is certainly not nothing, but we have to look hard at just what we can make of such a claim, how we are to assess it, and what conclusions we can draw if we do come to accept it. But that is a question we can come back to. For the moment, I want to continue in my zig-zag course and return to look at the historical changes that made the individualistic picture and its associated program of analysis so attractive.

Our job is to sort out myth from history and at the same time to try to identify those historical conditions and changes that gave a positive historical role to the myth of the Social Contract even though that myth had no basis in historical reality. And it is time the modern world made a thorough critique of that myth, that picture, and that agenda, discarding those problems, projects, and questions that no longer have to be addressed as soon as we banish the mythical and impossible view that generated them and required them to be solved. That individualistic picture itself was implicit in the mythical accounts of the "origins of society" that were meant to give justifications for and legitimacy to the new social forms that were struggling to be born out of the old feudal organization of society. (One can, of course, ask how a myth can give legitimacy or justification to anything at all. And that is an important question with contemporary relevance to, for example, Rawls' myth of "the original position," and we need to come back to it.) As a stop-gap we could say that the contract theories that had been put forward since the fifteenth century aimed at presenting a picture of humanity and the "origins of society" that provided a rival myth to the feudal myth of the origins of its particular arrangements of obligations and hierarchy, the bonding to the lord and his demesne.

Those contract theories grew in popularity among political theorists over the centuries until they became, with Hobbes, pretty well canonical; though they were still on the whole put forward by most theorists as mythical pictures and not historical events. Only Locke hankered after some sort of actual historical basis for the Contract and got soundly rapped for it by Hume.

Paradoxically, it was the feudal myth that could claim some sort of historical basis, as the Social Contract could not. There had been definite acts of prescribed form by which, in Carolingian times and after, one man rendered "homage" to another, making himself the other's "man" (the origins of the word "homage"). The other by this act became his "lord," and might grant his "man" (his vassal) "fees" of land or rents in payment for services past or anticipated. This granting of "fees" gave the name to the feudal system itself. So there seem to have been definite historical acts that had been the basis of the system of obligations that constituted feudalism.

But it could hardly be said that everyone who later found themselves bound by those feudal ties had done so in an act of homage or a swearing of fealty. Those bonds became inherited and instituted and the basis of a fixed social order that transcended those individual swearings. And in becoming inherited and institutionalized they changed their nature entirely. Originally the bond was the result of an individual act that was often the voluntary and unforced recognition of the advantage of becoming the protégé of someone, much like a Mafia boss, who could see that the tax collector did not oppress you or the magistrate would listen to your case and not decide arbitrarily against you, and so forth. But as soon as I inherit my subservience to you it is not an act of mine but a fact of birth that creates that hierarchy and maintains it. Even the appearance of the voluntary character of the original swearings is swept away and this newly transcendent system was given a transcendent source, God's ordinance. It was this necessary, natal, and inherited ordering that the Social Contract conceptions aimed to sweep away in its turn.

The attraction of contract theory, therefore, hardly lay in historical accuracy. Rather it lay in the theory's subversiveness of the feudal order and its customs and institutions. The feudal ordinances with their restriction on movement and change of "calling" were oppressive for the new form of economy that was displacing the subsistence economy of feudalism. For this new economy and new social life that it created, the market and the town were the dominant driving and drawing force. The Social Contract worked its subversion by reaching back beyond those personal swearings of feudalism and the later institutionalized obligations that defined a social hierarchy, back to a posited prehistory. The subversive spirit of that challenge is caught by the mocking couplet of those days: "When Adam delved and Eva span/ Who was then the Gentleman?" That couplet represents the "Golden Age" version of the myth, a pre-historical Golden Age from which sin excluded us but which would return with the Second Coming.

The secularizing atmosphere of the seventeenth century turned that picture around, and instead of what had been a sin that brought about exclusion from a golden age state of nature (eating from the tree of knowledge of good and evil) we have a myth of humanity emerging from a primal atomistic chaos and conflict, rescuing itself by the exercise of reason. Reason shows the advantage of combination, of laws and submission to an ordered political system. It was this secular vision of a human transition from barbarism to civilization by force of reason that generated the serious (and I should say, impossible) problems and projects which the philosophers of the seventeenth century undertook with great willingness, as though it were the most important task to show that this mythical picture was an actual possibility, whether or not any such event of transition had really taken place. In this they were showing solidarity with the era's secularizing tendencies and joining forces with the attack on the remaining feudal institutions and outlook that were acting as fetters on the development of commerce and trade and production for the market.

But the individualistic picture also reflected some new social realities that came about in the transition from the agricultural subsistence economy to a money economy. That new money economy not only involved the buying and selling of commodities but introduced the buying and selling of labor in the market place. A good illustrative example of this was the institution of the annual "mop fairs" for the hiring of domestic labor in place of the "house serfs" of an earlier time. The result of this was that, at least at an individual level, contracts, and not mythical oaths of fealty and acts of homage, were regulating the obligation of one person to labor for another and the other to pay a wage.

The fact that these individual obligations in specific circumstances were now governed by contract made it tempting to think that this new contractual relation could be generalized to encompass the whole of society, creating it in one grand encompassing contractual act as though all human beings were at the same time performing acts of homage to one another and to some single superior authority. This act would settle the obligations of individuals to one another and to the overarching regulating power to which they would henceforward, through all the generations, owe obedience either absolutely or in specified circumstances or under specified conditions.

Tempting though the picture was, perhaps, it is not tempered with any sense of realism or of logic, even when it is taken as myth. The notion of *contract* is the product of definite historical circumstances. It is an extension of the notion of *promising*, perhaps, and promising has a more ancient history. But *contract* is an extension of it. And the notion of *promising* itself already implies a social relation and framework of practices and obligations. The words "I promise" mean nothing where those practices have not been instituted. No act of promising can lift them off the ground at the same time as being lifted by them. So we are still left wondering what attractions hurried the contract theorists past these incoherences without so much as a nod of recognition. Again, to satisfy that wonderment, we are going to have to look outside logic, reasoning, and philosophy itself to the historical context and to the new social realities and trends that the contract theory and the individualistic paradigm reflected, however distorted, and helped move forward, however illogically.

The new social realities that the individualistic picture in some way reflected were symbolically captured by the Reformation redefinition of the relation of individual humans to God. God, it was now said, had His voice in each (the individual conscience), and it was not to be denied any more than God Himself. Individuals were being moved to the center of thought about humanity because actual people were in fact reaching a new separation and self-definition amongst the new possibilities, the new choices of life, and "calling." These were being offered in the growing urban environments that were drawing people from the horizonless, dependent life of a countryside only half-emerged from feudalism. This was an additional powerful inducement to take on board the individualistic way of looking at humanity without carefully checking its credentials and its logical consistency.

One could also say that Hobbes' picture of "Man in the State of Nature" as "the War of All against All" showed a sense of the direction in which humanity had been going over the previous centuries rather than where it was coming from. Those centuries that saw seizures and enclosures stripping away the peasants' means of subsistence forcing them to sell their labor also saw the vicious laws of vagabondage which had the same aim. This stripping away of consideration and care and social bonds continued in the highland clearances of the next century in which the clan chiefs sought to disencumber themselves of retainers who were not a productive asset in a newly commercial world. Those changes and those tensions are already portrayed in *King Lear* as Lear creates anger and resentment in his two daughters by traveling about with his retainers and companions like a feudal king or lord traveling among his vassals. Goneril and Regan represent the new consciousness and new calculation that had no use for those feudal marks of hierarchy and subservience that had no productive use or commercial value.

Despite Hobbes' fine historical sense, we can't say for sure that he saw those developments as *historical* developments, that is, as growing out of previous conditions. He may have seen that social relations generated by the market are essentially oppositional and reflected that in his description of what he calls "Man in the State of Nature." However, what comes out in his presentation is the opposite, an ahistorical way of looking at them as powered by something internal to each individual, something that might get the designation "human nature."

What Hobbes did was to reverse the historical order of development, so that humanity was pictured as emerging out of, rather than proceeding toward, the kind of separation and opposition and conflict that is generated by the market. In market relations there is an opposition of interest between buyer and seller and competition between different producers, as well as an opposition of interest between the laborer and the hirer of labor. But Hobbes' reversal of that order in his presentation by its own logic forced him to take that "human nature" as his starting point and to abandon any historical explanation in terms of the way the pursuit of money and profit were setting individual against individual in a way that would have been unknown, say, in earlier tribal societies. A tribal society could hardly have continued in existence containing such conflict.

But the notion of a universal "human nature" thrown into prominence by that historical reversal was also a great ideological weapon in the conflict with the old feudal order. The feudal economy and production was based on the villein bound by birth to the manor. The emerging need of the town and the market was for "free" labor to produce goods, labor that was free of just those bonds.

The notion of a "universal human nature" can hardly be made to encompass the idea of bonds that come with birth or the notion of a hereditary hierarchy of the sort that the feudal order imposed. That conception of a universal human nature proposed, and was part of, a grand new vision of humanity as equal participants in that nature. That notion and that vision stripped away all the bonds and commitments imposed by birth[4] leaving us with the bare individual to make its own way in the world with no inherited title to help it on and no servile bond to hold it back. The vision seemed a progressive and liberating one in those historical circumstances. We need hardly wonder at the enthusiasm with which it was seized on.

It was that liberating function alone that gave sense and force to the notion of "human nature." If we turn and look at the notion itself, its logical character, and explanatory function, we shall see that the notion of "human nature" is a blank with no explanatory force, despite the great use that is made of it.

It is a blank cheque on which anything may be written according to the whim of the writer, and there is no way of determining whether there are funds to meet it. That is no doubt the source of its popularity amongst those who make great appeal to it in their theories and their explanations. Unfortunately the notion of "human nature" can ground no theory and provide no explanation. Because you can put into the notion whatever seems convenient and necessary to explain whatever it is that you want to explain, it can in fact provide no explanation. The notion of "human nature" would advance things and give a genuine explanation only if there were some separate and independent way of testing for the presence or absence of the various abilities, characteristics, and tendencies that are claimed for it.[5]

But that does not mean that we are told nothing at all when we are told that something is "natural" or happens "by nature." Claims of that kind, though they are not themselves explanations of the thing, nevertheless have something to say *about* the explanation of the thing. From the perspective of the new conception of explanation and understanding as providing the means for manipulation and control, there is a whole range of expressions that could not be counted as real explanations even though they are used in ways that seem to be giving them that role: "natural," "by nature," "innate," "given," or "God given." One might call them "dummy" explanations in that they go into the place in which a genuine explanation might go. They do not give the prospect of manipulation and control and they do not tell us more about the thing than we know already.

But as "dummy" explanations that occupy the place where a genuine explanation might go they have the function of excluding any other. When we are told that something has a certain character "naturally" or that something else happens "naturally" we are being told not to look for an explanation because "that is just the way things are." To say that something is "God's will" is to express resignation and to say that we are not to look for human sense in it. It is not to offer an explanation of the thing. It could not be challenged except by rejecting the whole religious outlook and framework within which such an expression made sense. Or else one could reject the assertion by offering a genuine explanation and making the counter-assessment that it was an occasion for anger and action, not for resignation. "It's not God's will at all; it's the work of the IMF" or "British Nuclear Fuels," or something of that kind which may be a call to action, lobbying, campaigning or whatever.

"God's will," "God's gifts," "gift of Nature," "innate," "natural," or "given" all function in much the same way. Because we have no separate line into the source that will enable us to check the claim that it *is* the source, we are not being told something that leads beyond the things that we know already, the things that were to be explained. But putting expressions of that sort into the place where an explanatory term goes is in effect to make a claim, and, if you like, a warning off: "Don't look for such an explanation; there is none; this is a given, a starting point beyond which we cannot go." We don't have to accept that warning and that claim. We can go on to look for some separately identifiable thing, something that we could aim to produce or prevent (if it is in our power) by way of bringing about or obstructing the thing that is the subject of the explanation.

It is an underlying thesis of this chapter that humanity is not a "natural" but a social and historical species, and that the specifically *human* characteristics of humans are social in origin and that the societies themselves develop historically.[6] Because of the deep opposition between this view and the way of looking at humanity of the individualist program, which aims to start with the individual and the individual's claimed "natural," "innate," or "God-given" abilities, capacities, and tendencies, we need to carry the analysis of the notion of *nature* and *the natural* a bit further.

The natural and *the social* are opposed notions, just as *the natural* and *the historical* are. There has been throughout the above analysis also an opposition to the attempt to provide a "foundation," origin or absolute starting point for "society," social obligation or "the social" in general. *Nature* and *the natural* are designed for just that foundational role. They are supposed to provide the starting point beyond which, we are told, we cannot reach. One should always be suspicious of whatever is offered as "foundation" and "starting point." I am not saying that there are no such things, but only that their credentials need to be closely examined and that they should certainly not be allowed to pass "on the nod."

We have now to go back and look at the question and the concept that were put on the agenda in the attempt to undermine and "delegitimate" the feudal system of rights, duties, customs into which one was thrust at birth with little option. That question was the question of "the origin of society" which, while undermining the feudal picture of a "God-ordained" social order, at the same time generated the individualist picture and forced the appeal to "human nature" in setting out an alternative.

But the notion of "human nature" is one with a historical and if you like ideological function only, and has no substance. In addition, there is no such thing as an account of "the origins of society," any more than there could be an account of "the origin of language," and for much the same reasons. Anything that we try to offer in the way of such an account is going to turn out to be a mythical picture like that of the Social Contract, or a pseudo-explanation employing "blank-cheque" terms like "natural abilities" or "natural tendencies." As we have said, the use of these terms amounts only to a claim that there is no explanation, a claim that is dressed up and put forward as though it were itself an explanation.[7]

There is, and could be, no historic moment of transition, no act, no blinding flash, no individual or collective action or inspiration that marks an instantaneous change of logical category from herd to tribe, from natural or instinctive cries of alarm or pain to meaningful language use. There is no "baby's first word," in the sense of the first utterance of a word, despite the romantic notions of fond parents. The use of a word is distinguished from the mere making of a sound, not by the presence or absence of a "thought" (how would we tell that in a baby?) but by its use instantiating a skill or practice. A single instance does not show us that, even when the sound, if it is a word, would be apt, maybe even clever. That could still be accident. We need a bit of history to tell. The aptness, like that shown sometimes by a parrot's imitation of words, might be the result of conditioning and accident, not skill and intent.

The notion of a *society* involves a body of shared practices, including that of language. A practice and the mastery of a practice are distinguishable from luck and accident or from conditioning only by what is shown over a period. They are, one could say, "historical" notions. Neither a practice nor a society is the kind of thing that can come into existence at an instant or by a single act. ("I am hereby instituting a tradition" is at best a lame joke.)

And to try to give an account of such a mythical "logical" and instantaneous transition from a pre-social disorganization to the complex of practices and obligations that constitute a social organization is to be pushed necessarily into myth and pseudo-explanation because the "explanation" is trying to give an account of something that is itself mythical.

Genuinely to give an account of a mythical notion would be to do something of the sort we have been attempting, that is, to give an account of its symbolism, its function, or the historical reasons for its attraction. But to give an account that takes the myth as historical fact is to generate incoherence and confusion. Among the confusions generated by the myth of the instantaneous creation of society, we can point to how the notion of an *obligation* becomes impenetrably mystified if it is thought to be something that could be created in an instant, *ex nihilo*. Obligations can only arise in a context of practices and expectations, and these are not (logically) the creation of an instant any more than a tradition is.[8]

I hope it is clear that I am not using the word "myth" as a term of abuse. There is nothing wrong with myths: they can be deep and inspiring; they can provide a sense of identity and of how to live. They can do a great many things. What they cannot do is to provide an explanation of the things they are nominally about, for example, the origins of a tribe or of a practice. Nevertheless, the fact that a people hold a certain myth may help us understand and explain many things about them: their reverence for a particular animal, the solemnity of some activity or ritual.

Most societies have foundation myths, and perhaps it might be useful to look on the myth of the Social Contract as the foundation myth of our own society. This way it has a kind of sense that it cannot have as the myth of origin of *society as such*. That notion, we have seen, is one we can't make sense of. Perhaps we should look on the Social Contract as in its own way functioning for our society much as the myth of Romulus and Remus did for the Romans or the Blue Corn Woman, who was "mother of all" the Tewa tribe of New Mexico, does for them.

The Social Contract is a myth to which we refer regularly in seeking to articulate and give the sense of features of our own society and, in a sense to understand ourselves. But if we do that, we must still ask and press the question whether the picture is any longer a helpful one in the way it was in the struggle against feudal institutions; or whether now, in the contemporary world, it brings more darkness than light and inhibits real understanding. (My view is that it does the latter, but that is not our concern here.) Above all, we must not lose sight of its mythic character and set ourselves problems that take the myth as fact and would not be problems otherwise. The point of this whole analysis that we have been engaged in is to bring out how our era has done just that and framed questions and set problems on the assumption that they were dealing with realities and not merely articulating a myth. The result of that taking myth for reality is, as usual, a confusion that generates non-problems and senseless notions.

It is a fact about our era that it has been particularly concerned to find foundations, to seek out origins and starting points that stand outside any historical process. This search was forced on our era partly[9] by the individualism which it took as its starting point. Bringing those individuals together out of that separation required an external reality and a method of reaching it that would be available to all. This required the same starting point for all and the same method of proceeding. Hence the great search for "foundations" and for "scientific method" that has so occupied our time.

And the problem of "origins" was a problem for a secularizing era as it was not for the previous one. In the days in which one could talk about "Christendom," the problem had a ready answer: God was the origin and the fountainhead of everything. The new era took over that old ahistorical viewpoint and the old question of origins and foundations that could be posed within it, and then tried to manufacture a new answer by giving that originating and foundational role to an abstract and reified notion of *Nature*.

Nature was meant to stand over and above and outside of the happenings of this world in the way God had. This "Nature" was even endowed with causal powers to determine the happenings in the world from outside. At least they were *some* sort of powers that allowed what people came to call Nature's "laws" to determine the course of the happenings in this world below. Perhaps we should call them "Metaphysical" powers since the power of the "laws" to affect happenings is not one that any scientist would set about trying to investigate. The incoherence and illogicality of the notion of these phantom powers infects the determinism that has so occupied philosophers of our era. A picture has got them into a logical tangle.

Though there is no way of making secular and scientific sense of that picture of Nature and its laws standing outside and antecedent to the world and its happenings, and somehow bringing them about, many things conspired to hurry the secularizing philosophers past the incoherences and to seize on that picture and its associated pair of inverting spectacles. For one thing, they had to start from where they were, and that was within a biblically based world-view and a conception of explanation that was deeply ahistorical. After the seven days of God's creation of the world and everything in it, all the species of plants and animals, the world itself had been roughly as it is. One of the few real historical events in the Bible, events marking a historical change, was the expulsion from Eden. That marked a change for humanity and a change in humanity. All the rest, the stories of floods and plagues, the destruction of cities, the oppressions of one tribe by another, and so forth, did not mark any historical change. Apart from the expulsion only two events, Moses receiving the Tablets of the Law and the Coming of Christ, could be described as marking a historical change. But for that, humanity came as it is, and the world and the animals and plants too. There was no sense of historical development or change in humanity. Those moments of historical change were brought about by God, but no such historical changes are described that had their source within the world itself, no secular history.

This was the view of things that the philosophers of the seventeenth century were secularizing and adapting for the new mechanistic/scientific outlook. If your project is to create a comprehensive world-view out of the mechanical/scientific understanding of things, you can hardly escape giving to Nature a transcendental role and character like those of God in the world-view you are adapting and secularizing. The difficulty is that while God is, in the religious world-view, an object of awe and worship and ultimately mysterious and surpassing understanding, Nature is, in the secular scientific world-view, precisely the object of study by the sciences and their business to understand. This makes fatal the incoherences in the notion of a determining or causal relation between a transcendental Nature and concrete happenings. The relation between a transcendental God and the happenings of the world could be a matter of awe and mystery in religion. The relation between a transcendental Nature and those same happenings could hardly claim that same privilege of mysteriousness. Subjected to the tests of rationality appropriate to the secular, scientific view, that picture comes out as mere muddle and incoherence.

There is no real sense that we can give to the notion of "Nature's laws." The notion of *law* is an inappropriate borrowing that obscures more than it illuminates precisely because of the implication that goes with it of a separate legislator or legislature and of sanctions. That is what separates the notion of *law* from the notions of *custom* or *habit.* At first philosophers and scientists tended to talk about "God's decrees" or "enactments," but those phrases hardly bear much inspection either. How was God supposed to "legislate" for himself? Was He supposed to be binding Himself always to act in the same way? It is hard to see what could be meant by that notion, and it has the air about it of the old nonsense question whether God could create a stone too heavy for Him to lift. And, on the other hand, what sense are we supposed to give to the notion of "legislating" for plants, animals or minerals? Are they really supposed to be "kept in line" and forced to adhere to the path that has been laid down for them? We are here dealing with pictures and metaphors, and not very helpful ones either. They are inviting us to confusion and muddle if we take them at all seriously.

Perhaps the way out of these muddles is to go back to consider carefully the Aristotelian notion of *physis,* which, though it is normally translated as "nature," functions in an entirely different way from the notion we have been discussing. I have already discussed in chapter 10 the heroic measures Descartes took in an effort to transform or replace that notion and the associated notions of *essence* and *substance.* He is willing to decompose himself and the rest of the world into discrete moments with no connection or continuity so that nothing in the world is allowed its own internal source of continuity or identity through change. In fact, the result of this decomposition is that there can be no *thing* that changes, and therefore no change, though Descartes does not himself see or draw this consequence. That was left to others.

Descartes's project there was to make the notion of *Nature* as capable of playing for the mechanical/scientific world-view the role that God played in the theological view of the world that had been dominant in the feudal era. This required that *nature* be projected out of this world to become a transcendental Nature (which merited capitalization as an encompassing unitary thing). This turns the Aristotelian notion upside-down. The Aristotelian *physis* was no kind of "thing" that could be extracted or separated from whatever was said to have a "nature" or "an internal principle (*arche*) of movement or change." On the contrary, it was simply part of what identified the thing as of *this* sort. There are two elements in our identification of anything. One is its formation or construction. The second is its behavior. The *physis* of a thing is just that behavior we look for in identifying it as water, or a boomerang, or a human being. Generally, formation and behavior go together. When they don't it sets us a problem, as when some Russian scientists in the 1970s thought they had found a form of water that behaved anomalously. Until that turned out not to be the case, this anomalous form was given the provisional title "polywater."

The other important point about the Aristotelian *physis* is that it is in no sense an *explanation* of anything. It is not fitted for that role. Being simply the behavioral or developmental part of what we look for in identifying the thing, it can in no way *explain* that development or behavior, and it was not meant to.

There were two ways in which the seventeenth century made a nonsense of the notion of *nature*. One was in trying to give it the role of *explaining* anything. The other was in trying to project it out of the world as a transcendental something that stood over and above the happenings of the world, directing and determining them from outside. This introduced a second layer of nonsense since there can be no account of that would-be "governing" or "determining" relation between such an abstract, external, and transcendental entity on the one hand and the concrete things and happenings around us on the other.

But there is a subversive aspect to the Aristotelian notion of *physis*. Since the notion only records the behavioral and developmental tests that we apply in our identifications of types and sorts of things ("natural" kinds), the notion does not carry with it the implication of an external source of the identifications we make. The expression "natural kinds" now takes on a new and demystified sense. Working with the Aristotelian notion we can no longer read the phrase "natural kind" as something set up and visited on us by an "external" and transcendental "Nature." The Aristotelian notion won't let us give sense to that (if it ever had any). Nor will it allow us to give sense to the idea that those identifications are dictated to us by an internal "human nature" which would presumably be absolute, ahistorical, and species-wide.

This leaves it open to us to say that the kinds we recognize are a function of the projects and the interests that are bound up with the way of life of our particular society, or with features and projects of any life that is to be counted as "human" at all. But that remark opens up a whole range of issues that need a separate comprehensive treatment. In the meantime it will no doubt attract the dreaded epithet "relativist." Applying that label may give some satisfaction to those who affix it, but the act hardly advances things philosophically.

13 Newton, Euclid, and the foundation of geometry

For the seventeenth century and for some time afterward, Euclidian geometry was an ideal of knowledge that was both certain and objective. It was taken as giving us unassailable and universal truths about the world. As such, it was an inspiration that gave a hope, an example of what humanity was capable of, a standard of achievement, and a goal for other fields of knowledge. At the same time, it set the philosophers immense problems because they were working with an individualistic picture of humanity that laid on them the requirement that any account of knowledge had to trace its sources back to capacities and conceptions that were vested in each separated individual independently of any social relation or background. Any such program is faced with immense, even intractable, problems in trying to give an account of the two most striking aspects of geometry, its certainty and necessity on the one hand and its applicability to the things about us on the other.

Knowledge had to be shown to be, at least potentially, the product of an individual search and struggle that begins with materials available to each human being, unmediated, and undeveloped by social relations of cooperation, teaching or learning.

Descartes requires us to test and doubt all that we have received from others and not to accept it until we have proved it for ourselves. Hobbes is a bit more liberal in allowing us to learn from others and thus to advance further than we could on our own. But he insists that this learning from others (which language makes possible) is merely handy ("commodious" is his word) and not essential. We could each do it on our own, and, given additional time, would get to the same place that learning from and comparing notes with others makes possible.

This is the common background of picture and project that joined those two great combatants, the rationalists and the empiricists. In a sense, they differed only over details. Are we to seek the source and basis of knowledge in the native endowments of the individual, endowments of reason and ideas? Or are we to look for the beginning of our account of knowledge in the interactions between the individual and an external world, interactions mediated only by the senses and giving rise to what they called "sense experience?"

I have used the word "interaction," but the picture of the senses and sense experience with which the empiricists worked was of a passive receptivity. The raw materials of knowledge, sense experiences, were seen as wrought upon the individual by mechanical processes involving the impinging of various forms of energy on the various sense organs. Once those energetic emanations from the encompassing world had done their work, the resulting "experiences" were put into the hands of the individual, who was then allowed to work on them in various ways, "abstracting," "comparing," and so forth. From these activities, knowledge was supposed to arise.

Parts of this picture are very persuasive, mainly because there is still a bit of the mechanist in all of us these days, and we have not yet entirely let go of the great and seductive image of a single comprehensive picture and vocabulary that will describe and explain all things. The only alternative seems to be a kind of mysticism.

One trouble with the picture, however, is that it goes against many facts of common observation, facts which support a view that seeing, hearing and the other senses involve skills that are taught and learned, that the sense organs are not merely passive recorders but are *used by us* in an active process of inquiry and observation. Those activities also involve taught skills and training. We look and listen and observe; we don't just passively receive. And we are *taught* to observe, to pay attention, to see and hear and taste and discriminate. When we learn to speak, we learn to hear too. Native speakers of Japanese, in learning their language, do not learn to hear the difference between an "r" and an "l" as English speakers do. Being taught to hear that difference will involve, for a Japanese speaker, being taught to make those different sounds. And learning to draw is at the same time learning to see. Active and passive or receptive capacities are not so distinct as we have been led to believe by the empiricist program and by the mechanical world-view of which it was part.

The mechanistic picture pretty well reverses this fact of common observation, making the sense organs a passive part of that surrounding world and not something that really belongs to us as something that we can use and use with varying degrees of skill. According to that mechanistic picture, we use only the *results* of the passive, mechanical operation of the senses and not the organs themselves. One could even say that in this picture they are not properly speaking *our* organs at all, but only something through which the external world operates to produce experiences in us. The experiences would on this view belong to us all right, because we work with them and make them serve us. But, in the mechanistic picture of things, the same could not be said for the sense organs themselves in that they could not be described as being developed, trained or used by us and made to serve us. They are viewed as merely passive, indifferent and untrainable. This picture hardly does justice to common experience. It is not so much an alternative to mysticism as a variety of it.

But the unrealities involved in the empiricist picture have their counterparts in the rationalist. For the rationalist program was also shaped to meet those requirements to find the source and foundation of knowledge in what was available to the individual as individual and not as a member of a community with others. Our job will be to bring out the difficulties, even impossibilities, that result from that requirement when the program comes up against the agreed facts about geometry: its certainty on the one hand, and on the other, the fact that it applies to the world we inhabit, allowing us to work with it and to make predictions on the basis of it. Those two facts about geometry coming together in the one subject make difficulties for both sides of the rationalist/empiricist divide.

The rationalists were happy enough with the certainty and the universality of what geometry showed. So far as they were concerned, the certainty and necessity of geometry made difficulties only for the empiricists. Their own problems were seen as lying only with accounting for geometry's applicability. Experience and perception, they said persuasively, can in no way give us that certainty and that universality. Experience is finite and limited and cannot leap beyond itself to reach out to the infinite cases about which the universality of geometry gives us certainty. That universality and certainty must come from somewhere else. The rationalists, from their perspective, could point to the universality and necessity that attach to concepts and to reason in naming a source for that universality. Descartes even says in *Meditations* III "I have in me the notion of the infinite earlier than the finite."

Even if we accept that claim (which we need not, nor need we accept, as Descartes's project requires, that it be a universal truth about all humans), it still has to face the empiricist question how the presence of such ideas in the mind can tell us anything about the world outside us. It is this problem that forces Descartes's appeal to the Ontological Argument to give him an example of an idea whose very nature is supposed to supply a guarantee of the external existence of a referent. Whether or not the idea of God carries that guarantee contained in it, the ideas and the propositions of geometry pretty clearly do not. So we could not even attempt to generate that sort of argument to account for the certainty that we have about geometry and the complete confidence with which we apply it and work with it in designing, and building, and predicting the behavior of the things about us.

We require a second guarantee to be attached to the guarantee that Descartes wants to attach to the idea of God, a guarantee that the God guaranteed by that idea will Himself guarantee a connection to the world and a universal applicability of those geometrical truths which we discover by analysis of those ideas we find in ourselves (or that God is supposed to have put there). Those "native endowments" of mind that are claimed to be the birthright of each individual (claimed on no evidence beyond what it is that they are supposed to explain) are thus additionally claimed to be connected to a world outside the individual mind by a rope that is beginning to ravel pretty badly, if it ever did have any strength and reality. The whole enterprise is beginning to look like a misguided pursuit of a wrong-headed goal. We shall come back to that.

Kant hit on the ingenious solution of making the necessity that attaches to geometry a *conditional* necessity. Geometry describes the properties things must exhibit *if they are to be regarded or experienced as external*. That move solves one problem only to pose another. What is the source of that linkage, that conditional necessity? *Why* is it that we can see as external only those things that exhibit Euclidian properties? If we are then told in answer that it is part of the constitution or nature of the human mind, we are not being told very much. In fact we have not got any further than where we started, for the only facts that could be brought forward in support of this claim would be precisely those feelings of certainty and sense of necessity that were to be explained.

And, even if we were to accept that "constitutional" account, what then could be pointed to as the source of the certainty that we would have to have that human beings would continue to be constituted thus? If the "constitutional" account were taken as substantive, that question would be a legitimate one. Kant's usual move in circumstances like that would not really work here. He could not very well make that linkage between the Euclidian properties and regarding something as external a *constitutive* property of humanity or of rational beings as such. We would hardly be prepared to make that a *test* of humanity or of rationality and withhold those descriptions from anyone who did not mark a distinction between internal and external in that Euclidian way.

A similar move to ours is made by Locke against the rationalist appeals to *the innate* in explaining the certainty and necessity of geometry (or anything else, for that matter). Though he presents his argument as a denial of the existence of such innate notions and innate principles, the effect of the argument is to show that the notion of *the innate* is in fact an empty one with no explanatory value. It has no more explanatory force than the "dormative virtue" put forward by Molière's young man in explanation of the ability of opium to send one to sleep. It amounts only to a renaming of the thing to be explained (though, as I said in chapter 12, the naming can point enquiry in the right direction). That is, we could find no evidence to support the claim of the existence of "innate ideas," "native endowments," and the like, none beyond precisely those abilities that those supposed entities are supposed to explain.

[In the light of the contrary hopes of Chomsky and others that physiological advances may reveal common structures that will *explain* posited innate linguistic abilities, we have, perhaps, to take notice of the logical relation between the notions of *structure* on the one hand and *ability* on the other. That is, a structure may be the *condition* of an ability and of the possibility of exercising that ability, but the structure is not the *cause* or the *explanation* of that ability, its development or its exercise. At least not in the sense that the words "cause" and "explanation" bear these days. If we were talking in terms of the Aristotelian "causes" it would be different. In Aristotle's terms the structure would be the *material* cause of the ability, which would also have a *formal*, identifying cause. If we were talking about a human ability, and not just, say, the ability of gold to resist corrosion, there would probably be a *final* cause as well, some good that ability serves. And if we were to go on to talk about the development of that ability or its exercise on some occasion, we could talk also about what initiated that development or that exercise, the so-called "efficient" or "moving" cause.

But I am sure that Chomsky and the others have not got the Aristotelian senses of "cause" in mind, but rather the modern sense of "that which brings something about." And this does not characterize the relation between a structure and an ability. If we were to identify some physiological structure associated with, and a condition of, linguistic or grammatical ability, it could be identified in someone who had never learned to speak. The structure could not guarantee the ability, as a "cause" in that modern sense must.]

The upshot of all this is that the notions of "innate ideas," "laws of thought" and the rest are essentially "fifth wheels" whose turning is not connected with anything or doing any work. They certainly can't give us any real understanding of that difficult combination of necessity and objective applicability that geometry seems to present to us. They merely redescribe what it is that we are seeking to understand, what we know already, attaching to it a name or characterization that cannot be given a separate sense or description.

There are two functions to be served by this brief sketch of the nature of the difficulties facing the rationalists and the empiricists in giving an account of the facts about geometry on which they both agreed. The chief one is to make it possible to see the radical and subversive nature of the view of geometry that Newton gives us in the preface to the first edition of the *Principia*. The other, connected, function is to prepare the ground for the recognition that the source of the troubles which they faced, and Newton bypassed, was the requirement which both the rationalists and the empiricists laid on themselves that any account of geometrical knowledge trace the source and the foundation of it back to the individual, to materials and methods given to or available to each separate individual. This, I want to say, was the signpost that pointed them into the impasse.

Not only that, but that task which they took on themselves was a gratuitous one, gratuitous in the sense that it was a response to historical circumstances rather than to philosophical imperatives. [That is rather a long story, which I have tried to tell in the previous chapter. Roughly it is that the individualistic program was philosophy's homage to the new "mechanical world-view" and that it was also a necessary element in the Social Contract theories that were being used to subvert feudalism. Here I would only add that I don't regard responsiveness to historical circumstances as in itself a disabling failure of philosophical objectivity and detachment. On the contrary, I don't see how else philosophy is to have any function and significance in human life. Helping to identify and characterize "the sickness of a time" rather than merely contributing to it is, to my mind, philosophy's most important function. I would want to go on to characterize the individualistic picture and program as a contribution to that sickness rather than to its understanding.]

Before looking at Newton's radical dissent from the prevailing individualist program, I would like to look at one other approach to characterizing geometry, the formalist one. The formalist program marches boldly past all the problems of understanding the applicability and usefulness of geometry or any other branch of mathematics, and presents them as human creations. Mathematical entities are created by setting out a set of axioms that specify their properties and relations to one another. If some things are found to "satisfy" the axioms, to exhibit the properties and stand in the specified relations, well and good. Bertrand Russell mischievously said, "Thus mathematics may be defined as the subject in which we never know what we are talking about, nor whether what we are saying is true."[1] Of course, "defined" can hardly be allowed to pass, but if we modify the "know" to "care" we have roughly the formalist program. Hilbert, therefore, does not introduce definitions into his little book *The Foundations of Geometry*, and perhaps not surprisingly, finds Euclid deficient in the axioms he sets out in the *Elements*. [We shall come back to that because one of the central points I want to make is that a proper understanding of Euclid's definitions, particularly his definition of "straight line," which has so mystified the commentators, will support the view of geometry taken by Newton. And the two together present a view of the foundations of geometry that is subversive of the individualist picture and program.]

If we make axioms do the work of definitions, as Hilbert does, we have to face the question of how the axioms themselves are to get the sense that allows them to do the job of defining and characterizing. It is one thing to say that the terms "point," "line," "surface," "plane," and "straight line" can be left as blanks that will be filled in by the collective force of the axioms of *connection*, of *order*, of *congruence*, and so forth, but what about the other terms that appear in those axioms? How are we supposed to come to an understanding of terms like "distinct" as applied to points, or "determine" as describing their relation to a line, in particular, a "straight" line? How are we to understand those notions in advance of, and separately from, our understanding of those terms and notions that the axioms are set forth as characterizing? How can the notion of *distinct* as applied specifically to points be known or understood apart from an understanding of those things to which it is being applied? Or *in common*? It is not as though there is a completely general notion of *distinctness* that we can learn in some other context and then bring to these axioms that involve supposedly blank and undefined terms, in order to circumscribe and limit those blanks.

Hilbert's axioms cannot in any real sense carry out their assigned function of defining, or at least circumscribing, those blank terms, because the expressions whose meanings are assumed and given that job have senses that are specific to just those things that are to be defined. The expressions that are given the defining role have not got some general sense that can be understood apart from those particular applications to the things that are to be defined and delimited. The blanks are not really blanks at all, and the sense of the axioms requires, and is trading on, a prior understanding of the supposedly undefined terms that appear in them. Without that tacit understanding we would not know how to understand the terms that are supposed to be doing the real work.

Take the notion of *common* or *in common*. The sense of "in common" that is involved in "having a point in common" or "a line in common" is not to be got from knowing what it is to have an ancestor in common, or a love of horses in common. That geometrical sense of the word is specific and applies only to points, lines, angles, and so on. Though there may be some analogies and broad metaphorical connections with other uses, that sense cannot simply be found elsewhere and then imported to give the meaning and force needed for the axioms.

But of course, any definitions that we may want to introduce will have to face just these same questions that the axioms do. Where do they get their sense? We now have to try to deal with that question.

Perhaps we should start by noticing how the commentators on Euclid's *Elements* have struggled without much success to find *any* sense at all in Euclid's definition of "straight line." There is no doubt that at first sight it does seem to be impenetrably mysterious: "A straight line is a line that lies evenly along the points of itself." [We shall later give much attention to that definition because understanding it can give us an important insight into the nature of geometry – so long as we look carefully at the source of that understanding and of the sense that the definition has.] I think that the great Euclidian scholar Sir Thomas Heath and the other commentators on that definition of Euclid's had such difficulty with it because they were looking for its sense in the wrong direction. On the whole, they were looking for the sense *within* the words themselves and not in something beyond geometry itself which they might refer to and draw on for their sense.

As many have pointed out down the centuries, the attempt to define everything in words alone is bound to end by trying to eat its own tail. We have somehow to break out of the circle. The rationalists and the empiricists thought they could break out by having some words get their sense by directly referring to "simple ideas," whether these were original endowments or the offspring of sense experience. And in the early part of this century, G. E. Moore put into circulation the phrase "simple unanalyzable qualities" of which the exemplar was "yellow" and that to which he applied it was "good." It is, of course, tempting to take "straight line" in this way and say that we simply have to "intuit" it, or something of that kind. And, not surprisingly, some commentators did take that path.

I am not sure that the notion of *simple idea* and that of *simple, unanalyzable quality* are as perspicuous as their proponents have imagined. They have about them the air of the last resource of the desperate rather than the unforced discovery of the illuminating idea. And then we have to ask about the word "intuit": what kind of work it is being asked to do here?

In fact, all these notions create more problems than they solve. And harder ones too. But I don't propose to try to draw those problems out here and to show the impossibilities involved in trying to break out of the circle in that particular way. My aim will be the more positive one of trying to show another way of breaking out of that circle, one that actually makes sense of the Euclidian definition and one that helps to bring out the way in which Newton's view of geometry was radically subversive of the views and the program of his professed great admirer, Locke. Newton's account of the foundations of geometry was in fact subversive of the whole individualistic paradigm and program that governed the practice of philosophy in that era and continues its influence into ours.

Newton describes geometry in the preface to the first edition of the *Principia* as "founded in mechanical practice," and his account of the reasons for this only compounds the disagreement with his admirers and increases the distance between his view and the prevailing individualist program for philosophy. It also shows that Locke, despite his great admiration, can never have read the preface carefully or considered it deeply. For a *practice* is, after all, a social notion, something that is developed, refined, transmitted socially, like a language. It is not something available to the atomized individual with which modern philosophy has sought to start. [It is here also that the deeply challenging force of Wittgenstein's remarks about rules and private languages make themselves felt.] A practice is not something an atomized separated individual can engage in. The notion of a solecism or a mistake in practice is a social notion, as I have argued in chapter 9.

And it is that notion of a *solecism* or gaffe that gives us the notions of a *practice* or a *tradition* and shows that these are notions that apply to social groups and not to individuals. That it is a social notion comes out in the fact that the whole of a linguistic community cannot *collectively* commit a solecism. The group collectively *defines* what a solecism is. The individual, on the other hand, can commit one but cannot define one. A habit, which *is* something individual, is not a practice in the sense meant. A deviation from a habitual pattern is just that. It is not thereby a mistake or a solecism. An individual has habits or customs, not traditions. Though the individual may *share* in a tradition, the tradition is of the group. I may say that "It is my custom to . . ." and that will pass, but if I say "I have a tradition of . . .," I am being pompous and inaccurate.

In its very root, the notion of a *tradition* is of something "handed on" or "given," and this involves a social relation. Traditions are transmitted by the group, not invented by an individual. Though an individual may influence a tradition or a practice, as, for example, Shakespeare influenced the English language, it is not for the individual to found one. "I am hereby establishing a tradition" is at best a hackneyed joke.

These points have to be made because the shreds of mechanism that still cling to our era bring with them a nominalism that resists understanding of anything that cannot be attributed to or be found in individuals.[2] And if we say that the individual "participates" in the practice or tradition, but does not own it, we have to be careful to distinguish that notion of "participation" from the generalized and metaphorical sense given to it by Plato that allowed it to stand between even inanimate things and some transcendental entities, the Forms. There is nothing transcendental or mystical about the notion of a *practice* or a *tradition*. Practices belong to definite social groups and societies, and to definite historical periods. Practices may develop and change, and they may disappear or be displaced by other practices. We may hope, for example, that the primitive and repellent practice of female circumcision may disappear, along with the conception of property in the female, and especially her womb, that is embodied in it.

Plato made our task of getting a clear grasp of the notion of a *practice* or a *tradition* difficult for us by his generalized and metaphorical use of the notion of *participation* (*methexis*) to describe the relation of concrete objects to a mystified and transcendental "realm." We need to cut away that metaphor and get back to an original sense in which participation is something that humans do, a notion that is primarily a social notion. [*Methexis*, the word Plato uses for his own purposes, was used earlier to describe things such as "being a partner or accomplice with," "being a member of" a party, a conspiracy, etc., "sharing goods," "being in on the joke," "taking part in," all of them human activities, not logical or metaphysical relations.] The notion of *participation* can perhaps be extended to herd animals and the "social" insects, but it is only making trouble and mystifying things to try to extend it, as Plato wants, to the inanimate. I may participate in a riot or a rout, but the stone does not "participate" in a landslide.

Participation can perhaps be taken to be the most basic social notion. The games that parents play with infants and young children can usefully be seen as the beginnings of the process of "socializing" them, turning them into social beings. The reaction of the infant and the joining in of the game is perhaps the first step in that process. We know from the sketchy reports of "wolf children" that if this socialization does not take place within a certain period, it will have only a very limited success later on. That participation and that "joining in" that is the beginning of the socialization of the infant provides us with an utterly different conception of the beginnings of human society from the abstract and legalistic conception of the Social Contract. It also gives us a conception of how it is that something is outside the individual, something that is there for the individual to "participate in" which does not have to be consigned to some mystified, transcendental "world."

Practices are not embodied in the individuals individually. They are outside each of them individually. They are there for each individual to learn and to participate in. On the other hand, the practice is not outside the participants taken collectively and diachronically. The group, taken together, does not face the practice as something external and apart, excepting as something inherited from previous generations. That is seen in the fact that practices, like traditions, customs, institutions, and techniques, can change and develop, arise and disappear.

We may find it mysterious and difficult to understand how a practice or a tradition can stand outside each, so that each can be a participant in something that is in a sense external, while at the same time the practice and the tradition do not stand outside all collectively. But that is because we lose sight of the fact that the practice consists precisely in the *agreement* between the participants, and *agreement* is not something that an individual can do alone. Nor is it something external to those who are in agreement.

But we must keep sight of the historical element since it is that which reinforces and emphasizes that sense of the externality of the practice or tradition into which the individual is born or inducted. The agreement or the practice is not just a synchronic agreement amongst contemporary individuals, as the Social Contract myth had it pictured. Any practice or tradition will have a history and will have been transmitted and developed from generation to generation. But that handing on will give each individual a sense of it coming from elsewhere, a sense that can be misread as showing that the practice has its source and belongs, along with language or the sciences, to a world entirely outside and separate from humanity. That misunderstanding of the nature of the externality is the source of mystification and alienation in which what is essentially human comes to be seen as external and transcendent.

It is in just that way that we attribute to "market forces," for example, a life of their own as though they stood outside human practices that have developed historically. Because our era has generally rejected historical forms of understanding in favor of scientific forms, we have been unable to see the human creative force behind historical developments such as the domination of the market. That creative input is there even though the actual outcome was not something foreseen or intended. The scientific mode of understanding as it has been developed in the modern era requires that such things be shown to be necessary and inevitable, as having been waiting in the wings, implicit in nature, whether in something called "human nature" or in an abstracted "Nature" that has been projected outward and transcendentalized.

It was the business of the classical economists, for example, to present the market and the associated capitalist mode of organizing social, production and property relations as "natural" and "inevitable" rather than as the result of practices adopted and developed by humanity. It is ironical, though perhaps not surprising, that Marx, who regarded these as human and historical developments and not as coming from an eternal source, should have been so resolutely labeled "determinist" instead of those economists, past and present, who regard market relations as inevitable and eternal.

So both mystery and mystification have become attached to the notion of *practices*. Mystery comes from the fact that they will not fit into a certain program of explanation, and the mystification is the result of being told that certain practices and institutions like the market are "natural" and "necessary developments" in human life. That was one of the hidden messages in the individualistic program with its inevitable appeal to a notion of *human nature*, whether a sentient or a rational "nature." We have to unpick that mystery and loosen the grip of that mystification by getting an understanding of what it is that shapes the practices of different societies, coming to see them as generated by the activities and projects of a way of life rather than as something imposed by a mystified, transcendentalized "nature." But that is the project of another day.

We have had to take this long detour because of the great difficulty that the notion of a *practice* has for an era that has not quite given up its hopes for a comprehensive mechanical account of things. In fact, the two are incompatible. That is why it is ironical and unfortunate that Locke, who gave philosophy the role of "under laborer" to science, did not understand more deeply the Newtonian science to which he was proposing to attach himself as servant. Because, although Newton describes himself as giving the "mathematical principles" of "natural philosophy" (by which he here means mechanics and celestial mechanics), he goes on to describe the mathematics he uses as "founded in mechanical practice." So that practice lies at the root of all. And to make this completely explicit, he gives the following as his reasons for this view:

> the description of right lines and circles, upon which geometry is founded, belongs to mechanics. Geometry does not teach us to draw these lines, but requires them to be drawn, for it requires the learner be first taught to describe (i.e. *draw*) these accurately before he enters upon geometry, then it shows how by these operations problems may be solved. To describe right lines and circles are problems, but not geometrical problems. The solution to these problems is required from mechanics, and by geometry the use of them, when so solved, is shown; and it is the glory of geometry that from those few principles *brought from without* [my italics] it is able to produce so many things. Therefore geometry is founded in mechanical practice and is nothing but that part of universal mechanics which accurately proposes and demonstrates the art of measuring. But since the *manual arts* [my italics] are chiefly employed in the moving of bodies, it happens that geometry is commonly referred to their magnitude, and mechanics to their motion.
>
> (*Principia,* Preface to the first edition)

In giving this account of geometry and its foundation in practices and in the "manual arts" Newton not only brings geometry down from its pinnacle of abstraction standing "over and above" the world, but also sets himself outside the whole stream of philosophy of his time and its individualist tenor. Newton's view cannot be folded into that individualistic program for the reasons I have tried to bring out in the discussion of the notion of a *practice* or a *tradition* (and we could add Newton's term "art" to that list as something that the individual learns from others and participates in.)

Because of the importance I am attributing to it perhaps it needs to be brought out that the choice of the word "practice" by Newton is deliberate and appropriate. This comes out particularly in his saying, "To describe right lines and circles are problems, but not geometrical problems. The solution to these problems is required from mechanics." But this is brought out and clear only if we keep in mind that the word "describe" does not mean for Newton, as it would for us, "paint a word picture" of the thing or give a definition. It refers to the practical activity of *drawing* the line or the circle and to the skill and means for doing so, means that Newton says come from mechanical "art" and "practice." This will perhaps become clearer below, when we come to examine the definitions of "straight line."

Newton's account would have put Locke into a bind if he had taken note of and digested Newton's view of his own work. But Locke didn't. He saw Newton's work through the distorting spectacles of the great mechanistic program that fired the imagination of the scientific revolution. That great mechanistic enterprise did not see mechanics as Newton did. Its dreams of explaining everything "from outside" including human behavior would have crashed on the rock of the "mechanical practice" on which Newton founded geometry and thence the "mathematical principles" of his own great system. Those mechanical practices belong to humanity. They are something developed by humans.

We must add, however, that those mechanical practices are not developed in a vacuum but in a struggle to shape and live in a world that is by turns resistant and compliant. They are not, that is, arbitrary creations, but are shaped by aims and goals that are being pursued in that struggle. Nevertheless, they are not external impositions. There could be a form of life with goals sufficiently different from ours that its particular struggle would generate different practices. A form of life and practices that arose among dolphins, say, would no doubt be radically different from our own and would not give rise to those mechanical practices of building and fitting things together that lead to the discovery of straight lines. Their life wouldn't generate a need for the chalk line or the smoothing plane (or their underwater equivalents.)

Those discoveries, then, are not the external imposition of a "world governed by blind cause" as the grand poetical picture offered by mechanistic determinism would have it. That mechanistic picture and its engendered hope (or despair) are incoherent, as is the program of explanation they set in motion. It is the mother of mystery, not clarity.

Now let us turn our attention back to the definitions of "straight line" to see how this account of Newton's allows us to break out of the circle of definitions of words by words and, beyond that, to make sense of definitions that, taken by themselves, seem unhelpful or useless.

In antiquity there were three definitions of "straight line," and none of them make any sense or are of any use unless they are referred to practices. Two of them refer to methods of *testing* for straightness and one, perhaps the most famous, refers to a standard carpenter's way of *producing* a straight line. The oldest definition of straightness is Socrates' "that of which the middle obscures the ends." This doesn't puzzle us for long because we pretty quickly connect it with the carpenter's practice of sighting along something to test its straightness. The word "obscures" gives us that. But it is not a definition that can have a genuine role and function at the foundations of geometry itself, though it might have a role in geometrical optics. That is, it does not give us significant *geometrical* properties of straight lines, ones that would enable us to work with them geometrically. It relates geometry to optics.

The same is true of the classic definition of the straight line as "the least line between two points." This is the definition we all learned at school: "A straight line is the shortest distance between two points." Taken as a definition in words alone, it gives us no help. What are we to make of "least?" Some process of measurement seems indicated, and so we are already pointed in the direction of a practice and a technique alien to elementary geometry.

But in fact the derivation and reference of this definition is obvious, although its usefulness in geometry is not. It comes from the carpenter's chalk line as a way of producing straight lines, a technique which was known already in Homeric times. It is certainly true of a straight line that it is the least, but can that fact be used as a definition? It is not even certain that it guarantees uniqueness, since there might be a tie for shortness without our being able to show that this implied identity. Archimedes (*On the Sphere and the Cylinder*) makes this would-be definition into an assumption and a fact about straight lines, and Hilbert in *The Foundations of Geometry* felt it necessary to introduce a special axiom of uniqueness to the effect that "Any two points completely determine a straight line." The force of "completely determine" is not spelled out, but we can take it as aiming at guaranteeing uniqueness because of the theorems that Hilbert derives from that axiom.

The introduction of the practices of measurement and comparison that come with the notions of *shortest* and *least* makes that school definition not a suitable one with which to found geometry, or to do anything much in geometry itself. The measurement of the length of curves would have to be involved (since curved lines might be among the candidates for the title "least"), and that is already too difficult and sophisticated a problem for geometry. When Euclid himself comes to make comparisons of length, he does it by geometrical construction and appeal to his "common notions" about the addition or subtraction of equals, and so forth, not by measurement in the ordinary sense of applying a tape or a yardstick. The "shortest distance" definition is best left to the carpenters and their chalk line. (David Sherry has pointed out to me the etymological connection between "straight line" and "stretched linen," but this is not enough to give the school definition any geometrical use.)

So, now we are left facing Euclid's own definition and what to make of it. "A straight line is a line which lies evenly with the points of itself." If we set ourselves the problem of trying to puzzle out the meaning of it by examining the meanings of the words in it, we are lost. No amount of excogitation will get sense out of it. What are we to make of the key phrase "lies evenly with?" The early commentator Proclus attempts to expound it as meaning that the straight line "occupies a distance equal to that between the points on it" (whatever *that* might mean). And, having thus introduced the notion of *distance*, after floundering around a while, Proclus sinks gratefully, and not unnaturally, into the arms of the "shortest distance" definition.

Sir Thomas Heath, to whom we owe a perpetual debt of gratitude for his fine edition of *The Elements*, was entirely baffled by the definition, and says that "the language is hopelessly obscure." He tries to expound it as meaning a line "that presents the same shape at, and relatively to all points on it, without any irregular or unsymmetrical feature distinguishing one part or side of it from another." But all those notions of *shape, symmetry,* and *regularity* are more sophisticated and difficult and require the thing we are trying to define.

We need to break out of that word-circle. And in a sense, Heath sees this in saying, "The truth is that Euclid was attempting the impossible. As Pleiderer says, 'It seems as though the notion of a *straight line*, owing to its simplicity, cannot be explained by any regular definition which does not introduce words already containing in themselves, by implication, the notion to be defined.'"[3] This is the point at which the definition circle has begun to eat its own tail.

But if we look at Euclid as Newton did, we can see that he was not attempting the impossible. He was not attempting to define his basic notions in terms of notions that would have to be more basic still. Euclid's geometry is not a system of conceptions only, and the relations between them, conceptions that are generated out of the mind itself, or out of the air. It is, as Newton said, founded in practices and consists in the solutions to practical problems of how "to draw a line such that . . . ." "to cut a given straight line so that . . . ." The "propositions" are proposals of problems of "how to" and their solutions. There are, to be sure, propositions that simply describe relationships, such as the famous proposition 47 (Pythagoras' Theorem), but these are in fact adjuncts to the solutions to the practical problems.

Euclid is describing an art or a technique, not an abstract intellectual system of ideas as he was later taken to be by an era whose project was on the one hand too sublime and abstract, and on the other hand too individualistic, to be able to give space and importance to those earth-bound and essentially social notions of practices and practical problems. But if Euclid's geometry is rooted in practices and issues in practices, what particular practice can we point to by way of explicating and giving sense to that mysterious and baffling formulation, "A straight line is a line which lies evenly with the points of itself?"

Interestingly, Heath was in the presence of a solution to the problem that baffled him, but he couldn't see it because of a preconception that definitions could only relate words to words. He refers to an observation of Saccheri that an irregularity in a line could "be made perceptible" by holding two points fixed and rotating the line. But this was a perception that depended on an action and somehow must have seemed inadmissible.

That was unfortunate, because in that action lies the sense of that mysterious phrase "lies evenly with the points of itself." Euclid's definition is a rotational one. Having myself worked briefly as a draughtsman, I was able to recognize a reference to the practice of draughtsmen of testing the straightness of their straightedge by drawing a line and then rotating the straightedge through 180° and drawing a second line on top of the first. If and only if the lines coincide in every point is the straightedge (and the line) straight. That is what "lies evenly with the points of itself" refers to. It is that breaking out of the word-circle to a practice that gives sense to Euclid's way of setting out the notion of a straight line.

And perhaps we should notice too that Euclid's way of giving sense to the notion of a straight line makes redundant Hilbert's rather unclear uniqueness axiom. One could derive from the Euclidian definition a variant to the effect that a straight line was precisely one that "was determined by" any two points on it. By his definition, if two points coincide, then all must.

This same reference to practices will take the corresponding mystery out of Euclid's definition of a plane surface as "a surface which lies evenly with the straight lines of itself." Abstractly, one could conceive of this as generating a plane by a rotation of a line around an axis at right angles to it, but in practice one would test a surface by placing a straightedge on it randomly or in rotation around more than one point. Proclus' definition of a plane as "a surface which is stretched to the utmost" would hardly work. Apart from introducing the ungeometric notion of *stretching*, the "stretching" would give one a plane only if the perimeter over which the surface were being "stretched" already lay in a plane. However, Proclus has a second, more useful definition that would correspond to Euclid's and to the above practice of testing. It would also connect to the practice of those who lay concrete floors and aim to make them "flat." His more useful definition is "a surface such that a straight line fits on all parts of it." The floor layers achieve flatness by tamping the concrete with a straight board that moves along straight rails that have been made to lie in the same plane by making them level. We know this makes the floors flat, but it might take some theorems to show the connection to Euclid's definitions.

The seventeenth-century philosophers mystified geometry in trying to wrench it loose from its practical roots, roots that gave sense to its fundamental notions and a point to its pursuit. Geometry was given ideological work to do as an example of the "abstract and eternal truths about the world" that could be achieved by individual human reason. It was then supposed to be a way in which human minds could meet, reaching out of their separation to a common view of things and to agreement. Geometry was not able to carry this baggage, which required an inversion of the real order of things and robbed its basic notions of sense. Geometry was not the product of abstract excogitation that became the basis of theory. Practice preceded theory, though, as Euclid's work showed, that practice could be the basis of a beautifully elaborated theory that itself was aimed at a more sophisticated practice.

That ideological baggage still hangs about geometry like last season's snow. Geometry is still supposed by some to be something that is the pure product of rational intelligence itself and independent of practices and form of life. That belief is still there, for example, among those space scientists who have concerned themselves with "communication with extra-terrestrial intelligences" (perhaps our model, these days, of "other minds"). They have sent off their deep-space probes with diagrams aboard representing Pythagoras' Theorem. The assumption is that, however different their physical form or their form of life, if they are intelligent at all, the extra-terrestrials will understand Euclidian geometry and recognize the diagram as the product of another intelligence that is reaching out to them.

One might be tempted to say that the space program needed a

consultant philosopher to disabuse its designers of that conception of the nature of geometry and the belief that its origins lie in "reason itself." Unfortunately this pleasing suggestion founders on the fact that it is the philosophers on the whole who have made the greatest contribution to the prevalence of that mystified view of geometry.

Newton deserves all the praise and adulation that Locke offered him, not for the reasons Locke had in mind, but rather for being subversive of them, for standing out above the circling gloom and darkness with his clear-headed understanding and analysis of the foundations of his own enterprise, in the face of the prevailing contrary views. It is only a pity that Locke himself did not understand better that which he praised, so that he could genuinely have served Newton and science instead of trying to use them for his own ends and fold them into his own program.

The recognition that the Newtonian mechanics had its foundation in human practices might have gone some way toward curbing that poetic imagination of a grand mechanism of the Universe, a deterministic system in which humanity was trapped. That very trap had "Made by Humanity" stamped on it somewhere out of sight.

14 Coda: philosophy and history

We are told that we live in a "postmodern era," though the force and meaning of that claim are hardly clear and uncontentious. Even where there is agreement that this is the case, there is generally little agreement about just what it is that is supposed to *be* the case. Much debate has been directed toward the question of how to characterize post-modernity, or the "modernity" that it is thought to have superseded and supplanted. There have been deeper questions raised, too, about the nature and point of this proposed historical characterization and division. Just what is it dividing? Just what is its proper function and its area of operation? Is there indeed one notion at all, or a whole range of notions with different functions and with different criteria of application, trying to tell us different things? Even the reality of the notion of the "postmodern" has been questioned and the suggestion has been made that it is a piece of mystification and ideology only, a turning our eyes away from serious matters, a distraction in time of trouble.

None of those questions is going to concern us here. The notions of "modernity" and "postmodernity" come up for discussion only because I have made central use of the notion of *the modern era* in trying to describe the historical context that made certain assumptions and projects seem natural to the philosophers of the seventeenth century, without at all justifying those assumptions or those projects. This may seem to draw me into the debates about "modernity" and "post-modernity," and it is perhaps important to put some clear distance between my use of the notion of *the modern era* and what seems to be at issue in those debates. There are in any case some interesting and important issues involved in those notions, issues that need to be drawn out and clarified.

The term "modernity" itself seems to present an invitation to many to go off tracking the *Zeitgeist* with gun and camera, and the question we have to ask about that pursuit is what we are to do with the *Zeitgeist* when we have it bagged and mounted. Do we merely hang it on the trophy-room wall? Or is there some other use that our description of "the spirit of the age" can be put to? And how do we tell when we have it truly captured?

The sheer variety of the accounts of "modernity's" sources and its supposed moment of origin even suggests that the hunters may be pursuing different game rather than giving us rival descriptions and accounts of the same thing. "Modernity" has been dated from the invention of movable type and the resulting proliferation of learning, the rise of the secular state, the Reformation, the scientific revolution, the Enlightenment, the industrial revolution, the Renaissance, the discovery of America, the Copernican revolution, and humanist skepticism, and dated from the thought of any number of individual figures or schools back to and including the anonymous author of *The York Tracts* in the twelfth century.

Looking over that rich list of offered beginnings, we may get the idea that the proposed divisions of history are not being made for the same purposes and that each proposed division represents a different conception of "modernity" rather than a rival contestant for the title of "true account" of some one thing. There are, of course, connections between some of the items in the list, and some may be seen as "deeper" than others, and even as providing an explanation of others. Still, even when connected items are assimilated, the remaining variety is rich enough to suggest rival conceptions rather than rival explanations. If we were concerned to put some order into these accounts and to adjudicate between the different conceptions of "modernity" they represented, we would have to discover whether there was some one agreed function that the notion was meant to serve. Only if there was, would we be in a position to judge the relative success of each of the candidates. If not, we would have to say that they are playing different games tuned to different rules.

Sorting out that generous profusion of accounts of "modernity" is not a project I plan to take up, or even the problem whether there is a single function that the notion is aimed at serving. I am concerned only to differentiate between my own use of the notion of the *modern era* and any of those attempts to identify the "spirit of the age" and to date the moment when that spirit first made its appearance. Perhaps the first and simplest thing to say is that, as I want to use it, the notion of the *modern era* is not a matter of a single factor whose beginning can be dated, but a multiply interacting syndrome of factors that could be said to define an era only when, and in the sense that, they came to dominate developments and to erode and exclude previous arrangements, practices, institutions, attitudes, and ways of viewing the world and viewing humanity itself. In concrete terms, the division that I want to mark with the expression "the modern era" is between the feudal era with the complex of institutions and practices that were developed within it, and the period which succeeded it in Western Europe, a period with a revolutionary dynamic that, over some centuries and at different rates in different places, brought about the dismantling of the institutions and practices that had developed within that set of relations and that system which we call the "feudal."

I have used the term "era," and there is a danger in that word, one that would allow a confusion with one of the features of the common use of the term "modernity" from which I would most like to distinguish my own notion. "Modernity" is often spoken of as a state, status or condition that was entered into at some particular time or as the result of some particular event. At the heart of the notion of the *modern era* as I want to use it is not a state or condition, but a new dynamic of development and change, one that was in conflict with the institutions and practices that had developed under feudalism and was in that way in conflict with the dynamic that drove feudalism. It will take some time to make out what I mean by what I am calling that "new dynamic" and the nature of its break and conflict with the characteristic feudal institutions as well as what I may be referring to in talking about the changes in human self-image and values that were bound up with and part of those changes in the dynamic and the direction of development in what became the "developed world."

There are two important issues buried here which touch on our conception of historical explanation and understanding. One has to do with the changes in self-image and values that I have described as "bound up with and part of" that new dynamic which broke with and destroyed the feudal arrangements. I have deliberately used the expressions "bound up with" and "part of" to describe the relation of that new self-image and those new projects and values that arose with that new dynamic, because I regard the connections between them as too intimate to allow either to be taken to be "cause" of the other. We have not got two self-contained realms here: material life on the one hand, and mental life and ideas on the other, which could stand in causal relations to one another in either direction. The "life" that connects them makes that impossible and shows them to be in effect the same thing taken from two different sides. Though perhaps it would be better to describe the relation between them by saying that the material life gives sense and substance to the mental life and the mental side makes the material life into a "life." But this is a point that needs much expansion. I have had some things to say about it in the discussion of the incoherences of behaviorism in chapter 6, an incoherence that is the result of the impossibility of making that generic separation between thought and action which Descartes requires of us in adopting his new "method" of philosophizing.

The other issue that lies buried in the talk of a "new dynamic" and a "break" with feudalism is one with a certain analogy with the first. It arises out of the important recognition that the new dynamic did not come from outside feudalism. It was not the result of some new idea that suddenly struck someone or some group out of the blue, or some new force that arrived on the horizon, like the cavalry in the old Westerns, rescuing the situation. The forces and the dynamic which destroyed it grew up within feudalism itself. So it might perhaps seem we should have to say that the talk of a "break" is misplaced, because there is, after all, a kind of continuity, a line of development that stretches between the old and the new.

But we should notice that this will be always and necessarily so unless we are dealing with the irruption of something entirely external, an invasion of Tartar hordes, say, or the impact of an asteroid causing destructive climatic changes, or perhaps the impact in this century of modern developed capitalism on feudal Japan, or on dependent and underdeveloped Korea in the aftermath of the Korean War. The changes that those external forces might bring could easily involve major discontinuities and a break with the past line of development that could be given a date, or at least placed within a recognizable period.

But where there is no such cause of change that has been nurtured and developed somewhere outside the system which has been disrupted, a question is raised about the practice of dividing history into periods and talking of a "break" between one period and another. Raising that question certainly does not call into doubt the usefulness of the practice of marking such divisions. They have often enough shown their value by the illumination they have given. It is rather the basis of those divisions that needs to be looked at, and the meaning of talk of a "break" or of an essential change from one period to another where we can point to no external factor.

We certainly do want to say that the modern era moved and developed according to a different dynamic and different principles from those at work in the feudal era. And we should notice that both the Renaissance humanists and, later, the philosophers of the seventeenth century thought of themselves as breaking with a tradition and with a whole system of thought and of political organization.

And we should notice too, and draw out all the consequences of, the remarkable fact that the philosophers of the seventeenth century did not even try to refute or undermine the basis of the scholastic philosophy that had been associated with that previous era. They set it aside as irrelevant and started afresh. Hobbes simply made fun of it, though in making fun he came up with two very serious and important notions. The first, in chapter 8 of the *Leviathan*, was the notion of a *caste language*, a language that was cut off from the language of daily life and ordinary people. The fun he has at the expense of scholastic philosophy comes in setting about trying to translate scholastic dicta into "any of the modern tongues" or into that Latin that was spoken "when the Latine tongue was vulgar." The results are comic, and though the exercise is not exactly fair, there is a deep point there too, and one that all philosophers need to keep in the back of their minds when they are writing.

The other great and important weapon that Hobbes forged in his enterprise of bypassing scholasticism was essentially that of an *ideology*, that is, of a system of thought that expressed the point of view of, and benefited, one faction or section of society to the detriment of the rest. This comes out even in the titles of the two succeeding chapters of part 4 of the *Leviathan*, chapter XLVI, "The Darknesse from Vain Philosophy, and Fabulous Traditions," and chapter XLVII, "Of the Benefit that Proceedeth from such Darknesse, and to whom it Accreweth." The notion that the confusion sown by a system of ideas could benefit one institution or one section of society to the detriment of the rest is pretty well our modern notion of *ideology* and involves a sophisticated social analysis. The "Vain Philosophy" was of course the scholastic, and the foreign power it was being said to serve to the detriment of Britain was the Roman Church.

Descartes devised for himself a philosophical method that in a different way absolved him from dealing with his philosophical predecessors. And one may suspect that it was not an accidental feature of his method that it required Descartes to put aside everything that he had been taught at the school of La Flèche: "to rid myself of all the opinions which I had formerly accepted, and commence to build anew from the foundation." As a Catholic living in a Catholic country in the embattled Counter-Reformation period, he would have found the project of examining and rejecting the proceeding scholastic philosophy a hazardous one. And we know too that Descartes took note of the condemnation of Galileo and suppressed his unfinished work *The World* for fear of condemnation himself.

It is important to notice that Descartes's philosophical project of "building anew from the foundation" turned out in effect to be setting philosophy up as a rival to the theology that had dominated the previous era. And in doing that, he gave philosophy a theological cast.

In the thought of the previous era, it was given that God was the foundation and starting point for truth and existence and for morals and political obligation, the source of meaning, and the end of human life. In making the passage from that transcendent foundation to the concrete and particular truths and principles that were to be the guide and test for humans, the theologians made use of the Bible, revelation, the words of Christ, and those of the inspired Fathers of the Church. Descartes could call on none of those resources in his lonely project of finding those foundations within himself as though he were the only being in the world. The project of seeking transcendent and absolute foundations and articulating their connection with the concrete and the secular was a theological one, but the method and the resources that Descartes allowed himself gave that project a secular appearance.

What is important to note is that both Hobbes and Descartes managed to absolve themselves, in one way or another, from the task of examining and refuting the philosophy of that previous period. To that extent they made a break all right, and there was a discontinuity. But in making a break and aiming to start afresh, they stamped the philosophy of the modern era with a certain definite character, a characteristic problem that has shaped the philosophy of the past three hundred years – the search for "foundations."

Fresh starts need somewhere to start, and it was partly this need to find "foundations" that set the face of modern philosophy against historical understanding and helped to make scientific understanding the dominant mode in our time. History does not provide us with foundations. Wherever we are, there is always a previous history. And even where we may want to talk of "breaks," those breaks themselves always have some kind of history. That history may only be that of the collision of two disparate lines of development, but it is a history nevertheless. In history we don't have absolute starting points of the kind philosophers found themselves seeking. If, on the other hand, we want to make a clean break and a fresh start, we shall need to clear away all the rubble that history has deposited on our site. And that will involve clearing away history itself.

But we still have not yet got a clear account at hand of what we may mean by talking about a "break" between two historical periods when all the forces that are at work in the new era grew up within the old. At first sight that situation looks like something that would have to be described as a natural and continuous development, one that gives no purchase for the notion of a break or a division into periods. We shall have to come back to that and at the same time come back to demystifying and giving some substance to the notion of a *dynamic* that I have used in rather an abstract way above. We shall have to try also to identify the source and the repository of the energy that goes with the notion of a *dynamic*. But first it may be useful to switch our attention back to the notions of "modernity" and "postmodernity." There are also the associated terms "modernism" and "postmodernism," though the nature of the association is not always clear or handled in the same way by all.

"Postmodernism" and "postmodernity," when they are not used simply to designate an architectural style or an artistic impulse, tend to be used to refer to a disillusionment with the optimism of the Enlightenment, with its conception of the liberation of humanity from slavery and ignorance and its unlimited progress toward some final perfection. Something called "modernity" is then identified with those ill-founded hopes and that hopelessly partial Enlightenment view of the world.

The partiality of the Enlightenment view of things comes out as soon as one considers concretely the conditions of the conception, expression, and consumption of that view. When these things are looked at it can be seen that the Enlightenment view expressed little more than the sense of emancipation of one particular class from the constraining bonds of feudalism and a sense of the infinite possibility of the new order of society for that class, which was the motor and representative of that new order. That class has been called "the radical middle class." The term "radical bourgeoisie" would be more accurate, even though the word "bourgeois" has been somewhat damaged by being frequently used to abuse merely. The words "bourgeois" and "bourgeoisie" would be more accurate because the class whose view of the world the Enlightenment formulated and expressed was one that grew up within the towns and was created by, and associated with, the markets that had their home there. It consisted of the merchants, traders, and budding industrialists.

It was this class associated with the towns and created by their markets that was at the center of the historically transforming power of those markets, a power that on the one hand called for the transformation of the subsistence economy of feudalism, a largely agricultural economy with little division of labor. On the other hand, the market's call for products and commodities set the scene for the industrial revolution as the demands of the market outgrew the production capacity of the cottage industry and the "manufactories" that the market had itself called into existence. It was that infinite expansion of possibility that was reflected in the optimism of the Enlightenment picture.

But if to get clear about this, we ask just who that Enlightenment picture was painted for and whose portrait it was, we see that we have to eliminate large and important segments of eighteenth-century society straight away. It was not for them.

It was not the land-owning class that the Enlightenment was speaking to and whose portrait was being painted in those rosy colors. The importance of that class, its influence on historical developments and the shape of life, was on the wane, even though the land-owning class was able to fight its corner against the "free traders" well into the nineteenth century. But, most strikingly, it was not the peasants that the Enlightenment philosophers, the *Philosophes,* were speaking to, nor was it to the growing class of agricultural laborers, or the weavers who no longer worked in their cottages but in a "manufactory" on someone else's loom. These were not the classes for whom the books, poems, and pamphlets were written, the music composed, the paintings painted. It was not their liberation that was being referred to or their prospects that were being described, for the simple reason that liberation had not happened for them, nor was it about to.

If, *per impossibile,* it had been this class of peasants and laborers that was the consumer of literature and sustainer of the intellectuals, providing their living and their position, it would hardly have had that Enlightenment optimism laid out before it. There was nothing in the situation of the members of those classes or their prospects that would have corresponded to that Enlightenment view of the world and of humanity. The members of those classes would have recognized nothing of themselves in such a picture of liberation and unlimited progress. The books would have remained unsold and the intellectuals proclaiming that view would have been dismissed from their posts, their sinecures cancelled, and their support withdrawn for talking such nonsense. The Enlightenment would never have happened. And what then would have become of the "modernity/postmodernity" debate?

This little thought experiment can tell us a good deal about that debate. To begin with, it shows us that the debate has been about a partial view of humanity and history that reflected no more than the hopes and aspirations of one class that was feeling its power and saw its future as unlimited. That class was, to be sure, a dynamic class, and its power was real, and to that extent the Enlightenment view did reflect something real. It had to, or else it would have "fallen stillborn" and never been heard of after.

What was false about it was its claim to speak for humanity as such and for the whole of history where in fact it was the history and situation of just that one class which was at that time a dominant and shaping force in Western Europe. That class was the developing force of what has come to be called "the developed world" and so was clearly important. But though important, it was not the whole of the world or the whole of society.

One should not forget, also, that the Enlightenment view had its own role to play in rallying that class and giving it a sense of coherence and a sense of its own role. The Enlightenment view was itself thus a player, though, one must add quickly, not an independent player that could be detached from the individual human actors who held that view of things and whose actions were influenced by it. It mustn't be thought of as an autonomous force.

But still, we must come back to the fact that the Enlightenment claimed to be speaking for the whole of humanity when it was speaking for only a part of it. Most importantly, the liberation that it proclaimed was the liberation of that one class only. It could not be made to encompass the liberation of the others on pain of contradiction. The coming to dominance of the bourgeoisie, the merchants, traders, the budding industrialists, the hirers of those "hands" who provided the merchants and traders with something to trade, that new dominance itself meant the eclipse of the power of the land-owning class, as laws and institutions came to be shaped to the needs of this new dynamic class and its activities.

Most importantly, the liberation of the hirers of "hands" could not be made to encompass the liberation of the hands themselves. Quite the contrary. The "hands" that the hirers required had to be stripped of their common lands by enclosures, since those common lands had provided a peasant population with a means of independent subsistence. That part of the population had to be made dependent on those "hirers of hands" for the means of their subsistence. The liberation of some was hardly the liberation of all.

Those false claims of the Enlightenment to speak for the whole of humanity were also at the base of just that false optimism that recent history has undermined. It is now no longer so easy to think that humanity as a whole was being liberated, when whatever unevenly distributed prosperity that the developed world enjoys requires the impoverishment of the third-world suppliers of those goods we take for granted, the sugar, the tea, the coffee, the chocolate, the jeans, and the runners that we consume without a thought for the conditions of those who have labored to produce them.

And even within the so-called "developed" world, it now commonly takes the work of two to support a household. That recent development looks rather like a regression to those early nineteenth-century conditions in which a whole family, including small children, worked at the looms of the weaving mills.

The "progress" of the modern world has come increasingly to seem a regress to those willing to think about it, as we read of the small children in the third world whose eyes are destroyed making our carpets, or whose childhood is taken in other ways to provide luxuries for the developed world.

And there are the many threats to humanity itself from that very "progress" of the developed world, from the fearsome and vicious weapons it has generated and disseminated for profit through the world, turning tribal conflicts into genocidal disasters, to the threats from great environmental damage that is the by-product of its by-products. And we hardly see the liberation from ignorance that the *Philosophes* hoped to accomplish with the *Encyclopédie*. Certainly not in a time when "store-front" religions and the television healers "daily devour apace," and a struggle is going on to introduce Special Creation as a biological theory into the schools of the World's most advanced capitalist nation.

The question that we have to pose about the "modernity/post-modernity" debate is whether we are talking about an actual historical transition, a break between two identifiable historical periods, each with a different dynamic and direction of development, or about something that is better described as a "disillusionment," a change in our view of the history of our times.

It might seem to be pretty obvious from the above remarks which answer I would give. I have tried to make out the nature of the self-delusion that the Enlightenment view of things involved, the illusion that the one class was speaking for all. But there is a deeply important fact about that illusion, however, and one that it would be entirely false to leave out of account. The fact is that the illusion was an energizing one, one that gave that dynamic class a sense of mission and the coherence and strength to bring about some of the things that the members of it believed.

But not all of those things. And that is an important fact to keep in mind too. The Enlightenment view had some element of the self-fulfilling prophecy about it, but not all its prophecies and aims could be fulfilled equally. Particularly not those of universal liberation.

The relations between the classes in Enlightenment times, and our own, is such that progress for one will generally involve regress for the other, despite all the "trickle down" theories in the world.

This regress is sometimes obvious, as in the vicious "vagabondage" laws that were enacted through much of Europe in the sixteenth and seventeenth centuries with the aim of detaching the peasantry from any independent means of subsistence and driving them into the towns and the arms of employers. Sometimes the regress is masked, as when great changes in production and leaps in productivity allow a greater distribution of goods. I say "masked" because, despite a wider distribution of material goods, a closer look at the changes in the nature of work that the "hands" are required to do shows a progressive draining away of the skills involved and their incorporation into mechanical routines that require little training, call on little intelligence, and are a diminishing of the humanity of the person required to do that work.

That progress for some is regress for others shows itself most clearly in the relations between the developed world and the undeveloped, where any serious economic analysis shows "trickle up" rather than "trickle down" as each aid dollar finds two others to bring with it back to the developed world. In Latin American Spanish, the transitive verb "to underdevelop" has been introduced into the language to describe the first world's relations with the third and to characterize the changes that have been forced on the third world by the dominant first-world institutions such as the IMF or the World Bank (though you won't find the verb *subdesarrollar* in many Spanish dictionaries).

So we seem to be led to a position from which we may no longer wish to pose the alternatives so starkly as being between a genuine historical division or a simple change of perspective. A change of perspective is itself a historical fact of which we have to take note and becomes, for example, part of our understanding of the coherence and energy of the new class in its battle with the feudal practices, institutions, and laws that stood in its way. Even though it may not mark a change of the same kind as changes in material conditions, practices and institutions, scientific discoveries, and discoveries of new continents, a change of perspective needs to be ranged alongside those other changes, seen as something connected to them, rather than as something autonomous arriving from outside history and human life. The Enlightenment view had historical antecedents and it had historical consequences too. The philosophers who set it out were not visitors from another planet who came, formed their opinions, and then took them away with them. They were a part of the dynamic of that new social order.

But in seeing a change of perspective, outlook, hope or plan as embedded in and as one amongst other changes to which it is connected, we can see that a change of perspective is not in itself sufficient to mark a division between historical periods. Not, that is, if it is detached from that historical surrounding where it has antecedents which are the source of its sense and its moving power, and consequences that embody and demonstrate them. Abstracted from that context those views are nothing, nothing but wind and air. Much of the discussion of "modernity" and "postmodernity" seems to be caught up in that founding Cartesian assumption that thoughts, beliefs and doubts can be separated from their antecedents and from their consequences for action and still have sense. They cannot, and in asking us to separate our doubts from our life, Descartes is converting his "method of doubt" into a dumb-show.

The real historical force of the Enlightenment philosophy has to be understood by drawing out the conditions, the changes in material life that created possibilities, and energized those to whom the Enlightenment philosophers were speaking, those whose life and possibilities they were describing. Then we can understand how the very description of the new possibilities, and that optimistic picture that was painted, helped to consolidate that optimism and make those possibilities real.

The Enlightenment picture of endless progress and of human perfectibility then ceases to be a mysterious, abstract force arriving out of the air or the imagination. Understanding how that Enlightenment picture could have an actual historical role becomes no more difficult than understanding how drawing a plan helps a carpenter, or encouragement helps a child. We have only to put behind us the divorce between thought and action that Descartes so fatally enjoined and made a condition of the application of his method.

But what do we say about the waning of that confidence and the evaporation of optimism which is thought to be in evidence now? Frederick Jameson has talked of "late capitalism" as the ground and reference of "postmodernity." And there is some justification for that description, as we can see if we contrast our own with the atmosphere of earlier times.

In earlier puritan days display and consumption were wicked and ungodly, and this life was only a preparation for the life to come. That was the attitude and ethos appropriate and necessary to a time of investment and delayed enjoyment, of building up the capital base, the machines, the factories, and the infrastructure of railways, canals, ships, and ports, a time of colonizing and plantations.

By contrast, we now describe ourselves as a "consumer society," a society, that is, which no longer concerns itself with the future but with present enjoyments. It is a time when it seems natural to the managers of newly privatized public utilities to vote themselves large salaries and redundancy payments, to "take the money and run" in a way that shows little optimism or confidence in the future. Perhaps we have to consider that as a genuine historical break with the past, that waning of Enlightenment optimism and confidence in the class that has been the motor of historical change in our era.

One could certainly point to deep changes in many cultural areas that could be seen as the result of and evidence for that loss of confidence in future prospects and the consequent shift of interest from production and the means of production to consumption. Emblematic of this, perhaps, is one of the most radical innovations of that artist who has been described as "the first of the postmoderns," Marcel Duchamp. His outrageous innovation was the *readymade*, which scandalized the New York art world in 1916. The most famous of his "readymades" were perhaps his *Bottle Rack* and, above all, the urinal laid on its back, titled *Fountain* and signed with the fictitious name "R. Mutt." That piece produced, and still produces, much outrage amongst those who have been unable to see the joke and the comment he is making on art and the artist. In 1946 Duchamp even made a meta-joke and a further comment by issuing an "edition" of six *Fountains*.

With the readymade, Duchamp bows out of the production process and simply "elects" certain commercially produced objects to status of "art object." In effect, the artist becomes a consumer rather than a producer of objects. Their artistic status derives, presumably, from the status of the artist. Duchamp arrived at this point by about 1916 after a fairly rapid transition from paintings that echoed Lautrec, Cézanne, and the fauvists through a cubism with affinities with futurist attempts to incorporate motion, on to experiments with the role of chance in producing picture elements.

Some of the first readymades could be seen as having been chosen for certain formal or aesthetic qualities and thus to have analogy with *objets trouvés*. But Duchamp's later readymades could make no such claim, and the claimed elective power of the artist seems to have become absolute and arbitrary.

Much that is taken to be paradigmatically postmodern in painting, writing, architecture, and even music can be seen to have been foreshadowed there in Duchamp, though I don't propose to draw out those connections here except to point to the general change in the role and status of the artist from producer to consumer, simply adapting, recording, transferring, and assembling readymade elements with minimal or no reworking or transforming.

That change could be seen as reflecting the loss of that energizing optimism that could motivate the long apprenticeship and study, the careful work that went into the artistic production of earlier times. There was then also a sense of learning from, and pushing forward, the work of previous generations. Duchamp is again emblematic of a break from that tradition. In 1919 he took an iconic work of the past, a print of one of its most famous paintings, *La Gioconda*, and desecrated it, painting a moustache on it, and giving it the mocking title *L.H.O.O.Q.* (to be pronounced in French). It is tempting to see in this a mockery parallel to Hobbes' mockery of scholastic philosophy as part of declaring a new era. Though one would have to be careful to distinguish mockery of the quasi-religious status given those works housed in great temples of art in the capital cities of the developed world from mocking the achievement of the artists themselves, something that was hardly being laughed at.

But Duchamp is only one figure in a century of artistic manifestos and iconoclasm. All those manifestos aimed at making a break with the past, making a fresh start, and it is an interesting question why our century should have seen such a flourishing of fresh starts in the cultural area, and why it was that the artists so often set themselves the task of biting the bourgeois hand that fed them. The early part of the century was the time of riots and outrage at concerts and exhibitions. The *haut bourgeoisie*, who paid the bills, bought the paintings and went to the concerts, were being deliberately stirred up, their comfortable assumptions smashed by all the "isms" that proliferated then, with or without manifestos – fauvism, cubism, futurism, constructivism, vorticism, symbolism, dadaism, supremetism, atonalism, expressionism, and many others. One feels for the bourgeoisie of the time and wonders at their toughness to stand up to such an assault.

And the heirs of Duchamp are legion. Once one has embarked on the theme of artist turned from producer to consumer in a "consumer society," there seems no end to the schools and individuals that can be swept up in that net. Andy Warhol or Roy Lichtenstein and the whole of the movement known as "Pop Art" can be seen as consumers of icons and popular images and styles, which they merely repackage and represent to us. Christo, like a shopkeeper, will wrap up the Reichstag for us (or anything else he is allowed to and can manage), and Robert Smithson presents us with a Pacific island wrapped in pink net. In the Serpentine Gallery, the actress Tilda Swinton is offered to us in a glass case.

We could go on, but I'm not sure where we would get to. It may be an interesting fact that some artists and movements have taken a direction that has resonances with other features of life, for at least some classes in the developed world. However, to talk simply and without qualification of a "consumer society" is, of course, to leave out of account the unemployed, the low paid, and pretty well the whole of the third world. They don't get to do much consuming.

As in Enlightenment times, the state of one class of society is allowed to stand for the whole, the remainder being, somehow, invisible. Of course, it is not for the unemployed or for the people of the third world that the Reichstag is being gift wrapped, nor is the Pacific island being offered to its inhabitants, if there are any, as a present. It might be a touching gesture on the part of a departing colonial power in handing over to the natives, but a gesture that seems unlikely to be made by any, even in an effort to smooth the passage from a colonial to a neo-colonial form of exploitation.

However, we must again remind ourselves that though we may be talking about only one class, it is nevertheless the class that has historically been the dynamic part of what has been historically the most dynamic system and culture and society in the world, the one that sent out the explorers, the missionaries, the slavers, the colonizers to the rest of the world. So it is of no small importance if there is evidence that that class has lost its dynamism, its sense of direction, and faith in future possibilities so that it is no longer willing to forgo present enjoyment and consumption in order to invest in a future. We would have to say that the puritan ethos and the Protestant work ethic that were the shaping and driving force of that class during its greatest work of transformation are now not much in sight. Display, consuming, getting something for nothing seem to be their replacements. "Instant gratification," not investment, seems to be the driving force of capitalism in our time. Perhaps Jameson is justified in talking about "late capitalism."

Still, all this cultural analysis and the resulting impressions of spiritual malaise may nevertheless be a trick of the vision, a problem of perspective rather than a clear sign of the cataclysm, the end of an era, a call for a "post" this or that, a time to be building our ark. In checking whether an era has truly ended we need to look at more than its cultural production. No matter how important an indicator we take it to be, the importance of the cultural sphere will derive not so much from itself as from what it indicates. And we must remember that the disorientation and disillusion of some will not necessarily be the disillusion of all.

One thing that counts heavily against calling the end of an era is the continuity of the institutions, the legal framework, forms of property and their role in the organization of work and production, as well as in deciding the nature of the products and their distribution. All of those things that have developed in their characteristic form in what I have called "the modern era" and differentiated it from the feudal are still in place and operating more or less smoothly.

And if we look we shall still find the empire-building entrepreneurs of the old style, with a vision and confidence and determination. And no one has suggested that the Murdochs, the Gateses, and the Soroses of today would not be a match for the Rockefellers, Carnegies, and Fords or any of the earlier figures. Nowadays they may not hire armed gangs of strikebreakers or insist that their employees go to church, but times have changed and nowadays they do not have to. Things are organized differently now.

But there is a question hanging over Frederick Jameson's use of the phrase "late capitalism" to describe the state of that social and economic system that has grown up with and has characterized the modern era. It is, of course, notorious that Marx underestimated the staying power of capitalism, the work it still had to do in the world before its possibilities were exhausted, and one does not have to accept the tortured arguments of capitalism's theoreticians that it is the natural and eternal condition of humanity to think that there may still be enough fields to conquer to keep it going for some time. Certainly the directors of the various multinationals, Coca-Cola, say, or the tobacco companies, have been looking at China as one such vast field that will keep them expanding for a good while. There is no particular reason to think them wrong.

From the perspective of the use I have wanted to make of the notion of the *modern era* I think that there is no call to talk of a historical break, the end of one era and the beginning of another. In the cultural area we can point to breaks and discontinuities, all right, both in artistic production and discussion of that production, but there is no unambiguous conclusion that we can draw from those discontinuities, no clear conclusions even about that very restricted class, the consumers of those cultural artifacts in the developed world.

But the notion of a *historical break* and a *historical era* will only be made clear when we have gone back to face the question put right at the beginning and give an account of how forces that grew up within and were generated by the feudal system in the end produced essential changes and a new direction and dynamic of development. This question will have to be discussed completely concretely. There is no point in going on in abstract metaphysical phrases about "quantity transforming into quality" and suchlike formulas. Whatever sense those phrases have, they will have to draw from the concrete cases which they refer to. So we shall have to start with the concrete examples of essential transformations and let the Hegelian formulas feed on them.

If we are going to talk about an "essential change" from the feudal era to the modern, we shall have to give some account of the nature of feudalism as a form of social organization, and even what we mean by a "form of social organization." By a "system of social organization" I am going to mean a system of rights and obligations that shape and determine the lives of those who are counted as part of a given society, determine what work they must do, and for whom, determine the distribution of goods, determine who gives the orders and who is owed allegiance, determine where people live, and for whom they must fight, determine how disputes are settled.

From all this, it can be seen that I am already talking about some particular sorts of social organization and not offering some completely general notion, because most of the categories that I have given would have no application to many social forms, particularly to earlier tribal societies, for example. In earlier social forms, the obligations were generally not between individuals but between the individual and the tribe or community as a whole.

One important thing we must not be misled by is the expression "rights and obligations." This has a deceptively legal look when in fact what may be doing the obliging in a system may just as well be fear or force, hunger or other needs. That would be particularly true in the early period of feudalism before many of the relations of obligation had been codified into law or solidified into custom. Where it was not straight coercion, it would have been fear and hunger that drove many of the villeins into a life of service, into serfdom. They got protection and the use of a piece of land to cultivate and to build on. The vassals of higher degree got the use of larger tracts complete with serfs to support them in return for binding themselves to serve a superior lord or the king.

Taken in the large, one can say that the feudal system was a system of service, of direct obligation to serve standing between one individual and another. Initially that obligation would have been undertaken in a formal act of "homage" in which one man became the "man" of another with an obligation to bear arms when required and to do other services. In return he would receive protection and "fees" of the use of certain estates.

It is important to stress that the vassal only got the *use* of the estates which he "held of" the lord. The early feudal system did not have the institution of property in land as we know it. Being in possession of lands meant having the use of them only. One could not alienate them or dispose of them in any way. They could not be willed or inherited, and certainly not sold. That idea was unknown. Each contract of service, each act of homage, was between individuals, and though the superior lord might agree to renew the contract for one's child, that was in his gift and could be withheld. For the serfs and villeins it worked in the opposite way. If the father was bound, the son was bound, to the land and to service, even though his rights over the land were as limited and conditional as the vassal's.

It is important to stress this conditionality, this possession without ownership, not only because of the huge contrast with our own time, but because it helps to emphasize the personal nature of the relations, the rights and the obligations that formed the feudal system, at least at the outset. The rights were personal rights, not property rights. There was no such separate entity as property in land that intervened between person and person. Someone might be made a duke and have a duchy at his disposal to grant to vassals, but he held that duchy of the king and he might be dispossessed of it by the king, in theory anyhow; in practice it wouldn't be a simple matter of the king signing a paper and the thing was done. Legal theory and practical possibility rarely coincide so neatly.

I want to stress this conditionality in the possession of land at the heart of the feudal system because I want to suggest that the institution of ownership of land was one that was alien to and potentially destructive of that system, even though the institution developed by degrees within feudalism.

The point is simple. Originally, the use of the land and its serfs was granted to an individual as a fee for services and swearing fealty to the lord. But as the rights of the holder increased and he was first able to will the estate to his descendant and later even alienate parts of it, the estate took on a separate existence outside those personal relations and swearings that constituted feudalism. As something separate that could be disposed of in various ways, the land with its serfs took on many of the characteristics of money. And it was money that in the end made the fundamental transformation of relations that marked the finish of a system that had been based on fiefs and service, personal allegiance, and protection.

It was as early as 1037 that one of the first moves to make the fief heritable was taken by the king-emperor Conrad II, and it was taken with the specific aim of weakening the great nobles by giving that power to the lesser, the "vavasors." Conrad may have seen this as simply weakening the greater nobles so as to remove their threat, but the power that was taken from them was in one sense being vested in the land. That heritability became a property of the land itself, and the power that went with it belonged to the individual not individually and in himself, but only *as owner.* And *ownership of land* was a new relation that came into being at that time in mediaeval Europe. And this relation stood outside the form of relation between individuals that had characterized feudalism. It was a direct relation between an individual and the land, a relation that was no longer mediated by a relation to another person. It was thus one strand in the transformation and disappearance of feudal relations and their replacement by others that set the development of Europe in a new direction with a new dynamic.

The other strand was the growing importance of money. Its lack of importance in the early middle ages is perhaps symbolized by the fact that until the twelfth century the gold coins circulating in Europe all came from Greek or Arab mints.

There were many complementary and interconnected reasons for the growth in importance of money from the twelfth century. The rolling back or settling of the Huns, the Northmen, and the Arabs brought a relative stability that reduced the importance of the armed protection that had been, so to speak, the currency of the early middle ages. Markets and trade were growing, the Church looked increasingly for money donations, tithes in cash rather than kind, and taxes rather than armed service were required by the state. These demands spread throughout the system, as money rents, dues, tolls, imposts, license fees, *rachat,* and *mortmain* were levied to satisfy the new demand for money.

The substitution of rents and quit-rents for service, for work in the fields, for the *corvée* had the effect of transforming the feudal lord into a land-owning *rentier.* That was one essential transformation. But the greatest transformation, the one with the greatest consequences, came with the transformation of "fees" from conditional grants of land or other rights into money payments for services. The idea of wages is so natural to us that we can hardly see what a revolutionary development it was to interpose money ("which has no master") between master and servant. The feudal personal relation and allegiance is completely obliterated by the wage relation, and with that obliteration went the essential character of feudalism. The change did not prohibit feelings of loyalty and allegiance and personal connection between employer and employee, but those feelings were no longer essential duties as they had been in the relation of lord to vassal or to serf. The distance interposed by the new money-mediated relation makes those feelings of loyalty, allegiance, care, and concern into optional extras rather than the essence of the relation.

This change is well exhibited by the early institution of the annual "mop fair" at which domestic servants would be hired, an institution which replaced the keeping of domestic serfs. Just as the later Roman patricians found advantages in freeing their slaves and settling them as serfs on plots carved out of the *latifundia*, so the lords and *seigneurs* found advantages in freeing serfs and hiring them back as servants and laborers. The direct personal power that the master had over the serf brought personal responsibility with it. The master might neglect that responsibility and might even be cruel and sadistic, but those failings and those crimes would be personal and open to the eyes of everyone, including, and especially, God. The interposition of money, wages, as the mediating force between master and servant had the effect of dissolving those responsibilities that came with the direct and unmediated personal power. The master's responsibilities now ended with the payment of the wage.

Generally this change is presented as a great leap forward in freedom only from the point of view of the serf, who is presented as being liberated from a wicked and cruel bondage. The advantages to the master are little discussed, though they are hardly less. Along with what is regarded as the "freedom" of the serf, the power of the master was increased, and made in a way more absolute and arbitrary. In essence and potentiality, that is. For a long time the old feudal habits and paternalistic attitudes carried on despite the complete impersonal separation implicit in the interposition of the "masterless" money wage between master and servant, employer, and "hands." For a time, anyway. Nowadays, redundancies cause little heart searching in the boardroom. And we can ask, whose is the freedom now?

Though much more could be said about the transformation of the essential character of the feudal system as a form of organization of society, enough has been said to discharge the requirement to give an account of what is meant by a "break" or the passage from one era to another.

What had been a network of direct personal obligations that bound people[1] now began to be sundered and replaced by an exchange, not of vows, but of money. One can say "sundered" because the exchange of money, unlike the exchange of vows, carries no implications for the future beyond the work contracted for. Many of the old habits of paternalism and loyalty continued into the era of money wages and property in land, but merely as habits whose original source had disappeared and whose disappearance itself was a matter of time and convenience as they came up against the new requirements of money and profitability.[2]

One thing that may still cause confusion is the use of the word "essential" in describing the transformation that warrants us in talking of a break that separates two eras. Quite rightly, an essential transformation is seen as the destruction of one thing and its replacement by another, but if we allow our eyes to wander off the concrete changing thing and lift them to the heavens of abstract conceptual relations, it may look as though that transformation must be instantaneous. The logicians will wheel on the law of contradiction and tell us that the thing can't be both the one and the other, or else the law of the excluded middle and say that it must be the one or the other.

Powerful as those two weapons are, they are difficult to fire off without hitting one's own foot. The burning log is in danger of having to be either wood or ash but not both, and so forth. History, and life itself, rarely presents us with such neat boundaries, and where we try to impose them or the logical law apparently requires it, there is inevitable artificiality – as with "the moment of death" and suchlike. If the logicians want to trouble themselves with the Problem of the Bald Man or the Problem of the Heap, we can leave them to it and let them get back to us.

What we shall content ourselves with saying is that when, and in so far as, the practice and the possibility of buying the labor power of another began to replace the direct obligation to serve which was sanctioned by law or by custom, a new relation entered that had the power to displace the older one from the center, and in fact did so. And that new relation (or perhaps we should say "new separation") between people required and called forth new conceptions to encompass it and new moral principles to deal with the new problems that it posed. It also generated a new conception (and fact) of an atomized humanity and, for philosophers who felt they were faced with the problem of starting absolutely afresh, a new conception of the "foundations" or "origins" of society. (The scare quotes indicate my view that both are spurious notions answering to a false problem.)

There is an essential point that we need to concentrate on and be clear about because it has been the subject of much confusion and misunderstanding. It is the nature of the power that the new wage-relation had to displace the old feudal relations, the power of money to dissolve the feudal bond. One can take two roads here. One way is to try to represent the wage-relation and the counterposition of capital and labor and the creation of a market in labor as well as in goods as all of them having made those gains because they were part of a *natural way* of organizing human society, of settling what gets produced and by whom, of determining authority structures and the distribution of goods.

The problem with that story is to make out what is to be meant by "natural" and to say what that "nature" is meant to inhere in. I have spent much time in earlier chapters bringing out the incoherence of the notion of a disembodied "nature" inherent in nothing and operating in ways far more mysterious than God's. And I have had something to say also about the would-be notion of "human nature" as an all-purpose "explanation" of anything one wants to explain. Both are empty notions that don't advance things any, and the determinism they threaten is no more than a spook, the ghost of our own misunderstandings.

The other way we can go is to consider concretely the position of a feudal lord or a seigneur in the late feudal era at a time when the market and the money economy have grown, and to get money he has already been transmuting the duties of service on his estate into quit-rents and rents on peasant holdings, taking cash instead of a cow as inheritance tax from the villein, and so forth. The hiring of labor is the inevitable counterpart of the commuting of service to rents and other taxes, and the aim of the hirer would be to pay out less in wages than he gets in rents.

In this way we can see the attractiveness of the arrangement to a person from this background in these circumstances. We don't have to try to discover some abstract principle governing all human beings formed no matter how. That would be a fool's errand. The arrangement would be unintelligible to an Amazonian aboriginal and hardly attractive to the lord's ancestors whose main concern was defense against the Huns or the Northmen. In their circumstances, mutual ties were more important than money. And we should notice that as soon as we describe the situation concretely, we can understand the changes without any need to appeal to abstract and grand principles.

We have left ourselves one problem, and not a small one either. It is to say something to make out what was meant earlier by talking about a "new dynamic" of development that replaced the feudal and marked what could usefully be described as a "new era." What we have said already about the wage-relation severing the type of direct personal bond and obligations that characterized the feudal system gets us part of the way toward an account of that new dynamic and its sources, but it is only one part.

The other part is the growth of the importance of markets and trade and production for the market, a growth that was possible in the period of relative stability that came with the receding threat from the Northmen, the Huns, and the Arabs to the European core. In those earlier, embattled times, little more than a subsistence economy was possible when plunder was a recognized method of enrichment. Perhaps one could say that because plunder was a recognized way of enrichment, energies were given over to attack and defense rather than to production.

However that may be, in calmer times the markets and trade were able to grow, and that had three effects. One was the increased importance of money, which had the consequences we have already talked about. Another was that the market called out for goods that the largely subsistence, largely agricultural economy was not supplying, or able to supply without transformation. And so it was transformed. The third effect was that the market presented an alternative, more efficient, way of enrichment than the system of plunder that had earlier held back production and trade. The Venetians, for example, saw this clearly enough, though they still had to battle with the old system represented by the Arab corsairs that were a threat to the Venetian progress to wealth through trade.

The three effects together set Europe on a new course, generating new products, new industries, new wealth, and creating a new class that was at the center of this new movement, setting up the new industries, arranging the production of the new products, moving those products to market, selling them, and amassing the new wealth. Many of the new class would have been drawn from the old feudal hierarchy – those, anyway, who had the flexibility to abandon their old practices and attitudes and take on new ones appropriate to an active participation in the new order that was emerging. Those who held to the old ways ended by dragging themselves down by adherence to practices that had no useful role in the new order of things.

I have already called attention in chapter 12 to King Lear as an example of someone who keeps to the old ways in circumstances in which they no longer have a place, point or function. He insists on keeping his band of feudal retainers and companions as he travels around visiting his daughters as though they were his feudal vassals to whom his grant of parts of his kingdom was a conditional one based on a swearing of homage and service. The play is a perfect emblem of the split between the feudal and the new in several ways. Goneril and Regan treat their gifts in the division of Lear's kingdom as unencumbered inheritances, and one of the ambiguities of the play is whether the rights that Lear is insisting on are the feudal rights of the superior lord to be received together with his retinue by his vassal, or the rights of a father to love and respect. The play has much to say about loyalty and love at that moment of transition from the feudal to the new, and about Lear failing to make that transition at the cost of madness and death. In the background of our discussion of feudal swearings of loyalty and acts of homage, we can see that what Cordelia is refusing is not a declaration of love but a feudal act of homage, insisting on the bond of love over that feudal formal bond that comes into existence with the swearing.

The consequences were not so drastic for most of those feudal lords who did not change their ways and adopt the projects and enterprises of the new market-driven economy, getting into wool, joining the great bankers and traders like the Fuggers or the Medici, the land speculators like the Pastons, or the Companies of the Merchants of the Staple or the Merchant Adventurers. Those who stayed behind found themselves fighting a losing battle against loss of power, influence, and income as the new class and its activities grew in importance and made the running. It was this latter class, the new class of the bourgeoisie, that provided the dynamism of the new era and set the direction of its development. Not consciously, of course, but only in pursuing its own perceived interests. It was to this class that the new philosophers of the seventeenth century were speaking, and it was the world that they were creating which was being described.

It may seem strange and unwarranted to be drawn into such a long, though still superficial, historical discussion in a work whose real concern is philosophic. There are a number of reasons why this historical detour was necessary. The use I have wanted to make of the notion of the *modern era* required not only a characterization of that era, but that I try to give some account of how that era was in fact a new one that represented a break with the past. If that notion was to do any real work of clarification it also required that I give some account of what I meant by a "break" so as to give some sense of the reality of that historical break and therefore some understanding of the source of the conviction of the seventeenth-century philosophers that they had also to make a clean break and a fresh start. Since it was this conviction that made the search for foundations seem a necessary project for philosophy, it is important to understand the historical circumstances that gave rise to that conviction (without giving it any logical justification).

Those philosophers of the seventeenth century who started modern philosophy off on its special course made assumptions and adopted a project that had no sanction other than that it seemed natural at the time and in the circumstances.

To see that we do not have to make the same assumptions and adopt the same program, we have to go back and understand the time and the circumstances to see whether what was natural and seemed necessary to them is necessary for us. In particular, we can see the roots of their radical individualistic picture of humanity in the separation wrought by the sundering of the feudal ties by the limited contract of the wage-relation and in their attempt to fit all human relations to the market model in which individuals are represented as coming together as separate and equal participants in an interchange.

The force of my argument has been that though we may be able to understand how the "new" philosophers came to that view and took on that project through an understanding of what was happening around them, we can at the same time see that neither their view nor their project was given justification or foundation by those circumstances. The best one can say is that they came to their view by taking an aspect and a trend and cutting it loose, abstracting it, generalizing it, and projecting it into the empyrean, where it was made to work as an absolute founding principle of radical individualism on which their whole project of understanding humanity, knowledge, society, and morals was to be based.

Of course, nothing could give what was only a picture the strength and solidity to do that work and justify that project. And in addition, that "hyperbolical individualism" could not be justified, for the simple reason that in being abstracted and universalized, it ends by inverting reality in putting the individual before the social. Actually, it would be better to say, as I have argued above in chapter 9, that in the end sense can't be made of that radical individualism because in the end sense can be made of language only on the assumption that it arises out of the communion of humans sharing practices in communities.

Most important, perhaps, we need to examine the new project, freely undertaken then, of searching for foundations, and the associated assumption that nothing is really understood until those foundations have been found.

It was for this reason that the Euclidian geometry was the model of knowledge that was laid before us. But that model that all knowledge was meant to imitate was one that had been misunderstood and mystified, as I have tried to make out in chapter 13. Euclidian geometry was not, as it had been represented, a purely intellectual edifice that rested on truths that had some claim to "self-evidence" (whatever that mysterious notion might turn out to be when tracked to its lair). An

understanding of the grounding of Euclidian geometry as shown by
Newton sees it as deriving from the practices of carpenters and other
"mechanics."

To give itself a starting place in its project of inventing itself out of
nothing, the new philosophy invented a false world of ideas (or concepts, or "whatever is before the mind in thinking") that stood apart
from human life and from the practices and the usages of the language in which human life was conducted.[3] Descartes's method of
"clear and distinct ideas" required us to look on ideas as prior to language rather than as something embedded in language and generated
by the usage and practices that constitute it. To try to answer seriously
the question where those "ideas" are meant to reside and how they are
meant to get their sense is inevitably to be pushed in a theological
direction. Descartes needs to make appeal to the help of God in more
places than he admits.

And that is not surprising. As soon as one lays on oneself the
requirement of finding absolute foundations and absolute starting
points, beginnings that stand outside history, having no history, no
cause, no antecedents, one is in theological territory, asking a theological question with only a theological answer. I have argued this
point in a number of places in the preceding chapters. That search for
absolute foundations is itself a theological search, a search for the
transcendent. The secular world and everything in it has, by definition,
a history. Only the transcendent and the theological is without history
and without context and background. In this everyday world foundations themselves have to rest on the ground and can't hover in the
mid-air of "self-evidence."

In all the discussions in the preceding chapters I have tried to make
the arguments as concrete as I could, to root them in ordinary life and
the language of ordinary life. In that way I hope to have made my style
of philosophizing an alternative to, and subversive of, that style of philosophizing that the modern era was seduced into by the Cartesian
search for "foundations," foundations that in the end turn out to be
abstract and insubstantial. I have tried to show how that conception of
philosophy as the search for a "higher truth" and the methods associated with it have led us repeatedly into blind alleys and traps,
have mystified things, and caused us to lose our bearings and end in
confusion.

At the same time I have felt that it was of the greatest importance to
see how the "new" philosophers were not being perverse and idiosyncratic in taking on the particular assumptions and the projects that
generated the problems and confusions I have tried to address in this

book. I have tried to show the philosophers as reacting to and reflecting the new realities and new needs of a revolutionary time, to show them as a part of that history. It is, however, a history that we now have to transcend by understanding the part it has played in forming our assumptions, projects, and perspectives.

Notes

INTRODUCTION: PHILOSOPHY AND MYSTIFICATION

1 In referring to the manner of grasping or referring rather than the thing grasped or referred to, I have deliberately made a practice of using the rather loose and vague word "notion" instead of the more common philosophical words "idea" or "concept." This is because "notion" has not had the long history of philosophical use that has attached to the words "idea" and "concept" such a weight of philosophical baggage. The use of "idea" and "concept" in the history of philosophy might give one the impression that they referred to objects of some sort, entities that could be implanted or removed, perhaps transferred from one site to another.

Descartes so used the word "idea" that he thought it made sense to talk of ideas being "innate," and Locke described them as "whatever is before the mind in thinking" and in that way gave them the status of *objects*. Without that history, the word "notion" carries none of that baggage and is therefore more open to being grouped with skills and practices rather than with entities and objects.

2 The transcendental and essentially mysterious character of the empiricist starting point, *experience*, is not so obvious since experience can seem such an ordinary thing, known to all. There is such an ordinary notion. But it won't do the work the empiricists require. Their notion is abstract and mysterious both in its nature and in its origins. Locke thought he could appeal to the language of physics, the talk of "impacts" to reach outside the enclosed world of "experience" to what is, from that point of view, an "external" and "transcendental" world of ordinary things. But of course, the language of physics will have to be unpacked in the same way as everything else, in terms of just those enclosing experiences he is trying to transcend. Locke might as well make Descartes' appeal to God to get him out of his bottle.

3 It was in this moment that the "problem of the uniformity of nature" was born.

4 It is for this reason that we get those baffling definitions of "substance," definitions with a theological flavor that reflect the theological use to which the notion was now being put. "Substance is that which needs no other to exist" or is "*causa sui.*" Those definitions succeed only in making us dizzy. We have no idea what to make of the phrase "needs no other to

exist." And "cause of itself" can be given no sense that accords with any normal use of the word "cause" or is even connected legitimately with our ordinary senses of that word. We have no idea what to make of the word "cause" in that phrase.

That is where the vertigo begins.

1 UNDERSTANDING NONSENSE

1 In chapter 8 I remark on the debilitating effect on philosophy of the habit of discussing heatedly propositions that no one actually believes but are put forward simply to be argued about. One is reminded of Lichtenberg's remark, "His theories are only good for arguing about."

2 In the introduction to the *Grundgesetze der Arithmetik* (pp. 14–15 in Montgomery Furth's translation of 1964 published by the University of California Press) Frege makes an argument for the basic principles that parallels Aristotle's exactly, though expressing it in slightly different language. That is, he argues, not for the *truth* of the principles, but for our *need* to take them as true if we are not "to reduce our thought to confusion and finally renounce all judgment whatever." And he says of people who might be said to reason by laws that contradicted ours: "we have here a hitherto unknown type of madness."

3 In fact I think it takes us backward, sowing confusion by treating ideas as candidates for implanting, something a bit like pacemakers, perhaps.

4 *The Realistic Spirit* (London and Cambridge, Mass.: MIT Press, 1991), p. 106.

5 These things get discussed in chapter 12, "History and Human Nature."

6 I try to bring out these points in chapter 4, "Miracles," criticizing the attempt to define "miracles" in ways that would make them out as points of contact or overlap between the practices of scientific understanding and religious understanding and a source of rivalry. If we are to get an adequate understanding of either of these practices, it is essential to see them as incompatible and as having incommensurable vocabularies. The great secularizing movement of our era has generated much pressure to make of the scientific enterprise something that could supplant the religious. Much confusion has been generated by this, and many false trails laid for both scientists and philosophers.

7 Bernard Harrison has pointed out that the frequently misunderstood use of the word "game" by Wittgenstein was introduced by him only to emphasize the fact that the sense of certain words that may look as though they refer to independent properties of things (length, color, shape) in fact is tied essentially to practices and systems of operations such as measurement or comparisons and classifications for certain purposes.

8 Galileo had used an inertial theory of the tides to prove the motion of the Earth, and though Newton's gravitational account supplanted this, his appeal to the rotating bucket of water in establishing his distinction between relative and absolute motion can be seen as homage to the Galilean account. And we need to keep in mind that the great and essential Copernican change of view required the distinction between relative and absolute motion that in turn seemed to require a conception of absolute space.

9 Though this notion may strike us today as a bizarre one that mixes the theological and the physical in an unacceptable way, it does have the great merit of avoiding exactly that conception of space as a kind of substance, stuff or medium, a physical existence – precisely that conception which later caused all the trouble. Newton's conception puts a stop to asking questions about space (or later the *aether*) which implied that it was a sort of physical stuff – and it was questions of that kind which ended by requiring that "stuff" to have contradictory properties. With his conception, Newton can refer his distinction between relative and absolute motion to a point of view outside the system instead of being stuck with the notion of an immovable stuff within it. He is in effect saying simply: "There is a 'correct' description – one that comes from outside the system, from God, and is not defined as relative to anything within it." One might be tempted, but not for long, to use Newton's corollary IV to the axioms to make "the Center of Gravity of the Universe" an immovable reference point. But that notion could not in the end be given sense without an external gravitating body that the Universe as a whole attracted and was attracted to. That would also require something outside the system, but something physical.

10 In this, he is differentiating his system from, though in a sense relying on, that of Euclid, who does take us through the construction of the various figures and operations that are used and so grounds them in practices. Newton is well aware of this, having in his preface described geometry as "founded in mechanical practice." And that foundation helps to found his own system, except in relation to *time*, for which no mechanical practice is provided.

11 If we take seriously Newton's observation about the foundation of geometry lying in mechanical practices, we can solve a famous difficulty and make sense of Euclid's deeply mysterious definition of a straight line, "A straight line is a line that lies evenly on the points of itself." Without making out a relation to "mechanical" practices we are left in a fog that even the impressive Euclidian scholar Sir Thomas Heath was unable to pierce. He describes the language of the definition as "hopelessly obscure" as he sifts through the ancient and modern glosses in a search for its sense.

But the sense becomes plain when we see the definition as deriving from the common practice amongst draughtsmen of testing their straightedge by drawing a line and then rotating the straightedge through 180 degrees and drawing a second on top of the first. Only if the lines coincide in all their points is the straightedge straight.

We can also see why that definition is particularly apt and useful for Euclid. It removes the need, which Hilbert later felt, to introduce as a separate axiom that "Two points completely determine a straight line." That axiom would be needed for the chief rival to Euclid's definition, the chalk-line "shortest distance" definition, which brings with it no guarantee of uniqueness as Euclid's does. On Euclid's definition, rightly understood, that axiom is redundant. A straight line becomes one that is determined by any two points lying on it. These matters are discussed more fully in chapter 13.

12 Newton makes this clear in a very interesting Wittgensteinian remark

toward the end of the famous Scholium to the Definitions: "And if the meaning of words is to be determined by their use, then by the names time, space, place, and motion, their (sensible) measures are properly understood; and the expression will be unusual and purely mathematical, if their measured quantities themselves are meant." Unfortunately, he couples this clear distinction with a Platonic view that the "measured quantities," the "absolutes," are the ultimate realities. That caused the trouble since it seemed to legitimate asking just those questions that turned out to be senseless. The view that progress implies an ideal approached has much to answer for.

13　(Hassocks, Sussex: Harvester Press, 1977.)

2　FOLLOWING AND FORMALIZATION

1　The core of it was written in 1958/9 and was published in *Mind* in 1964.

2　*Remarks on the Foundations of Mathematics* (Oxford: Blackwell, 1956), pt I, §18.

3　In "What the Tortoise Said to Achilles" (*Mind* (1895) Carroll has the Tortoise trick Achilles into writing down as a premise every inference rule that would enable him to make the transition from premise to conclusion. Achilles is then unable to work the passage from premises to conclusion because he has nothing but premises to work with.

4　We shall be looking next at Aristotle's argument for what looks like an exception to this. He makes an argument for the impossibility of *denying* the law of contradiction. Roughly the argument is that for the denial of the law to have sense it requires that very law that is supposed to be getting denied. The denial trips itself up. But to say that it is not possible to deny the law is not to say that it is necessary in some absolute sense to adopt it.

5　*RFM*, pt I ,§128.

6　*The Later Philosophy of Wittgenstein* (London: The Athlone Press, 1958).

7　"Wittgenstein's Philosophy of Mathematics," *Philosophical Review* (July 1959). Dummett makes even more use than Pole of the tag "conventionalism" in his presentation of Wittgenstein. The serious trouble with the word "conventionalism" here is that it cuts off discussion just where the particular force and interest of Wittgenstein's analysis begin to show themselves and leaves us with something sounding like a Social Contract theory of language. Wittgenstein may have been interested in why humans, who are born, so-to-speak, "linguistically free," are everywhere found in linguistic chains, but his analysis goes deeper than the notion of a *convention* or a *contract*. Even the notion of an *institution*, which comes closer, must be treated carefully if it is not to be turned into an empty tag in the way that "conventionalism" and "convention" have.

8　*Op. cit.*, p. 329.

9　*Ibid.*, p. 320.

10　*Ibid.*, p. 337. Since this paper was written there has appeared Joseph L. Cowan's crisp attack on Dummett's paper (*Philosophical Review* 77 (3) (July 1961). Although I agree with much in the article, I think that Cowan has grasped rather too firmly the nettle offered him by Dummett that rules might disappear and communication be left in danger of breaking down. He does not seem to see just what is entailed by this view which is being attributed to Wittgenstein. That is, Cowan seems quite happy with the consequence that one could never commit oneself in advance, even though this would seem to make it impossible to have intentions or to make honest promises. In resisting the setting up of *rules* as separate and external entities (a resistance we would all approve), he seems to have rejected every sort of "given" – even the "forms of life" that Wittgenstein offered as candidates.

11 *Posterior Analytics* 76b23.

12 Wittgenstein takes up the similar problem (not of whether there are things we *must* think, but its converse) of whether there are things we *cannot* think (in *RFM* I §116).

13 This is not to ascribe to Aristotle a view like Hare's in *The Language of Morals* that someone's principles can simply be deduced from their actions. Aristotle views the situation as much more complicated than that, for example, in the chapter on intemperance in the *Ethics*.

14 Since this piece was written in the late 1950s, Montgomery Furth's translation of the *Grundgesetze der Arithmetik* appeared (Berkeley: University of California Press, 1964). In Frege's introduction, p. 15, there is a crucial passage that is remarkably similar in force to Aristotle's argument. The suggestion there is that when we come to the end of logical argumentation and reach a basic law we can only "step outside of logic" and say "we are compelled to make judgments by our own nature and by external circumstances; and if we do so, we cannot reject this law – of Identity, for example; we must acknowledge it unless we wish to reduce our thought to confusion and finally renounce all judgment whatever." Frege is not there arguing for the *truth* of those laws, but for their *necessity*. Necessity for life and for judgment.

15 The possible exception is the practice of rationality itself, which for Wittgenstein would count as a way of life. There is perhaps something incoherent in the notion of *choosing* or *rejecting* rationality. The notion of *rationality* is implicated in the notions of *choice* or *rejection* themselves. One could simply *cease* to be rational, but that is a different thing. There is a sense in which we cannot even "renounce all judgment" (in Frege's phrase), as is shown by Aristotle's example of the man walking to Megara and avoiding the well. That "renouncing" is itself an act and therefore the product of one's choice and rationality. Cratylus' and Carneades' attempts to "act out" their denials of the law of contradiction are just that: a piece of play-acting that is still connected to the reason and judgment that they are pretending to forgo.

16 *RFM* V, §32 (1st edn), VII, §39 (3rd edn) This remark also carries the suggestion that those who have worried themselves with the problem of reducing Aristotle's "practical syllogism" (in which acceptance of the premises simply issues in action) to the theoretical syllogism have been turning things on their head. Perhaps we need to see the practical syllogism as the more fundamental with "accepting the conclusion" as the action that issues from the acceptance of the premises.

17 It may be worth remarking that the successful completion of the ideal language program would have enabled us to do without jurists. The law's

interpretation would be manifest and could be settled mechanically by reference to clear and unambiguous interpretation rules.

Given this potential saving of time and expensive expertise, it might seem surprising that none of its proponents thought of approaching governments for a research grant.

3 INFINITY

1 *Paradoxes of the Infinite* (London: Routledge & Kegan Paul, 1950).
2 *Contributions to the Founding of the Theory of Transfinite Numbers* (New York: Dover, n.d.).
3 *Op. cit.*, p. 96.
4 But he had to provide an extended (and attenuated) definition of *limit* here. See the letter of 1886 quoted by P. E. B. Jourdain in his introduction to Cantor, *op. cit.*, p. 78.
5 That conflict is nicely dissected by David Sherry in "The Wake of Berkeley's Analyst: Rigor Mathematicae?," *Studies in the History of the Philosophy of Science* 18 (4) (1987): 455–80.

4 MIRACLES

1 G. E. M. Anscombe, "Times, Beginnings and Causes," in *Metaphysics and the Philosophy of Mind* (Minneapolis: University of Minnesota Press, 1981).
2 R. F. Holland, "The Miraculous," *American Philosophical Quarterly* 2 (1) (January 1965).
3 It is hard to see what one might mean by "contingent" in combination with "permanent" even though one might balk at following Diodorus Cronus in making a definitional connection between "permanent" and "necessary."

Of course, there are plenty of things that we are certain *won't* get or even *can't* get scientific explanations simply because they were not recorded carefully enough, or even remarked at all. Perhaps no one was interested enough. Or maybe no one was around at all, or no one with the right observational skills. But nothing of that sort presents the sort of challenge that the proponents of "secular miracles" are looking for.
4 Such a conception has been fathered onto Newton, wrongly, I think. It has been wrongly assumed that in talking about his "absolute time" and "absolute space" he was talking about concrete realities rather than mathematical ideals. The title of his book *Mathematical Principles* goes against this, as does his view of the mathematics he was working with as "founded in mechanical practice."
5 In chapter 3 I discussed a crucial distinction we need to make here between two senses of "whole." One of these has the notion of *parts* answering to it and applies to things that might lack a part and so be *not whole*. This would be true of functional or organic wholes, as well as accidental or "material" wholes such as *The Complete Works of William Shakespeare*. The other sort of whole, what one might call a "classificatory" whole, has members rather than parts and will be indefinite in extent.

5 HOW TO TELL YOUR FRIENDS FROM MACHINES

1 *God and the Soul* (London: Routledge & Kegan Paul, 1969), p. 41.

2 This is one of the consequences of the condition that Descartes has laid on our use of his method, namely, that we avoid *eso logos*, that is, that we do not discuss real beliefs that are connected to life and have consequences for action. This leaves us in a kind of shadowland where things have no hard boundaries.
More is said about this in chapter 7, "Skepticism about Skepticism."

3 Both the android and the independent intelligent being it turned into were played by Julie Christie in the television adaptation, with only a change of hair color to mark the difference.

4 When I wrote this I did not know of the work of Harry Braverman. His classic *Labor and Monopoly Capital* was published several years later in 1974 (New York: Monthly Review Press). Vividly relevant is his account in it of the process of "de-skilling" – the analysis by management of the work of the skilled worker so as to incorporate it into routines that could be performed by the unskilled (or by machines). What is particularly relevant is Braverman's analysis of the work of Frederick Winslow Taylor, whose *Scientific Management* (1911) was the handbook of this process. Taylor's ultimate aim was to reduce the worker to a mere automaton by producing rules that would define the worker's tasks in terms of the movements of the worker's limbs. Where has the purpose gone there? It hardly belongs to the worker.

5 *Oppression and Liberty* (London: Routledge & Kegan Paul, 1958), p. 111.

6 *Leviathan*, pt 1, ch. 8.

6 NATURE AND NECESSITY

1 Even Popper (who comes the closest to carrying on that empiricist tradition) gives an ambiguous role and status to experience. For him, what he calls "basic statements" carry the real logical load, and he describes the relation of experience to them (in successive sentences of the *Logic of Scientific Discovery* (London: Hutchinson, 1968), p. 105) as "causing" and as "motivating" the acceptance of basic statements. What experience does *not* do, for him, is to *justify* the acceptance of basic statements, or, presumably, the whole scientific edifice constructed with their help.
There is much to be said about, though perhaps not so much *for*, that view of Popper's. On the one hand, the idea of experience *causing* an acceptance of "basic statements" would, on the conceptions of experience that have underpinned empiricism, lead quickly to a pervasive determinism that would call into question Popper's claims themselves. And on the other hand, it is hard enough to make out just what might be meant by describing experience as "motivating" (giving a motive for?) acceptance.

2 *An Enquiry Concerning Human Understanding*, section VIII, pt 1. That conclusion is in itself a very dark saying. It is hard enough to understand what can be meant by calling necessity "a quality in an agent," but to call it a "quality of" or "in" an onlooker seems beyond unraveling. One should note also Hume's bland substitution of the preposition "in" for the preposition "of" that normally connects qualities and their subjects – a change

that tends to blur, if not obliterate, the distinction between things and qualities.

3 In "Semantics for Propositional Attitudes," in *Models for Modalities* (New York: Humanities Press, 1969).

4 (Oxford: Blackwell, 1980), p. 264.

5 "Modality de Dicto and de Re," in E. Nagel, P. Suppes and A. Tarski (eds), *Logic, Methodology and Philosophy of Science*, p. 630.

6 *Objective Knowledge* (Oxford: Oxford University Press, 1972), p. 195.

7 *The Philosophy of Leibniz* (Oxford: Oxford University Press, 1986).

8 (Oxford: Oxford University Press, 1973).

9 (Oxford: Oxford University Press, 1974).

10 *Counterfactuals* (Oxford: Blackwell, 1973).

11 One is reminded of Pope John Paul's condemnation of birth-control programs devised by the first world for the third as discriminating against "the unborn poor." There may be good arguments against those programs, but this sorrowful picture of a world of hopefuls and rejects in an anteroom of existence is not one of them.

12 "On What There Is," in *From a Logical Point of View* (Harper, 1963).

13 A hilarious near-example of this is Flann O'Brien's *At Swim-Two-Birds*. There the characters, disliking the parts they have been given, stage a revolt against the author and begin writing a part for *him* in which they confine him to bed, afflicted with boils, so that they can get on with their "lives."

7 SKEPTICISM ABOUT SKEPTICISM

1 *Proceedings of the Aristotelian Society*, Supplementary Volume LI (1977), to which this chapter was originally a reply.

2 In *Steps Toward an Ecology of Mind* (St Albans: Paladin, 1973).

3 *Treatise*, Book I, pt IV, sec. 1: "Neither I, nor any other person was sincerely and constantly of that opinion [skepticism]. Nature, by an absolute and uncontrollable necessity, has determined us to judge as well as to breathe and feel."

8 FOOL'S INTELLIGENCE

1 Since Gödel's theorem has sometimes been pushed onto the stage to do specific battle against A.I and machine intelligence as well as against determinism (giving Heisenberg's uncertainty principle a well-earned rest), I should perhaps say that I think it has no relevance at all to either problem and have sketched some arguments to this effect in a review (*Mind* (1973)) of John Lucas' book *The Freedom of the Will*.

2 The Genesis story of the Fall carefully avoids the conceptual pitfall of trying to present human intelligence as God's artifact, or even as His gift. It is shown, on the contrary, as the result of Eve's act of defiance in eating and offering the Forbidden Fruit of the Tree of Knowledge. Symbolically, one might say, humanity is presented as seizing its own intelligence, and in that act of defiance passing from the Eden of the world of natural existence to the hard world of human existence where goals are set, not

species-given, and struggled for consciously, where the struggle has become *work* and work has become a struggle with a nature that is now something outside and confronted.
3 *German Ideology* (Moscow: Progress Publishers, 1964), p. 31.

9 LANGUAGE AND THE SOCIETY OF OTHERS

1 G. P. Baker and P. M. S. Hacker, *Rules, Grammar and Necessity* (Oxford: Blackwell, 1985), ch. 4.
2 Colin McGinn, *Wittgenstein on Meaning* (Oxford: Blackwell, 1984), ch. 4.
3 (Oxford: Blackwell, 1956), p. 57.
4 *Grundrisse* (Harmondsworth: Penguin 1973), p. 83.
5 *Ibid.*, p. 496.
6 *Ibid.*, p. 485.
7 (Moscow: Progress Publishers, 1964), p. 42.
8 (Oxford: Blackwell, 1953), p. 226.

10 *DEUS SIVE NATURA*: SCIENCE, NATURE, AND IDEOLOGY

1 (Oxford: Oxford University Press, 1982). Also in Winch, *Trying to Make Sense* (Oxford: Blackwell, 1987).
2 *The Philosophical Works of Descartes*, tr. E. S. Haldane and G. R. T. Ross, (Cambridge: Cambridge University Press, repr. 1969), p. 168.
3 For Descartes the concept of *the light of nature* also had a political, polemical, and secularizing role. It may even have been a quite conscious parody of the notion so often appealed to by the Jesuit theologians who denounced Galileo's works – *The Light of Faith*.
    The concept of *the light of nature* had a political dimension too, and an important, revolutionary one. Since it was something in the possession of each individual and was not mediated by the keepers of the Faith, the Church, and the clergy, Descartes was thus striking a blow for that swelling individualism whose rise marked the seventeenth century so distinctively. *The light of nature* was being proposed as standing to the natural order as Luther's *inner light* or *conscience* stood to the moral. One can hardly overestimate its historical importance, despite the fun I have made of it above in Descartes's bludgeoning use. It had a central role in the development of the new world-view that was growing out of the struggle of the new social and production relations mediated by the market to replace the feudal forms of social organization. That new world-view, appropriate to market-mediated relations, had individualism at its base, democracy as its natural political form, and science as the key tool available to the individual in trying to understand the world.
4 Though some cosmologists seem to think that the Universe could create itself *ex nihilo* by "borrowing from the future," so to speak. This seems to me to be a desperate attempt to turn science into a free-standing religion.
5 In *The Man who Mistook his Wife for a Hat* (London: Picador, 1985), ch. 2.
6 What is this but to tell us not to take these doubts seriously? Are we then to take seriously a philosophy raised on this base?
    I have already in chapter 7 ("Skepticism about Skepticism") commented

on the oddity of, and the assumptions underlying, this notion of Descartes's of "*making use of*" our doubts in this way or that. What are we to make of this notion? I can make perfectly good sense of the idea of "making use of" someone else's doubts, as Iago used Othello's and worked on them, but not of "making use of" my own doubts. I may refrain from, or hold myself back from, acting in some way in which my doubt moves me. But that is something quite different. The impulse may be resisted, and that is where the choice comes in. But when the impulse is not resisted it is both inappropriate and gratuitous to describe that as "using" my doubt, or my fear, my admiration or my hunger (or whatever), and Descartes should not be allowed to get away with it.

It would be nearly as bad to say that my doubt "used" me; though one might have at least *some* idea what someone might be getting at in talking in this misleading and totally inappropriate way. Perhaps she just meant that I was out of control, irrationally paralyzed by the doubt, or whatever.

It is here that the famous split between thought and action, between the "inner" and the "outer," is introduced. It turns out to be a presupposition of the Cartesian method, not a consequence of it.

7 "*Lusus Naturae*," in *Wittgenstein: Attention to Particulars: Essays in honour of Rush Rhees*, ed. D. Z. Phillips and Peter Winch (London: Macmillan, 1989). And "Naturalism and Preternatural Change," in *Value and Understanding: Essays for Peter Winch* (London: Routledge, 1990). As Holland points out, these expressions have (and had originally) a perfectly ordinary, and I should say, unproblematic sense to describe, for example, those "sports" that the plant-breeder seizes on and those sideshow freaks that may make the bumpkin's jaw drop but do not challenge science as a whole or limit the run of its writ.

8 In *The Open Society and its Enemies* (London: Routledge, 1962). This sort of view would lead to a ridiculous regress. If we took nature to be really some kind of internal entity distinguishable (almost like an organ) from the thing itself in a way that allowed us to talk of a causal relation, to say that this internal entity *caused* the thing to behave somehow, then we would be able to ask questions about that entity's nature and just how it was that the entity caused its host to behave in *this* rather than *that* way. And so on.

In his 1908 Gifford Lectures, the biologist Hans Driesch did a similar job on Aristotle's concept *entelechy* turning it into a phantom organ, a director of operations in the reconstruction of the unfortunate polyps he cut into bits or turned inside out, something that would *explain* their remarkable ability to regenerate. See also chapter 6.

9 "Creation" implies an agent, but Descartes needs an agent (not of this world, like his parents) to bring him into existence out of nothing. The disappearance into nothing he can manage himself without help, so that "destruction," the normal opposite of "creation," would not be appropriate here.

10 *Trying to Make Sense, op. cit.*, p. 105.

11 In *Science and Hypothesis* (New York: Dover Publications, 1952.) (Readers of this edition should be warned that in the penultimate paragraph of the essay there is a serious, even ridiculous, mistranslation or misprint which transposes "start" and "end," making a nonsense of Poincaré's argument. The sentence *should* read "We see that we start with an experiment that is

very particular and as a matter of fact very crude, and we end with a perfectly general law, perfectly precise, the truth of which we regard as absolute.")

12 Proposed concretely, that is, as a basis for testable theory building, not just speculatively as with Democritus and his seventeenth-century followers, whose atoms had hooks and sharp points and all sorts of marvelous properties that could not be brought to the test. The seventeenth-century atomists had only the dogma of Transubstantiation in its militant Counter-Reformation formulation by the Council of Trent to contend with. Not quite the same thing as an empirical test.

11 ON MISUNDERSTANDING SCIENCE

1 And it is no good shifting the ground and saying that the philosophical "theories" and "theses" are not really about the world but about language as a reflection of the world. Any *facts* about language – those things that are but might be otherwise – would not be a matter for philosophy but for linguists, the historians of particular languages, morphologists, etc. Philosophers will be interested in the aspects of language that are variable and not necessary, but in a negative way, as Michelangelo had to interest himself in those parts of the block of marble that were obscuring the statue imprisoned within. What is hidden behind the changeable in language could be called, in Wittgenstein's term, the "grammar" of the notion of language itself.

2 Kuhn later told me (1994) that he doubted that he was making that point at the time of our meeting sometime in the mid 1970s, but that he agreed fully with it and thought it important.

3 It is just here that we have to resist the pull to specify the relation between paradigm and practice in logical or causal terms. It is just here that the image of model and drawing is perhaps most useful. That image helps to emphasize the two-sided nature of the relation. The model does not determine the drawing or cause the movement of the artist's hand and the relation of the lines. But those movements are not unconnected with the model either. The connection involves the aim and the skill of the artist. The skill and vision that goes into making that connection has itself a history of development that may be long and complex. And anyone who looked for a causal connection between that history and that skill would convict themselves of fatuousness.

The story is told that when someone asked scornfully of one of Matisse's simplest and most pared-down charcoal drawings, "And how long did that one take to produce, M. Matisse?" Matisse answered: "Fifty years."

4 (New York: Dover, 1952). Readers of this edition should be warned that there is a transposition of "start" and "end" that makes nonsense of the final paragraph of that chapter and does not reproduce the French. That transposition may itself be evidence of the strength of the older model and its influence on the translator.

5 *Reason, Truth and History* (Cambridge: Cambridge University Press, 1981), ch. 5, "Two Conceptions of Rationality."

6 Partisans of The Real have not, to my knowledge, settled accounts with

relativity theory. Perhaps they would say that relativity theory removes temporal relations of priority etc. from the ambit of The Real (on analogy with the theological treatments of the problem of the conflict between human freedom and God's foreknowledge). Would that leave us unable to say that the Battle of Waterloo really came after the French Revolution?

12 HISTORY AND HUMAN NATURE

1 Rousseau does make a gesture at realism by making the nuclear family a "natural" (and presumably primordial) society. But on inspection it turns out not to be a "social" unit at all but rather like parent birds or animals feeding and protecting their young according to "natural" and presumably instinctive behavior. There is no question there, in that behavior, of social bonds or obligations. These may arise within his "natural" family, though he does not tell us how. So there seem to be, in Rousseau, social bonds that antedate any "contracting" and do not depend on a contract.

2 Hobbes also makes appeal to this unlikely claim, and it is not obvious what meaning is to be put on it that would make it in the slightest way plausible or save it from plain falsehood.

As it happens, I have a great deal of sympathy with that claim, so long as it is construed negatively, as a claim that on the whole people have to be (and are) taught to be stupid (leaving aside the damaged and traumatized and those with congenital problems).

Somehow I don't think that that is what Descartes had in mind. His appeal to "lack of complaint" as an argument for equable distribution does not give one much confidence in the depth of his meaning or his analysis. It seems that he simply needs that claim to be true in order that his individual meditation should have universal significance and application.

3 Aristotle, consistently with his view of humanity as *zoan politika*, social animals, denies this possibility in his, at first sight paradoxical, first sentence of the *Posterior Analytics*: "All teaching and all getting of knowledge by reasoning involves already existing knowledge."

4 The Anabaptists, consistently with this vision, swept away even membership in a particular church as something one was born into or could be baptized into without mature consent.

5 Materialists of various kinds will, of course, claim that the abilities and tendencies attributed will be independently discoverable in certain neurological structures or in patterns of neural activity that will variously "explain" the abilities or "be identical with" them. Unfortunately, the materialists have not paid careful enough attention to the logical relations between the notions of *ability* and *tendency* on the one hand and the notions of *structure* and *pattern* on the other. Those relations are too intimate to be causal and explanatory and not intimate enough to constitute identity. The expansion that point needs will have to wait.

6 The possibility of human separation and differentiation, of individuality and individual self-image, is also the product of a history and of a particular social development that sets before us choices and puts a value on individuality and separation that would be unimaginable and even

abhorrent to a stone-age tribesman or to the members of many human communities even now. Setting oneself apart would, in a tribal society, have meant setting oneself outside the tribe to become a solitary, brutish thing, something frightening, to be avoided, perhaps even to be hunted.

7 Perhaps we should note also that the words "instinct" and "instinctive" have only a negative sense given by what they exclude, not what they attribute. When we say that the spider spins its beautiful symmetrical web "by instinct," we are not pointing to some separate something that accounts for that ability. We are claiming only that there was no process of conditioning, imitation or learning that would account for it. (And we have to keep reminding ourselves that any biological structures we may find associated with the ability do not "explain" it. They are a condition, not a cause.)

8 The feudal era provides us with what looks, at first sight, like an interesting counter-example to this. At a certain period when a king or superior lord made a request for help and his vassal complied, the superior thereafter tried to claim this as a right of his and a duty of the vassal. This came to be so oppressive that no one would give such help without a written guarantee that the particular instance of help did not create such a duty.

The right way of looking at this is to say that there was in existence a second-order practice or tradition of allowing one instance to create a right and a duty.

9 Over and above this particular reason for the search for foundations to bind back together an atomized humanity, there is the need of each particular social order and system to legitimate itself by presenting itself as the fixed, immovable, natural order of things, the end of history. And that requires foundations that themselves are fixed and immovable.

13 NEWTON, EUCLID, AND THE FOUNDATION OF GEOMETRY

1 "Mathematics and the Metaphysicians," in *Mysticism and Logic* (London: Allen & Unwin, 1950).

2 In chapter 6 I have tried to give an account of Aristotle's way of giving a fundamental importance to the individual and the concrete individual without falling into the difficulties caused by the nominalist refusal to recognize the existence of anything else. We could go beyond what is said there and trace the nominalist impulse to a faulty theory of meaning, one that requires a concrete referent for each meaningful word. Words are seen only as "names" – hence the term "nominalism."

3 *The Thirteen Books of Euclid's Elements* (New York: Dover, 1956), p. 168.

14 CODA: PHILOSOPHY AND HISTORY

1 Not only individuals but families had been bound in this way by the vows, and a family might have to make good the default of or answer for the crimes of one of its members. Law and custom made little distinction between individual and the clan. That clan identity was being eroded by the same forces that were separating individuals previously bound, and

that erosion in turn, abstracted and generalized, helped support the philosophers' founding image of radical individualism.

2 We can see an act of this drama, maybe the last, being played out in splitting the Tory party between those with a remnant of that old feudal paternalism (*noblesse oblige*) and those representing the new hard-nosed Thatcherism.

3 Hobbes could have helped here with his insistence on "the vulgar tongue" as the repository and test of genuine sense. I would regard that notion of a *vulgar tongue* as meaning one that grows out of the needs and practices of everyday life and retains that connection even where there may have been a sophisticated articulation that makes it difficult to see.

Index

298   *Index*